The Natufian Encampment at Beidha

The Natufian Encampment at Beidha
Late Pleistocene Adaptation in the Southern Levant

by Brian F. Byrd

Foreword by Diana Kirkbride

with contributions by John Field, Suzanne K. Fish,
Howard M. Hecker, and David S. Reese

Jutland Archaeological Society Publications XXIII:1, 1989

Jysk Arkæologisk Selskab, Moesgård, Århus
Distributed by Aarhus University Press

The Natufian Encampment at Beidha

Brian F. Byrd © 1989

ISBN 87 7288 054 6
ISSN 0107 2854

Layout: Elsebet Morville
Cover: Elsebet Morville
Drawings: Lykke Johansen, Line Juel, Elsebet Morville and Brian Byrd
Photographs: Diana Kirkbride

Printed by Special-Trykkeriet Viborg a-s
Type: Baskerville 11/12
Paper: G Print 130 g

Published by:
Jutland Archaeological Society
Moesgård
DK-8270, Højbjerg
Denmark

Distributed by:
Aarhus University Press
DK-8000 Århus C
Denmark

The publication of this book has been supported by:

The Aylwin Cotton Foundation
The British Institute at Amman for Archaeology and History
The British School of Archaeology in Jerusalem
The Danish Research Council for the Humanities
The H.P. Hjerl Hansen Mindefondet for Dansk Palæstinaforskning
The Society of Antiquaries of London
and
The Wainwright Foundation, University of Oxford

Contents

Foreword

by Diana Kirkbride

Awe inspiring is the only term that comes to mind as I launch the first of a series of volumes that will contain the final report on the Beidha excavations.

The work on this site has occupied a very large part of my working life, and the site is peculiarly a part of myself, as I not only found it originally, but also directed the excavations from the first season in 1958, until the last in 1983, and am now spending my declining years presiding over the publication.

The history of the excavations at this remarkable site will not be detailed in this volume which is dedicated exclusively to the Natufian element at Beidha, a subject I delegated to Brian Byrd in 1983. However, it is appropriate at this time to acknowledge those institutions which have given us financial support for the excavations, and here I stress that these apply only to the excavations and not to those who are supporting the publication.

The Beidha excavations were sponsored by the British School of Archaeology in Jerusalem, until 1983, when the sponsorship was taken over by the British Institute at Amman for Archaeology and History in conjunction with the Department of Antiquities of Jordan and the Yarmouk University.

I am grateful to the following institutions for their support of the excavations:

American Philosophical Society (1961)

Ashmolean Museum, Oxford (1958, 1959, 1961, 1983)

Bollingen Foundation of New York (1963, 1964, 1965, 1967)

British Academy (1961, 1963, 1964, 1965, 1967, 1983)

Palestine Exploration Fund (1961)

University Museum of Archaeology & Ethnology, Cambridge (1958, 1959, 1961, 1963)

Wenner-Gren Foundation for Anthropological Research (1963, 1964, 1965, 1967)

Two Private Donors (1967)

Society of Antiquaries of London (1983)

Gerald Averay Wainwright Foundation, University of Oxford (1983)

University Museum, Manchester (1983)

I also held the Wainwright Fellowship for fourteen years, and Wainwright himself was fascinated by Beidha but he would not allow his fellowship to be used for any field work. So the fellowship became a personal one and Wainwright himself was content with my letters describing the excavation progress and indeed ordered me back to Beidha every time I worked elsewhere.

The excavations took place with the help and encouragement of the following Directors of Antiquities: the late Gerald Lankester Harding, C.B.E.; the late Dr. Aioni Dajani; the late Said Dura, who kept the permit for me while I was working in Iraq 1969-1975; and Dr. Adnan Hadidi, who gave us much practical help in 1983 as well as co-sponsoring the excavations. He also provided fenced protection for the site, and gave us every possible help and encouragement, a service he continued to perform when I last visited Beidha in 1988. He retired in 1988, soon after my visit.

I should also acknowledge gratefully the loan of tents and equipment from the following:

British School of Archaeology in Jerusalem (1958, 1959, 1965, 1967, 1983)

Gerald Lankester Harding (1958-1967)

The Palestine Museum (1961, 1963, 1964, 1965, 1967)

Netherlands Expedition to Deir Alla (1965, 1967)

The Jordan Army (1965, 1967)

École Biblique & Archéologique de Jérusalem (1967)

British Institute at Amman for Archaeology and History (1983)

Center for Jordanian Studies, Yarmouk University, Jordan (1983)

Department of Antiquities, Jordan (1983)

In addition, the work on the final report is taking place at the Forhistorisk Museum, Moesgård, Denmark and I acknowledge the generous support of its director Peder Mortensen. Furthermore, I am grateful that the Jutland Archaeological Society has agreed to publish this series on the Beidha excavations.

Although I have delegated the Natufian element at Beidha to Brian Byrd, and have handed him all the notes, flints, photographs and records available, the fact remains that he was with me in the field for only a single season, 1983. As the director of the project, I feel I should give some account of my discovery of Beidha in 1956 and the initial work at the site.

Seyl Aqlat (my original name for the site) is a seasonal torrent bed situated in Wadi el-Ghurab. The seyl begins as a vertical drainage fault high up in the sandstone cliffs that line the northern side of the Wadi Ghurab and descends in a series of steep drops and deep water holes until it finally floors out into first Wadi Ghurab, secondarily to Wadi Slehsil and from there into the Wadi Araba.

The west bank of the seyl was formed by isolated sandstone cliffs set back at a slight distance and the eastern side was formed by a high steeply sloping bank composed primarily of sand. On top of this bank was a low, but clearly defined tell. Considerable erosion has taken place in this eastern bank, and consequently some of the tell has disappeared. Dry-stone walls with their tops only a few cm. below the surface were clearly visible in the side of the eroded bank.

During the initial finding and search of the site, the tops of some straight walls were seen, and we picked up a large number of unpatinated fine quality flint artifacts of the type known as Pre-Pottery Neolithic B. A Natufian element was also present, the artifacts all very shiny, and a milky blue colour with whitish streaks of patination.

At the beginning of the first excavation season, 1958, I took the men to the highest point of the tell and there put down a small cluster of five meter squares. Cleaning the surface sand carefully, we found we were dealing with a series of large stone-walled Neolithic buildings and the depth of the deposits were considerable.

As it was obvious that the Neolithic would take a long time to excavate, and as that part had to be finished before we could tackle the Natufian, I decided at once to put trenches into the talus and sample the Natufian from there. I simply started down from below the Neolithic walls as seen from the seyl side and dug straight down. Two trenches were dug which I called M1 and M2 and so marked the artifacts. The M1 sounding was subsequently widened toward the north by going up to the top and descending to the Natufian level in slice after slice, thus taking several cuts to reveal in 1959 a huge Natufian hearth, roughly circular and partially outlined with stone slabs. A fine selection of animal bones and horn-cores, and a tremendous number of flint artifacts were recovered.

The M2 sounding was made a little further north of M1 along the talus. It also just cut the edge of a hearth area and the end of an irregular pit, with slightly undercut edges and floored by wadi pebbles, about three levels of them, and below came more loose sand. I thought I had found a pit-dwelling, but now being vastly more experienced I realize it was, in reality, an erosion gully, such as are appearing around Beidha today. The 'pit' tantalizingly disappeared into the section under the Neolithic village, and I erected a wall of stones against this section in order that the loose sand should not be blown away, and thus bring down the Neolithic village above.

Only very limited work was done on the Natufian element at Beidha during the subsequent seasons prior to 1983, as I concentrated on excavating the Neolithic village levels. The report on those more extensive excavations will be the subject of the subsequent volumes on the Beidha project.

Acknowledgments

The research at Beidha has been conducted with the permission and support of the Jordanian Department of Antiquities and we gratefully acknowledge their strong and continued backing under the directorship of Dr. Ghazi Bisheh. In particular, Dr. Adnan Hadidi, the Director General of Antiquities until 1988, graciously gave permission for the Natufian chipped stone material from the 1983 season at Beidha to go to the University of Arizona on loan, facilitating the analysis phase of the Natufian research.

I am indebted to Diana Kirkbride, director of the Beidha excavations, and Peder Mortensen, who has been in charge of the analysis of the chipped stone assemblage, for allowing me to study the Beidha Natufian. The director's support of my excavation of the Natufian horizon while I was a field supervisor under her direction in 1983, and assistance while studying the artifacts and archives from the earlier seasons was vital and is gratefully acknowledged. Peder Mortensen, director of the Forhistorisk Museum, Moesgård, provided generous support (and considerable time and effort) during my various stays at the Museum between 1985 and 1989. The Museum's lodging, office and lab facilities, and other material support during the various stages of the project, particularly during the final preparation, are deeply appreciated.

The analysis of the chipped stone assemblage from the Beidha Natufian was written in partial fulfillment of a doctoral dissertation under the direction of Arthur Jelinek in the Anthropology Department at the University of Arizona. This research was supported by an American Schools of Oriental Research Shell Foundation Fellowship (1984-1985), and grants from the Aylwin Cotton Foundation (1986), the Educational Fund for Archaeology, Department of Anthropology (1984-1986) and the Graduate Development Fund at the University of Arizona (1984). Analysis of radiocarbon samples from the Beidha Natufian were conducted by the Accelerator Mass Spectrometer facility at the University of Arizona through NSF grant EAR-8512761. Institution support has been provided by the American Center for Oriental Research, Amman, Jordan; the Center for Jordanian Studies at Yarmouk University, Irbid, Jordan; and the Forhistorisk Museum, Moesgård, Denmark. A special word of thanks must go to Moawiya Ibrahim, director of the Institute of Archaeology and Anthropology, Yarmouk University, for allowing me to participate in the 1983 season while employed at the Center for Jordanian Studies, Yarmouk University, and for the loan of equipment during the 1983 field season. Furthermore the full support, hospitality and unending enthusiasm of Niazi Sha'ban during the 1983 field season when he served as Department of Antiquities representative at Beidha and in subsequent journeys back to the site and the Petra area, are fully remembered and appreciated.

Study of Palestinian Natufian collections stored in Great Britain was facilitated by E.W. MacKie and Sally Drummer at the Hunterian Museum; Dr. Sieveking and Penny Robinson at the British Museum; P.L. Carter at the University Museum of Archaeology and Anthropology, Cambridge; and Mark Newcomer at the Institute of Archaeology in London.

The photographs were printed at the Forhistorisk Museum, Moesgård, and the excellent artifact illustrations were produced by Elsebet Morville (figures 19:d, 20:b, 23:b, 32:a-c) and Lykke Johansen (the remainder). Line Juel drafted the majority of the plans and sections. Fig. 1, drafted by Elsebet Morville, was first published in the *Journal of World Prehistory* (see Byrd 1989 for reference).

The publication of the volume was coordinated by Poul Kjærum, editor of the Jutland Archaeological Society, and P.J. Crab proofread this volume. The layout and final preparation work for the publication was conducted by Elsebet Morville, Jens Kirkeby and Line Juel of the Museum's illustration department. The Arabic summary was translated by Khairiyeh 'Amr and Sabri Mohammed.

Publication subvention support has been

generously provided by the Aylwin Cotton
Foundation, the British Institute at Amman for
Archaeology and History, the British School of
Archaeology in Jerusalem, the Danish Research
Council for the Humanities, the H.P. Hjerl
Hansen Mindefondet for Dansk Palæstinaforsk-
ning, the Society of Antiquaries of London and
the Wainwright Foundation, University of
Oxford.

I have benefited considerably from advice and
discussion with the following scholars: Søren
H. Andersen, E.B. Banning, Ofer Bar-Yosef,
Phillip Edwards, Nigel Goring-Morris, Michael
Faught, Paul Fish, Andrew Garrard, Arthur
Jelinek, Mujahed Muheisen, Deborah Olszew-
ski, Robert Netting, John Olsen, Gary Rollefson,
Glenn Stone, Allan Sullivan, and Katherine
Wright. I also thank Jens Andresen, Ole Ditlev,
Gert Gram, Flemming Højlund, Helle Juel Jen-
sen, Kirsti Leth, Torsten Madsen, David
McCreery, Anne-Marie Mortensen, and last,
but most importantly, my parents for their
support and encouragement.

Finally, the assistance and good humor of the
B'dul and Amerin Bedouin excavators and siev-
ers is fondly remembered and acknowledged.

1. Introduction

There has been immense interest in the late Pleistocene "cultural complex" termed the Natufian ever since Dorthy Garrod (1932, 1942) defined it, based on excavations at Shukbah Cave in the Wadi en-Natuf and Mugharet el Wad in Mount Carmel (fig. 1). Additional investigation in the 1920s and 1930s by Turville-Petre (1932) at Kebarah Cave, Neuville (1934, 1951) in the Judean desert, and Rust (1950: 119-121) in western Syria confirmed the distinctiveness of the Natufian complex and also revealed stratigraphically earlier microlithic industries.

In characterizing the Natufian, Garrod used the terms "industry" and "culture" interchangeably. Microlithic backed lunates were the key "fossil indicators" for the Natufian chipped stone industry, and other characteristic chipped stone tools included triangles, burins, perforators, end scrapers, core scrapers, and backed blades which often displayed sickle polish (Garrod 1932: 258). The use of the microburin technique to segment bladelets and of bifacial (Helwan) retouch subsequently to blunt or back these bladelets was viewed as distinctive of the industry.[1] In addition, large chipped stone tools (often made of chert) such as picks, choppers, and round scrapers were also recovered. Equally important characteristics of the Natufian included bone tools (particularly points, harpoons, gorgets, sickle hafts, and pendants), ground stone vessels and pestles, limestone mortars, sculpture in stone and bone, burials, construction features such as walls and pavements, and thick cultural deposits.

These early researchers characterized the Natufian as the first agriculturalists based on the presence of sickles (to harvest the cereals), and mortars and pestles (to process the grain) (Garrod 1932: 268; Neuville 1934: 254). However, no direct botanical evidence was available. Whether or not agriculture was practiced during the Natufian has been a major point of disagreement ever since then (e.g. Childe 1935; Perrot 1962; Moore 1982; Henry 1985).

Recognition of the apparently pivotal position the Natufian holds in the developmental sequence from mobile hunting and gathering societies to sedentary village communities quite naturally led to an intense amount of research in the ensuing fifty years (e.g. Garrod 1958; Perrot 1962; J. Cauvin 1978; Henry 1981; Bar-Yosef 1983; Valla 1988). Research and discussion have emphasized the sequence and underlying causes of events leading to the emergence of sedentary communities and domesticated plants (particularly cereals and legumes) and animals (especially sheep and goat). The role of particular variables in this fundamental development in human adaptation has been the subject of conflicting interpretations – models variously emphasizing changes in the environment, population size, settlement patterns, economic strategies or social organization in attempting to explain the initial steps toward fully sedentary villages depending substantially upon domesticated plants and animals (e.g. Braidwood 1960; Binford 1968; Flannery 1969, 1973; Wright 1971; Bender 1978; Henry 1981; Moore 1982; Redding 1988).

The venue of the pioneering research of Garrod and her contemporaries was Palestine, and primarily western Palestine, with the major exception of Rust's work in southern Syria. Jordan remained *terra incognita* in regard to the Natufian, with the exception of a little known excavation by Waechter (1948) at the rockshelter of Ala Safat on the eastern edge of the Jordan Valley. This geographical bias towards western Palestine began to change in the 1950s and 1960s with an increase in the number of prehistorians working in the Near East. New Natufian settlements were identified in a broad range of geographical and environmental settings including the Jordan Valley, the hills of northern Palestine, southern Syria and southwestern Jordan (e.g. Bar-Yosef and Tchernov 1966; M. Cauvin 1974; Kenyon 1981; Kirkbride 1966; Stekelis and Yizraely 1963).

---

[1] The microburin technique is now known to occur in a variety of earlier Epipaleolithic chipped stone industries in the Levant (e.g. Bar-Yosef 1981).

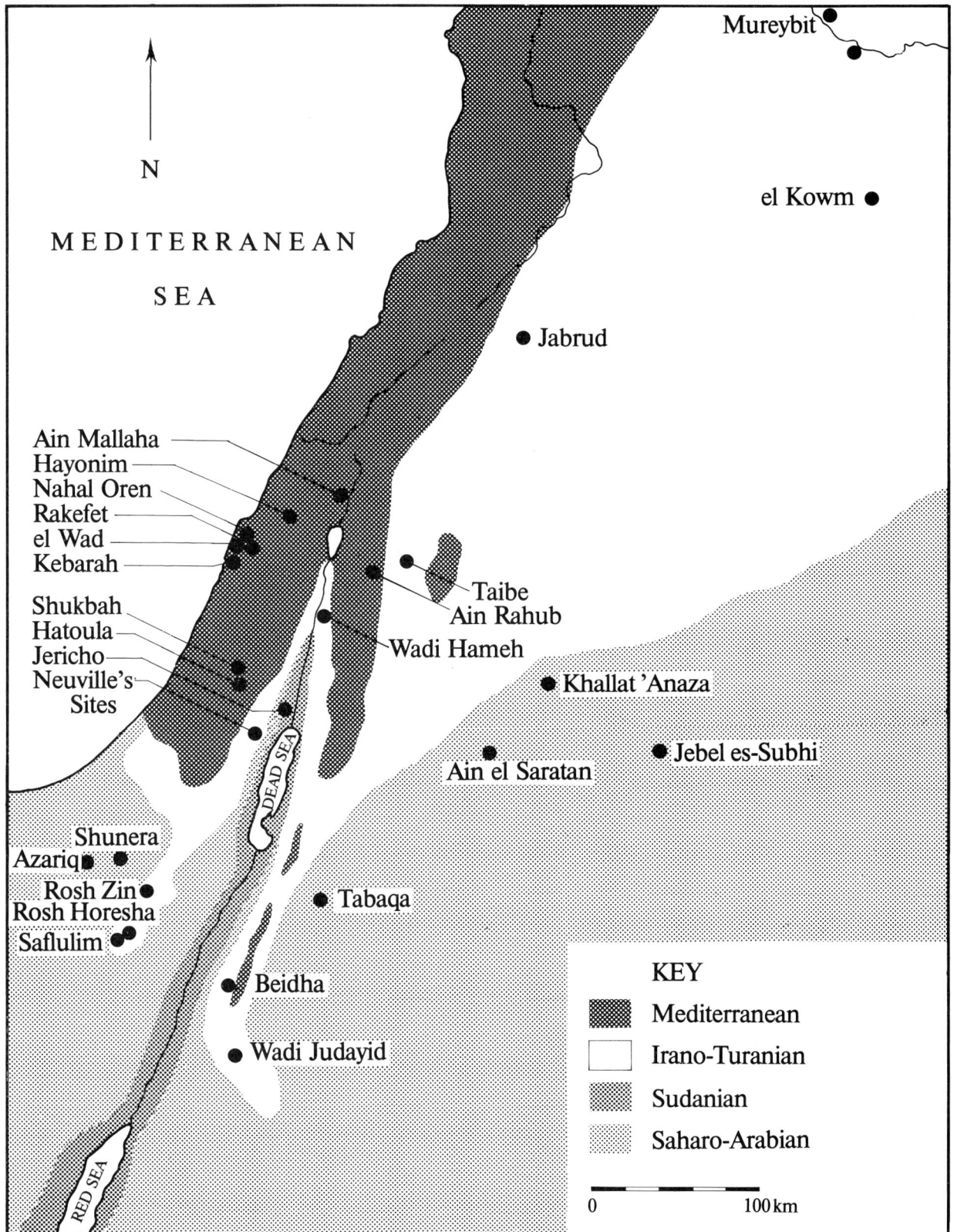

Fig. 1. Natufian site locations and the distribution of modern plant geographic zones in the Levant.

Diana Kirkbride's research at Beidha (initially termed Seyl Aqlat), in the rugged sandstone area of southern Jordan, was the first of its kind at a Jordanian Natufian site (Kirkbride 1960). In fact, for almost a quarter of a century Beidha stood as a solitary point in Jordan on distribution maps of Levantine Natufian settlements (cf. Bar-Yosef 1983). Hence, it provided the first insights into Natufian adaptation in the eastern half of the southern Levant and to whether adaptive strategies were similar to those in the better known western Levant.

Kirkbride's research goals at Beidha were threefold: (1) to investigate the economy of the early Neolithic occupation at the site by conducting broad horizontal excavations, thereby facilitating examination of the relationship between domestic buildings, (2) to examine the relationship between the Beidha Neolithic and contemporary occupation in the Levant and broaden the knowledge of this culture, and (3) to study the relationship between the Neolithic and the Natufian at Beidha (Kirkbride 1960: 137). With Kirkbride working as the only supervisor for the first three seasons, the excavations at Beidha proceeded slowly, but by the end of the 1967 season she had exposed the largest area of any aceramic Neolithic site in the Levant (Redman 1978: 146) and a considerable area of the Natufian.

During the last two decades the pace of field research on the Natufian has increased sharply, producing data on many new sites in a diversity of geographical settings, particularly in the southern and eastern Levant. Excavations and surveys have continued in the highlands and coastal regions of northern Palestine (e.g. Bar-Yosef 1983; Henry and Leroi-Gourhan 1976; Noy et al. 1973; Lechevallier and Ronen 1985). In addition, projects have been conducted in the Jordan Valley (Crabtree et al. 1987; Edwards 1987), in the highlands of Jordan (Muheisen et al. 1988) and in the northern Levant (J. Cauvin 1977; Moore 1982). Further afield, projects have been undertaken in the steppe and desert areas of the Negev and Sinai in the south (Goring-Morris 1987; Goring-Morris and Bar-Yosef 1987; Henry 1973a, 1976; Marks and Larson 1977), and eastward along the edge of the Syrian-Arabian desert (Betts 1986, 1987; Byrd 1989; Byrd and Rollefson 1984; Clark et al. 1988; Garrard et al. 1987, 1988; Henry 1982). The

preliminary results of these projects reveal a rich mosaic of varying settlement and subsistence strategies during the Natufian, and distinct regional variants are emerging which challenge earlier interpretations of Natufian economy and organizational adaptation. In addition, the abundance of radiocarbon dates now available suggest the Natufian began prior to 12,500 B.P. and persisted until almost 10,000 B.P. (Byrd 1989: 167).

After a sixteen year hiatus, initiated by the 1967 Arab-Israeli war, Kirkbride returned to Beidha for a final season (Kirkbride 1984). I participated in this field season with the research objective of gaining a fuller understanding of subsistence strategies, and the degree of settlement intensity and duration of the Natufian occupation. The new excavations emphasized sampling for ecological data and gathering evidence of temporal and spatial intrasite variability (Byrd 1987, 1988). The procedure included: (a) fine scale recovery of a sample of the chipped-stone assemblage, (b) detailed mapping of in situ artifacts and features, and (c) sampling for botanical, sedimentological, palynological and radiocarbon material. This monograph is the result of that field research and laboratory analysis of the material and archives from the excavations of the Beidha Natufian prior to 1983.

2. Geographical and environmental setting

Geographical setting

Beidha is situated in southern Jordan (fig. 1) about four and a half kilometers north of the well-known Nabatean site of Petra (fig. 2). Four kilometers to the east of Petra lies the modern town of Wadi Musa, located next to the strong spring of 'Ain Musa (the Biblical spring of Moses). Geographically, Beidha lies on a rather narrow – about four kilometers – north-south trending shelf which interrupts the rapid wester-ly descent from the Jordanian plateau to the Wadi Araba, the southern portion of the Jorda-nian Rift system. This shelf is dominated by steeply faced Cambrian sandstone remnants that were the medium for the famous Nabatean temple carvings. It is a region of dramatic changes in topography, geology and plant communities.

The site, at an elevation of approximately 1020 meters above sea level, lies in an alluvial valley which is drained by the seasonally flowing Wadi el Ghurab, "Valley of the Ravens" (fig. 3). The wadi originates northeast of the site, on the slopes of Jebel Shara (maximum elevation 1700 meters), which forms the western edge of the Jordanian plateau. The wadi flows generally from northeast to southwest and near Beidha it runs along the sandstone cliffs on the southern side of the valley. Less than a kilometer down-stream from Beidha it joins the Wadi Slehsil and after another kilometer it drops precipitously over 400 meters before joining the Wadi Musa and flowing more gradually into the Wadi Araba (Kirkbride 1985: 8).

Geomorphologically, Beidha is situated in a remnant alluvial fill terrace abutting the sandstone cliffs on the north side of the valley (Field, Appendix A). If this cliff face is followed for about three-quarters of a kilometer to the northeast, one encounters the Siq al Barrid, which served as the northern caravansarai for Nabatean Petra. Evidence of Nabatean occupa-tion is abundant in the area, the series of ag-ricultural terrace walls constructed across the site of Beidha being but one example.

The Neolithic settlement at the site has created a low tell that rises above the general level of the alluvial terrace. The terrain slopes down to an intermediate terrace on the southern edge of the site, while on the west the site has been cut by the Seyl Aqlat, a seasonal water-course which drains the area west of Siq al Barrid (fig. 4). The steep bank, over eighteen meters deep, created by the Seyl Aqlat appears to have cut away a considerable portion of the Natufian settlement (Kirkbride 1985: 118; Field, Appendix A).

Modern environmental setting

Due to the rather abrupt changes in elevation and geology, three major environmental zones occur today in the local Beidha area. They include the forested Cretaceous limestone high-lands of Jebel Shara (Mount Seir of the bible), the more steppic sandstone shelf and its inter-spersed alluvial valleys where Beidha is situated, and the desert lowland wadis adjacent to the Wadi Araba (Kirkbride 1985).

The modern potential plant geographic zones have been reconstructed for the area. The word "reconstructed" cannot be emphasized enough, given the amount of environmental degradation that has occurred over the last 9,000 years. The effects of overgrazing and forest clearing for herding, farming, firewood, and building mate-rials, along with subsequent erosion, have drastically affected the plant communities. Steppic vegetation, especially certain species within that community, have invaded areas that had been inhabited by more mesic plant species. Toxic plants, particularly of the succulent family, have increased in quantity due to their unsuit-ability as fodder for sheep and goats. Hence, researchers have been forced to reconstruct what they believe the modern climax vegetational regime would be like with the aid of remnant

14

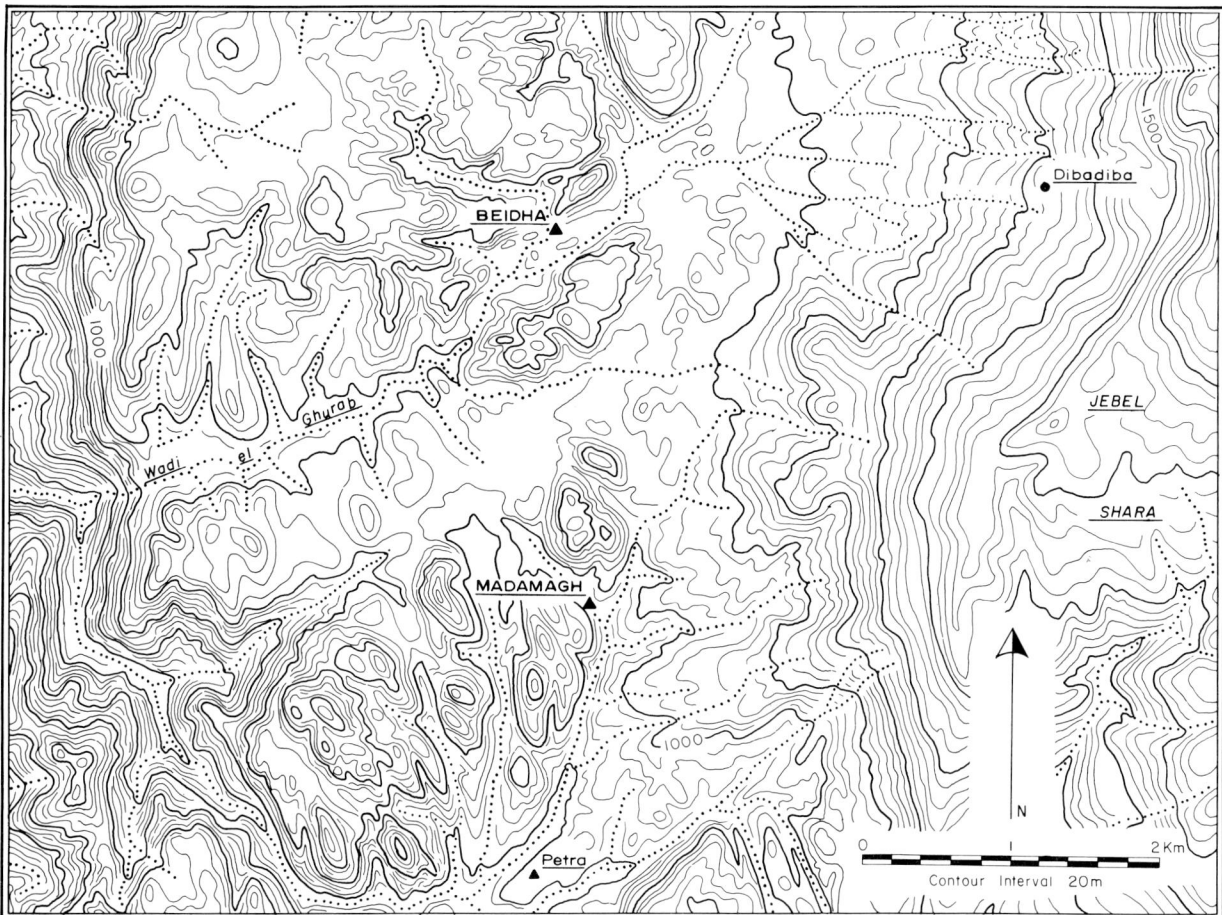

Fig. 2. Topographic map of the Beidha region.

stands and occasionally single finds of species (Zohary 1962; Al-Eisawi 1985).

Zohary reconstructs the modern plant community of the general upland around Beidha as being of the Mediterranean vegetation zone: evergreen maquis and forest association (Zohary 1962: 112-115). It is a unique climax distribution of oak, *Quercus calliprinos*, and juniper, *Juniperis phoenicea*, and two associations occur, each dominated by one of these two species. The evergreen oak forms relatively dense stands primarily on the highland calcareous limestone soils directly east of Beidha, while junipers occur in very pure stands on the Nubian sandstone in the highlands further to the north (Zohary 1962: 102; Atkinson and Beaumont 1973: 309-310). In addition, *Crataegus azarolus*, *Pistacia palaestina*, *P. atlantica*, *Rhamnus palaestina*, and *Daphne linearifolia* (which occurs only in this area) are present (Zohary 1962: 102). Steppe and desert shrubs occupy the underwood.

Rainfall in the area varies considerably. At Shaubak, 20 kilometers to the northeast of Beidha, mean annual rainfall for a twenty year cycle (1940-1960) was 342 mm per year, while at Al Hai, on Jebel Shara directly to the east of Beidha, rainfall averaged closer to 300 mm (Raikes 1966: 69-72). In contrast, mean annual rainfall at the town of Wadi Musa during the same period averaged 170 mm, and Raikes has suggested that the rainfall in the immediate environs of Beidha probably averaged between 170 and 200 mm. In contrast, in the Wadi Araba, west of the sandstone shelf, mean annual rainfall drops to less than 50 mm per year.

Given the lower elevation and rainfall of the alluvial valleys situated in the sandstone shelf in contrast to the highlands, the modern climax associations probably would be characteristic either of the transition zone between the Mediterranean forest and the Irano-Turanian steppe or possibly steppic. The geological contact between the Cretaceous limestone of the

15

Fig. 3. View of the Beidha area from Jebel Shara on the west (site is located on the terrace below the arrow).

uplands and the Cambrian sandstone lies at 1320 meters and only the juniper component of the Mediterranean forest extends downhill onto the sandstone derived soils (Helbæk 1966: 65). No trees occur in the alluvial valleys; however oaks and junipers exist in the better watered small catchment basins in the sandstone massifs of the sandstone shelf.

The alluvial valleys contain a dwarf shrub steppic vegetation (Gebel and Starck 1985). Further west on the extremely rugged pre-Cambrian granite slopes which drop into the Wadi Araba, a strip of the Irano-Turanian steppic vegetation occurs, but the precise community association is not well described (Zohary 1962: 115). In general, these two areas of steppic plant communities are related to the Irano-Turanian vegetation zone east of the forested hills, where a dwarf shrub steppic environment of the *Artemisietalia herbae-albae* order (primarily a variety of sage) occurs. Further east in the sandy hamada and sand desert of the

Wadi Araba area, *Haloxyletum salicornici* and *H. persici* of the Saharo-Sindian plant geographic territory are present (Al-Eisawi 1985).

Paleoenvironmental reconstruction

Several lines of evidence have been used to reconstruct the southern Levantine environment at the end of the Pleistocene including deep-sea cores, pollen cores from lakes and swamps, geomorphological data from sedimentary and lacustrine sequences, and pollen and faunal remains from archaeological sites. This research has clearly shown that temperatures rose at the end of the last glacial maximum and that this trend continued through the Natufian (Valla 1987a: 274). Deep-sea cores indicate that this was a worldwide trend (Luz 1982) and this is further supported by the composition of faunal

16

assemblages at Natufian sites, both in terms of the presence of more temperate-adapted species and the increase in the size of mammals (Davis 1981, 1982; Kurten 1965; Pichon 1985, 1987; Valla 1987a). With the retreat of the glacial ice sheets, air circulation patterns changed world-wide, and in the Levant storm tracks began to shift northward, creating regional climatic differences, until they reached their present day patterns (Bintliff 1982). In the southern Levant small changes in the climate seem to have had significant effects during the late Pleistocene and there is considerable disagreement regarding the timing, length, and amplitude of these changes, as well as what effect these changes had on the distribution of plant communities.

At present, there are two conflicting interpretations of the southern Levantine climate during the Natufian. Henry has argued, based primarily on pollen and faunal samples from archaeological sites and on Tsukada's pollen diagram from the Huleh Basin, that from 13,000 B.P. to 11,000 B.P. rainfall increased in the southern Levant (Henry 1987a: 10-12). Alternatively, Goldberg has asserted, based primarily on the deposition of wind blown sands and stony colluvium sediments associated with archaeological sites in the southern Levant, that there was increasing aridity from the onset of the Natufian (Goldberg 1981; Goldberg and Bar-Yosef 1982; Bar-Yosef and Vogel 1987). It is difficult to resolve these conflicting opinions at present, but this may be because attempts to generalize on the climate of the entire southern Levant are still too ambitious and, hence, over-simplified. Instead, more localized regional reconstructions are needed – and these may reveal that climatic conditions were more varied with respect to local situations.

Despite these differences in interpretation, it was colder during the Natufian than at present and effective moisture may well have been greater (Pichon 1987: 147; Valla 1987a: 276-277). This would have allowed open forest and steppe areas to be more extensive than today. Furthermore, a more complex mosaic of plant communities may have existed which included associations of species not directly analogous to modern plant communities.

Reconstruction of the paleoenvironment during the Natufian in the Beidha region is very limited. However, Field's preliminary geomor-phological study has found no indication of erosion or large scale deposition of wind blown sands or stoney colluvium (Field, Appendix A). Rather, sedimentation, fed by ephemeral streams, was causing the Wadi el Ghurab to aggrade during the Natufian occupation. This may suggest that during the period the site was occupied, the early Natufian, ground cover was more extensive in the alluvial valleys and that the open forest and transition zone to the steppe extended further down the slopes of Jebel Shara than today.

The nearest permanent water source to Beidha at present is situated at an elevation of 1320 m, three kilometers up the slopes of Jebel Shara. Here the slow-flowing spring of Dibadiba emerges near the contact between the Cretaceous limestone and the Cambrian sandstone. Travertine deposits, however, occur near Bir Abu Roga, slightly downstream of Beidha, and it is possible that a spring may have been active at that location during the late Pleistocene (Raikes 1966: 71). In addition, excavations along the sandstone cliff face in area AA-15 at Beidha have revealed a possible travertine deposit. The existence of a localized spring is further supported by the presence of pollen from plants that require standing water in the Natufian deposits (Fish, Appendix B). Hence, it appears that a water supply was available in the immediate vicinity, and may have been a major determinant of settlement location.

Given the nature of the climatic regime and the marked zonal nature of the plant communities, a diverse range of resources would have been available within a limited catchment area around Beidha. These would have included edible wild plants and a wide range of herd animals, particularly ungulates, whose distribution would have varied considerably between ecological zones.

The Mediterranean forest would have been the source of acorns, pistachios, and cereals, particularly emmer wheat and barley, (Helbæk 1959; Flannery 1973). *P. atlantica* and barley will, however, extend into the steppic area in certain environmental situations (Zohary 1973). A wide range of legumes are found in both the steppic and forested regions. Almonds would have been present in semi-steppe and steppic settings and fig trees in rock crevices, springs and wet gorges in the steppe (Zohary 1973;

Zohary and Spiegel-Roy 1975: 324; Helbæk 1964).

As most cereals and legumes are annuals, they ripen in the spring and early summer after the winter rains (Flannery 1969). The perennials, mostly nut, oil and fruit plants, generally have a more varied seasonal distribution. Nuts ripen in the autumn and are harvestable until late winter (Flannery 1973: 274). The precise time that plant resources ripen varies altitudinally, hence, resources could have been collected moving up the topographic gradient, and thereby extending the season of availability.

The environmental distribution of herd animals would also have been quite varied. In the Mediterranean zone wild cattle, *Bos primigenius*, probably inhabited open woodland and grassland areas. Of the three species of gazelle recognized in the Levant, mountain gazelle, *Gazella gazella*, prefers the Mediterranean forested area, and goitered gazelle, *Gazella subgutturosa*, prefers steppe and semi-desert areas (Roberts 1977; Garrard 1980). It is, however, dorcas gazelle, *Gazella dorcas*, which has its primary habitat in semi-desert and desert areas (Harrison 1981; Dorst and Dandelot 1970), that has been identified as the main gazelle species recovered at Beidha (Hecker, Appendix C). Within the steppe and desert region, equids, either Asiatic wild ass or Syrian onager (*Equus hemionus*) and wild horse (*Equus ferus*), would have been present (Roberts 1977; Groves 1974).

The sandstone shelf and its rugged rocky areas would have been the habitat of wild goats. Whether both species of goat – wild goat (*Capra aegagrus*), which is now extinct, and ibex (*C. ibex*) – were present in the immediate area around Beidha are unclear. Both species inhabited rocky locales in a wide range of vegetation zones and altitudinal situations; however, the precise microenvironments which the two species may have exploited is open to debate (see Hecker 1982). Yet, on analogy from research in Pakistan, where a variety of different species of *Capra* occur, there was probably no overlap in niche habitat in the Levant (Roberts 1977). It is possible that ibex inhabited the most rocky areas of the sandstone region, while wild goat, which preferred larger social groupings, inhabited less rocky upland portions of the sandstone shelf (cf. Schaller 1977).

A number of other animal species undoubtedly were indigenous to the local area including residential game birds (such as partridge, sand grouse, coursers, chuckar, bustard and, perhaps ostrich), and small animals such as hyrax, hares, foxes, badger, and small rodents (Garrard 1980; Meinertzhagen 1954). Predator species, including leopard, cheetah, panther, lion, wolves, and jackals, also inhabited the region in the recent past (Kirkbride 1985).

Other resources are readily available in the local area (Kirkbride 1985). Flint occurs both in tabular form at the contact with the limestone and the sandstone geological formations on the slopes of Jebel Shara, and today as flint cobbles and pebbles in the wadi beds near the site. Hematite for use as pigment is present immediately east of Beidha in the hilly regions of the Wadi Araba and also in the wadis of the sandstone shelf, while malachite can be found in small quantities near the precipice into the Wadi Araba and in large deposits in the rocky areas of the Wadi Araba such as near Feinan.

The rich and varied nature of this semi-arid portion of the Levant, typified by the extreme altitudinal zonation of the environment, provided a rich source of varied resources – particularly plant and animal species.

3. Excavation and stratigraphic summary

The site of Beidha was brought to Diana Kirkbride's attention while she was employed at Petra by the Jordanian Department of Antiquities. She began conducting a reconnaissance survey of the Petra area in her free time and inquired of the B'dul Bedouin workmen about the location of archaeological sites with flints, bones and ash but lacking pottery (Kirkbride 1968a: 263). They brought her to a site, initially called Seyl Aqlat, in the Beidha area – the stone walls and Neolithic flints eroding out of the upper talus slope and, further down the slope, white patinated Natufian artifacts, revealed the research potential of this aceramic tell. In 1958, the first of seven excavation campaigns, which were to last until 1967, were initiated at Seyl Aqlat – later the site was only referred to as Beidha (Kirkbride 1966: 8). In 1983 Kirkbride returned to the site for an eighth and final season (Kirkbride 1984).

Generally, the excavations were organized within a five by five meter grid system with one meter balks (50 cm per square) separating the squares. The excavations were supervised by Kirkbride and conducted primarily by trained Jericho pickmen, and screening was rarely used. Excavation was by stratigraphic unit, finds were provenienced by these units, and emphasis was on the exposure of complete buildings. Small scale soundings were used to preview the stratigraphy and guide the broad scale excavation. Although primary attention was placed on the aceramic Neolithic village, a series of soundings were made into the Natufian horizon. It should be noted that the small size of the artifacts recovered from the Natufian horizons shows the considerable care, particularly in 1958, that was taken by the excavators to insure recovery of Natufian microliths.

Early excavations: 1958-1967

Three Natufian soundings were made during the first season. Initially, a small excavation was conducted in area C-2 to obtain a preview of the depth and nature of the stratigraphy at the site (fig. 4). The 5.55 meters deep sounding revealed, from top to bottom, a little over a meter of sterile sand and a possible soil horizon associated with a Nabatean terrace surface, followed by about 2.3 meters of Neolithic occupational debris, and then 2.25 meters of loosely compacted culturally sterile sediment before reaching the Natufian horizon (fig. 5). The trench was abandoned with the exposure of the top of the Natufian, as the loose sand directly above the Natufian threatened to collapse the trench. Subsequently, two excavations were initiated on the western talus slope in order to explore the Natufian horizon (fig. 6).

One trench, 3.5 by 2.5 meters in size, was located in area K-2 near the southern end of the site.[2] Here the excavations revealed a little over 1.6 meters of very pale brown sand separating the Neolithic from the Natufian. The Natufian deposit was almost 0.60 meters thick and consisted of three distinct layers (fig. 7). The uppermost deposit was a light brown sediment with dense quantities of microliths. An intermediary gray ashy deposit included a roasting area with sandstone slabs placed around it and abundant animal bones. The third and earliest Natufian deposit was a brown sand, less dense in microliths. Below the Natufian horizon was a loosely compacted very pale brown deposit similar to that between the Natufian and the Neolithic.

A second excavation unit, 4.5 by 3.5 meters in size, was centrally placed along the the western slope in area F-1. The uppermost Natufian horizon was a compacted light brown sand, with its upper surface containing heavy traces of calcium carbonate. Cutting into this deposit was an elongated pit, 1.5 by 0.7 meters in length (fig. 8). The pit had, in places, undercut sides, and

[2]Originally the terms Mesolithic 1 and Mesolithic 2 were used to refer to the excavations in area K-2 and F-1 respectively. Hence, the artifacts were labeled as such – M1:2 (the second number indicating the deposit).

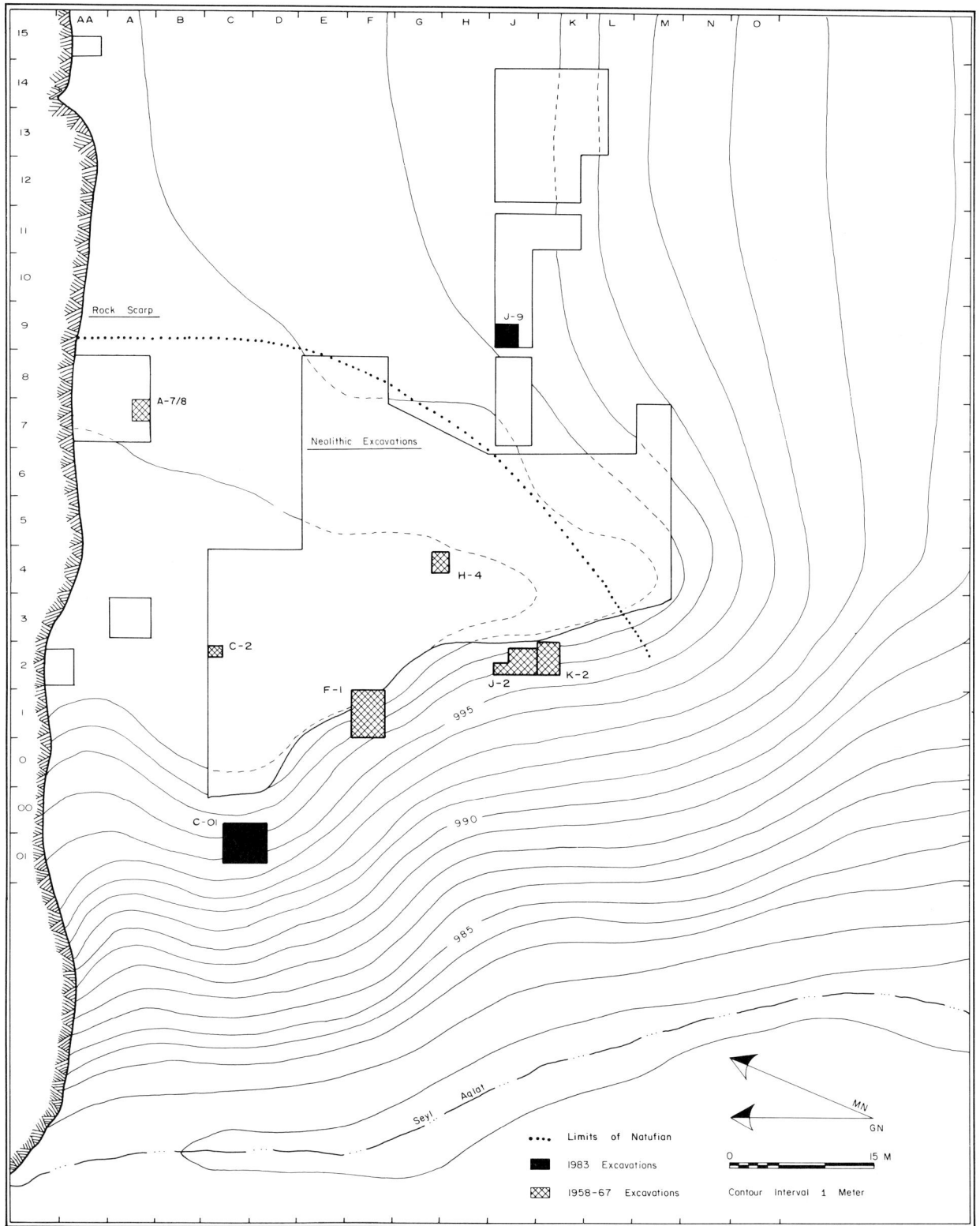

Fig. 4. Topographic map of Beidha, showing the location of Natufian excavation areas.

along the western end it was more gradually sloped. Much of the base of the pit was covered with large wadi cobbles, gravels and a few small sandstone slabs. Near the west end of the pit were several burnt stones. The pit continued into the east section of the trench. Kirkbride suggested that this feature may have been a pit dwelling (Kirkbride 1968a: 264). However, given the absence of cultural material within the pit, and since the pit is cut from the top of the Natufian deposit, or slightly higher, it appears that this feature is not a man-made Natufian pit dwelling. Instead, it may represent the head, or nick point, of an erosional gully.

The size of the excavation in area F-1 was then reduced to a trench, 0.85 by 3.25 meters, that cut through the 0.4 meters of Natufian occupation (fig. 8). The uppermost deposit was 0.3 meters thick, rich in microliths and contained several sandstone slabs. Below this layer was a thin gray deposit containing a small hearth. The earliest Natufian deposit was very thin and less dense in artifacts, and below the Natufian horizon was the culturally sterile sand.

In 1959 the Natufian was excavated only in area J-2 immediately adjacent to area K-2 (fig. 4), in order to explore the large sandstone slab in the north K-2 section (fig. 7). The resulting trench, approximately 3.25 by 2.75 meters in size, was subsequently extended 2.0 by 1.5 meters further to the northwest. The excavations revealed a stratigraphic sequence similar to that of area K-2. In addition, an extremely large roasting area was uncovered.

In 1963 a small sounding in area A7/8 revealed the top of the Natufian horizon, thereby providing further information on its areal extent (fig. 4).[3] Another small sounding was made in 1964 into an unexcavated portion of the Natufian in area F-1. The objective was to allow Hans Helbæk, who was studying the paleobotanical material from the site, to look for Natufian carbonized plant remains (Helbæk 1966). The results, although negative in this respect, exposed another small hearth and a limited sample of artifacts.

Excavations in 1965 revealed the probable remnants of mud brick architecture directly below the floor of a phase VI house (XVIII) in area L-

[3]The presence of the Natufian in area A7/8 has only recently been brought to my attention, and hence the estimate of the extent of the Natufian has been revised (contra Byrd 1987, 1988).

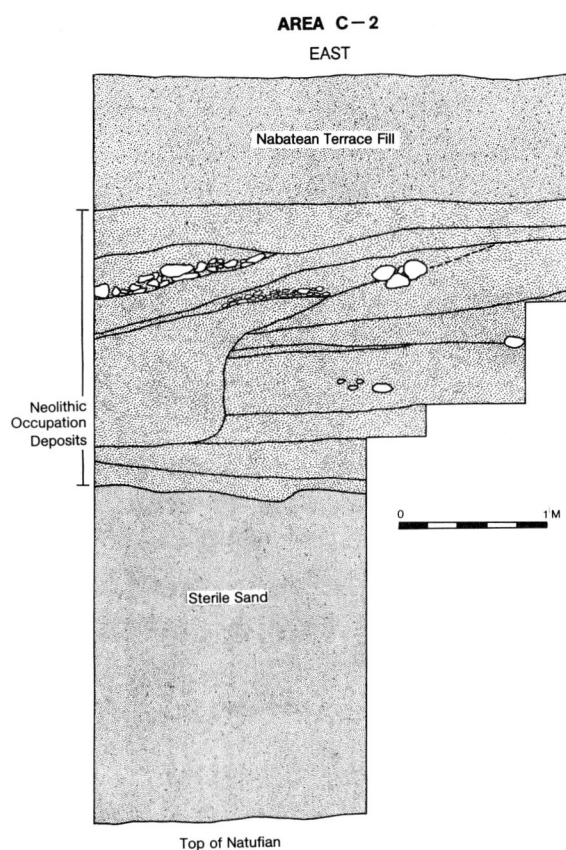

Fig. 5. East section of sounding in area C-2, revealing depth of deposit above the Natufian.

4/L-5. The chipped stone artifacts were designated as Natufian, thereby implying temporal continuity between the Natufian and the Neolithic (Kirkbride 1967: 10-12). Re-examination of the very small quantity of material recovered from this sounding reveals that the artifacts, including a few bladelets and bladelet cores, have a slight white patina, but lack the polished, glossy nature so characteristic of the early Natufian assemblage. There is also an absence of microliths or other tools characteristic of the Natufian (almost no tools were recovered). When these observations are combined with the fact that the Natufian is separated by a minimum of 1.5 meters of sterile alluvial deposit in area K-2, only ten meters away, it seems clear that this is not an early Natufian horizon, and, therefore, there is no evidence of mud brick architecture in the Natufian of Beidha. It is more likely that this represents a somewhat earlier Neolithic horizon, or possibly a very late Natufian occupation, that awaits the clarification of further excavation.

21

Fig. 6. View of Beidha from the southwest during excavation of the Natufian in areas K-2 and F-1 (location of later excavatons in area C-01 indicated by the arrow).

A broad scale excavation through the court-yard levels in the center of the site, primarily areas G-4, H-4 & J-4, was initiated in 1967. The ultimate objective was to expose, over several seasons, a large area down to the Natufian (Kirkbride 1968b: 90). During this penultimate season, however, only a small trench in area H-4, 2.0 by 1.75 meters at its maximum, was excavated through the alluvial sand to the Natufian. Furthermore, the sounding was not continued to the bottom of the Natufian horizon. This excavation did show, nevertheless, that the Natufian occupation extended somewhat further to the southeast than previously demonstrated.

Renewed excavations in 1983

The research objectives of the new Natufian excavations at Beidha were aimed at placing the settlement in an ecological context, gathering

further data on intrasite spatial patterning, and obtaining absolute dates for the occupation. These data, when combined with the results of the earlier campaigns, would then provide a clearer understanding of the nature of subsistence strategies, settlement intensity and occupational duration during the Natufian at Beidha.

Initially, a sounding was placed in area J-9, between the eastern edge of the tell and the out-lying structures exposed in 1967 (Kirkbride 1968b), to determine whether the Natufian horizon extended that far to the east (fig. 4). If the Natufian was present in this area, outside the tell, a broad horizontal excavation could be undertaken with little difficulty and danger. The results of this 2.6 by 2.4 meters sounding were negative. At a depth of three meters below the surface (93.58 meters absolute elevation) a thin lens of wadi gravels, pebbles and loose sand was uncovered. In this deposit were a small number of white patinated, polished artifacts similar in

22

AREA K−2

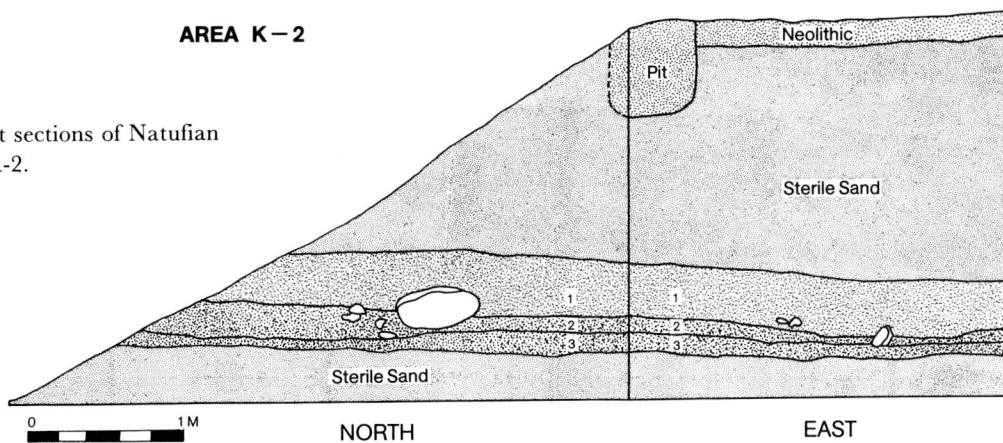

Fig. 7. North and east sections of Natufian excavations in area K-2.

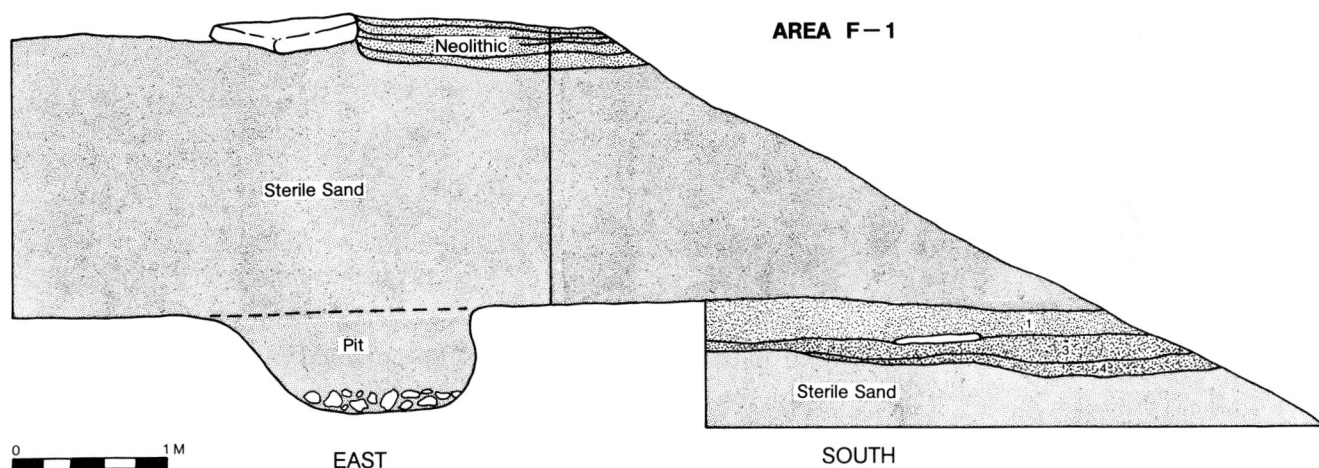

Fig. 8. South and east sections of Natufian excavations in area F-1.

AREA C−01

character to the Natufian. These may represent material which had been eroded from the Natufian horizon further to the north or west. No additional occupation evidence was identified, despite excavation to a depth of almost four meters below the surface and three meters below the base of the Neolithic (92.88 meters absolute elevation). This sounding did help, however, in delimiting the extent of the Natufian horizon.

A sounding was then undertaken on the western slope of the site. A trench, 2.5 by 1.0 meters in size, was excavated in area C-01 to determine how far the Natufian extended to the northwest.

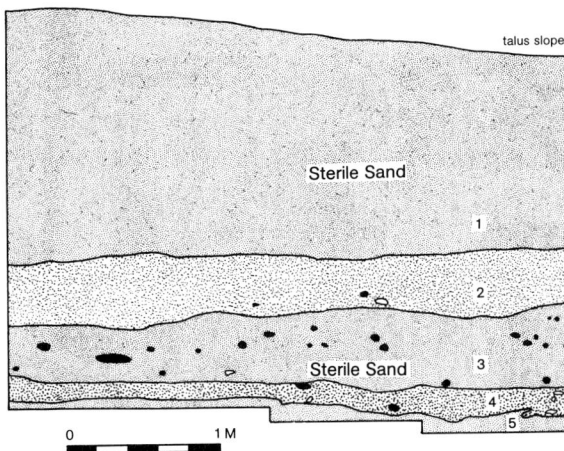

Fig. 9. East section of Natufian excavations in area C-01.

Fig. 10. Photographs of north and east sections of the Natufian excavations in area C-01.

The results were positive and a larger area of excavation, 4.0 by 4.0 meters, was opened up (fig. 4).[4] This excavation when combined with the excavations in areas K-2 and F-1 provides a well-spaced sample along the western talus slope. This has been the only location where sizable excavations could be conducted, avoiding the deep Neolithic deposits and, in part, the loose alluvial sand below the Neolithic which often collapsed into the trenches.

The excavation proceeded by one meter squares. All tools, cores and non-flint artifacts that were found *in situ* were plotted in three dimensions. The sediment was dry sieved using a 1 mm mesh, and artifacts recovered in the sieve were bagged by the meter square. Given the extremely loose nature of the sandy sediment and the distinctive white color of the artifacts, dry sieving worked well, and the recovery rate was probably almost equal to wet sieving and sorting

[4]The new excavation covered portions of four squares; C-00, C-01, D-00, D-01, and all artifacts were recorded with respect to meter squares within these areas. For the purposes of this report, however, the entire excavation is referred to as area C-01.

24

in the lab. Pollen, soil, flotation and radiocarbon samples were taken where appropriate. Flotation samples were recovered from hearths and areas of ashy occupational debris.

The excavations in area C-01 revealed five main deposits, two of which represent Natufian occupation episodes (fig. 9; see Field, Appendix A for a detailed sedimentological discussion). The most recent deposit is a culturally sterile, very pale brown (10YR 7/4) loosely compacted sand extending over 1.5 meters in thickness between the Natufian and the Neolithic (fig. 10). This material is alluvial and deposited from ephemeral streams. Near its base, alternating lenses of trough cross bedded sands and thin gravel beds occur. Underlying these lenses is the Natufian horizon of deposit 2, some 0.40 meters thick, consisting of compact light yellowish-brown (10YR 6/4) sand with a very low frequency of chipped-stone artifacts and one small stone-filled hearth. This deposit grades into deposit 3 which is a culturally sterile layer, 0.40 meters thick, of very pale brown (10YR 7/3) compact sand. This is underlain by a second

occupational horizon of brown (10YR 5/3) sand, layer 4, which averages 0.15 meters in thickness. It contained moderate densities of chipped-stone artifacts, some gray ashy areas and two small hearths. The lowest deposit exposed by the excavations is layer 5, a culturally sterile loose, very pale brown (10YR 7/4) sand. In layer 5, at the west edge of the area, was a lens of pebbles and gravels indicating the presence of an old drainage rivulet.

This excavation exposed several hearths, a control sample of the chipped-stone assemblage, and a number of radiocarbon samples suitable for tandem accelerator dating. However, no evidence of architectural features, well-made large grinding stones, or burials were found. In addition, faunal preservation, unlike the earlier excavations, and botanical preservation were extremely poor.

No radiocarbon dates were available for the Beidha Natufian prior to the 1983 excavations. This was due to the absence of large pieces of charcoal in the deposits, but with the development of the accelerator mass spectrometer technique for radiocarbon dating, the very small fragments of charcoal recovered during the 1983 excavations were suitable for dating.

Five radiocarbon samples of charcoal have been analyzed by the accelerator mass spectrometer facility at the University of Arizona, and the results are presented in table 1. The dates from the lower Natufian occupation, level 4, fall between 12,130 and 12,910 B.P. Although the dates on the wood charcoal may be slightly older than the occupation, they suggest habitation during the beginning of the early Natufian (Bar-Yosef 1983: 13). This confirms Kirkbride's initial designation, which was based on comparative stylistic grounds (Kirkbride 1960: 141). The range of the dates is consistent with recent results from two other early Natufian sites in Jordan, Wadi Judayid in the Ras en Naqb (Henry 1982) and Wadi Hammeh 27, in the Jordan Valley (Edwards 1987), both of which are dated prior to 12,000 B.P. The two dates from the upper Natufian deposit at Beidha, level 2, do not overlap with each other, but both are considerably later than those from level 4. It seems probable that sample AA-1461, 8,390 B.P., is intrusive from the Neolithic levels. If the other date of 10,910 B.P. obtained from level 2 can be considered accurate, then that would suggest occupation near the juncture between the early and late phases of the Natufian.

25

Lab	Provenience	Date
AA-1463	C-01-24 level 4	12,910+/-250 B.P.
AA-1465	C-00-16 level 4	12,450+/-170 B.P.
AA-1464	C-01-23 level 4 (hearth 2)	12,130+/-190 B.P.
AA-1462	C-01-24 level 2	10,910+/-520 B.P.
AA-1461	C-00-16 level 2	8,390+/-390 B.P.

Table 1. Accelerator radiocarbon dates on charcoal from the Natufian at Beidha (conducted by the Accelerator Mass Spectrometer facility at the University of Arizona).

Summary

Natufian occupation has been identified in six areas of the site. In four localities consisting of approximately 54 square meters at their maximum, the excavations continued into the Natufian horizon and yielded cultural remains. In the two main excavations of the early seasons, K/J-2 and F-1, the depth and nature of the deposit are similar – the thickness of the Natufian ranged between 0.4 and 0.6 meters and three depositional phases were distinguished within a continuous sequence (i.e. no occupational gaps were observed in the depositional history).

In contrast, the recent excavations, further to the north in C-01, revealed a different stratigraphic sequence. Here only two occupation horizons occurred with a hiatus in occupation occurring in between. The thin lower occupation phase appears similar to occupation deposits from the other excavation areas, both in terms of the density of artifacts and their character, while the upper phase is dissimilar – it has an extremely low density of artifacts with a different character. The full implication of these distinctions with respect to the nature of the Natufian settlement at Beidha will be explored in Chapter 6.

4. Analytical approach to the Beidha chipped-stone assemblage

Chipped stone artifacts represent the overwhelming majority of cultural residue throughout most of human development, their pre-eminence in the Old World spanning over two million years, until their gradual replacement by the broken fragments of ceramic vessels. Given the ubiquitous nature of chipped stone artifacts and given that they represent the primary evidence of variability in human activity, they have been subject to intensive research. It is fortunate that the intrinsic nature of chipped stone manufacture, a reductive technology, enables us to make inferences about the steps involved in the production and use of these artifacts.

A number of factors affect the final appearance of a chipped stone assemblage. These include the available raw material, the steps in the reductive technology and the range of artifacts which were produced, the tasks for which these artifacts were then used, the effect of settlement pattern variability (including length and intensity of occupation, and the organization of tasks) and the influence of style on the appearance of the assemblage (e.g. Binford 1978, 1982; Jelinek 1976; Odell 1981; Sheppard 1987). The frequency of different classes of artifacts and their relative ratios (such as debitage, cores, cortical flakes, and tools) are affected to different degrees by the interrelationships of these variables (Sullivan 1987).

The Beidha Natufian chipped stone analysis focuses on the nature of the reduction sequence, the types of retouched tools that were produced, and the identification of intrasite spatial or temporal patterns in the distribution of different artifact types. The results of these analyses are then evaluated in terms of the implications they have for the range of tasks which were conducted at the site.

Technology and the reduction sequence

The examination of the techniques used in the production of chipped stone artifacts has been a major focus of prehistoric research during the last 20 years (for example, Crabtree 1972; Brezillon 1968; Tixier *et al.* 1980). In the analysis of Epipaleolithic assemblages from North Africa and the Near East, interest has concentrated on the classification and morphological description of flakes removed from cores, the cores themselves, and the steps involved in the manufacturing and resharpening of tools, particularly in the retouching and backing of bladelets (e.g. Tixier 1963; Bar-Yosef 1970; Marks 1976, 1977, 1983). In addition, there have been detailed studies of the core reduction process either by analysis of the flake scar patterns (for example, Suzuki and Akazawa 1971) or, more recently, by the laborious strategy of backfitting flakes removed from cores (Volkman 1983).

The study of Natufian assemblages has paralleled these general trends. Henry's study of 11 Palestinian Natufian assemblages was the first detailed study of Natufian debitage (Henry 1973b: 56-69). The research mainly involved a description of debitage attributes and their relationships to technological trends. The range of attributes studied for the Beidha Natufian debitage builds directly on Henry's study, with only limited modifications.

Recently, two monographs on this topic have been published. Valla studied the Natufian assemblage from Ain Mallaha with comparative analyses of material from el Wad, Hayonim Terrace and Nahal Oren (Valla 1984: 21-32). Although this research mainly emphasized tool manufacture and typology, debitage and core manufacturing techniques at Ain Mallaha were also examined. In addition, Calley conducted an attribute analysis of the debitage and cores from

Mureybet, including an examination of the manufacturing techniques of the late Natufian occupation phase IA (Calley 1984, 1986).

Analysis of the manufacturing techniques of the Beidha Natufian chipped stone assemblage entailed consideration of the raw material used, the nature of the cores and initial reduction pieces, characterization of the debitage produced, identification of the major debitage categories of the industry, the selection of blanks for tool manufacture, and the techniques used for segmenting bladelets prior to their shaping into microliths. In addition, the process of manufacturing backed bladelets was studied, and is included in the context of a discussion of microliths.

The nature of the raw material, its quality, size and possible source location can contribute important evidence for understanding a number of characteristics of the assemblage, including the maximum size of artifacts and variation in the degree of utilization. Examination of variability in the form of relative frequencies of different classes of debitage provides insight into the relative emphasis on different types of manufacture and the steps within these manufacturing processes. Primary elements and crested elements indicate the degree and nature of initial core reduction. Core tablets, a product of the rejuvenation of platforms on cores, can impart evidence of a particular way of extending the life of a core, the reduction technique, and occasionally the original size of the raw material and the intensity of its reduction. The presence of blades and bladelets demonstrates the use of a specialized form of reduction, and they are an important feature of Natufian industries. Exhausted cores can also deliver information on raw material sources, the intensity of reduction, and the nature of the final debitage types that were removed.

The debitage classes, their subcategories, and the definitions used to distinguish them appear in Appendix E. Most of the terms used are standard in Old World prehistoric research and have been consistently employed for some time. In particular, this study relies heavily on the terminology and definitions of debitage classes presented by Marks (1976: 371-383) and Henry (1973b: 60-61), supplemented by the excellent discussions of Tixier (1963: 24-42) and Brezillon (1968: 69-105). The only category that may be

treated somewhat differently is that of fragments. Considerable attention was given to the distinction between flakes, blades, and fragments as a result of difficulties encountered in separating the debitage classes of blades and flakes in this assemblage.

The term "blade" is used throughout this discussion to include bladelets and blades, except when otherwise noted. The standard definition of a blade as a flake with length (on axis of flaking) greater than twice its width (Tixier 1963: 37) was used, and there was no difficulty in placing complete pieces in the blade or the flake category. Questionable pieces were simply measured. The blade and flake categories were further subdivided into complete pieces, microflakes/blades, and large fragments (Appendix E). Microflakes/blades were defined as complete pieces less than 1 cm in maximum length.

Classification of broken pieces of debitage (identified as debitage based on the presence of a recognizable interior and exterior), however, presented a major difficulty. If a broken piece had an extant length twice as great as its width, it was classified as a blade, while if the estimated original shape was of flake dimensions (i.e. the converging laterals made the original size apparent), it was so classified. These large fragments were then further subdivided depending on which segment of the original piece they represented (Appendix E: 1b, 2b).

If neither of these conditions was met, the broken piece was initially placed in the indeterminate debitage category. This category is subdivided into small fragments with parallel sides and flake scars, and other, indeterminate, fragments. This distinction was made in an attempt to estimate what portion of these fragments were originally blades or flakes.

After the classification of the debitage from each deposit was complete, samples were drawn from the categories of complete blades, complete flakes, and small fragments of indeterminate debitage (those with parallel sides and flake scars), and analyzed for variability in a number of metric and morphological features. The primary objective was to identify patterned variability related to the reduction sequence. In addition, blades were sampled in enough detail to reveal any spatial or temporal variability in metric and morphological features. Seven random samples of complete blades were selected from the main excavation areas. They included samples from each occupation level in areas J-2 (levels 1, 2 & 3), and C-01 (levels 2 & 4) for an examination of changes in the nature of blade manufacture over time. Two more random samples were taken from area K-2 (level 1) and area F-1 (level 1) to facilitate examination of spatial variability in blade characteristics. Three random samples of flakes and indeterminate fragments were selected from area J-2 (level 1) and area C-01 (levels 2 & 4). The total number of artifacts studied was 995; including 620 blades, 229 flakes and 156 indeterminate fragments of debitage. Appendix F presents a list of the features and categories examined: length, width, thickness, completeness of the blank, cortex, platform type, lateral profile, exterior flake scar pattern, distal shape, skew class, and raw material type.

Microburin products were also examined in some detail. This involved recording the same features examined for the debitage, along with the location of notches and type of retouch used (Appendix F). These additional features were examined in order to identify recurrent patterns in the use of the technique.

During the analysis of the tools, observations were made regarding the nature of the blanks selected for retouching. Although many tools had been retouched so extensively that none of the original features are discernible, some tools still retained evidence of their original size. Completeness of blank, tool blank category, length, width, thickness, and raw material type were recorded (Appendix F). This information was then contrasted with the results of the study of the debitage that had not been selected for retouching to provide insight into the variation between the debitage that was selected for tool manufacture and that which was not selected.

The cores were also studied, although not in as detailed a manner as the debitage. The analysis included classification as to core type (Appendix G), cortical features, and raw material (Appendix F). Length, width, and thickness measurements were also made.

Tool typologies and analysis of retouched pieces

The study of retouched chipped stone artifacts has been an important component of prehistoric archaeology, and emphasis has been placed on the study of the shape (or morphology) of artifacts, and on the manufacturing techniques that produced them. Bordes's classic study of lower and middle Paleolithic retouched artifacts emphasized typological analysis and the use of a type list for ordering and describing lithic assemblages (Bordes 1961). This approach has facilitated the quantitative comparison of different assemblages. There has been, however, discussion on the merits of chipped stone tool typologies. Researchers have pointed out that accurate typological work requires considerable experience, and that comparisons between assemblages should take into account the geographical region, the time period in question, and the type and origin of the raw material (Fish 1981; Cahen and van Noten 1971).

Comparative typological studies of Near Eastern Epipaleolithic chipped stone tools have been undertaken only relatively recently. The first was Bar-Yosef's (1970) dissertation which built on the detailed comparative studies of similar industries outside the Near East, particularly Sonneville-Bordes and Perrot's (1953) research on European Upper Paleolithic assemblages, and Tixier's (1963) detailed study of the Epipaleolithic of the Maghreb, North Africa. Tixier's study has been particularly influential since a number of Near Eastern prehistorians have used it as a starting point for developing their own typologies.

Bar-Yosef's study of the Epipaleolithic industries of Palestine focused on developing an adequate regional type list, examining indices of chipped stone tool morphology and technology, and emphasizing microliths as the "fossile directeur" of the time period (Bar-Yosef 1970: 2). Recognizing the need for a regionally specific typology (Bordes 1950), Bar-Yosef attempted to define locally distinct microliths, to emphasize their trend toward geometric forms over time, to increase the list of problematic tools (particularly carinated, nucleiform, and core scrapers), and to include distinctive Natufian tools in the type list for comparison with the earlier Epipaleolithic industries (Bar-Yosef 1970: 17).

Ninety six tool types were defined, and these were divided into twelve tool groups: scrapers, nosed, carinated and core scrapers, multiple tools, burins, retouched and backed blades, truncated pieces, points, microliths, geometric microliths, microburins, notches and denticulates, and diverse other tools (Bar-Yosef 1970: 19-20, 202). Overall, emphasis was placed on the earlier Epipaleolithic industries of the Kebaran and Geometric Kebaran.

Henry, in his dissertation research on the Natufian of Palestine, built on Bar-Yosef's study, placing more emphasis on characteristically Natufian tools (particularly geometrics, notches and "massive pieces"), and a category for utilized pieces (pieces which showed evidence of tool use, but were not intentionally retouched) was added (Henry 1973b: 53-56). The utilized pieces include pieces with sheen and use retouch, and hammerstones. In addition, microburins were removed from the tool list and classified, more appropriately, within the debitage categories. Although no explicit definitions were given, presumably the definitions provided by Bar-Yosef (1970) and/or Tixier (1963) were used. Henry's analytical procedure involved calculating percentages, conventional indices, means, standard deviations, and metric data on the tool assemblages (Henry 1973b: 75-79). Covariation analysis was used to identify degrees of similarity, and cluster analysis was used to measure distance between different assemblages.

Hours, focusing on Upper and Epipaleolithic assemblages, presented the results of the 1969 London Symposium on Near Eastern chipped stone tool types (Hours 1974). The use of two tool type lists was proposed; a long, detailed list and a short one for comparison and preliminary reports. The long list consisted of 121 tool types (including four microburin products) subdivided into 13 groups: end scrapers, burins, borers, knives and backed pieces, truncations, notches and denticulates, composite tools, retouched pieces, special tools, nongeometric microliths, geometric microliths, diverse, and microburins. It was asserted that previously the tool groups of backed pieces, multiple tools, burins on truncations, and carinated scrapers had been subdivided too finely.

The Negev Prehistoric Project, which included excavations at two Natufian sites, provided a glossary of the technological and typological terms used (Marks 1976: 371-378). The list emphasized new types. In general, the other categories were based on Tixier's definitions (Tixier 1963).

More recently, Valla's study of the chipped stone tools at four Natufian sites in Palestine attempted to identify chronological divisions within the Natufian. This was done by analyzing variability in chipped stone tool types in relationship to stratigraphic data (Valla 1984: 21). Both Bar-Yosef's (1970) and Hours's (1974) typologies were used, although some modifications were made. Among Valla's modifications of Bar-Yosef's typology were elimination of types 16-19 (now recognized as cores), and classification of the infrequent tool types of micropoints as Falita points, fragments of backed truncated pieces as geometrics, and massive pieces under their specific types. Modifications of Hours's typology included classification of the infrequent micropoints as pointed bladelets, backed and truncated bladelets as Kebarah points, and fragments of backed and truncated pieces as bladelets with two truncations. Two new categories, end fragments of tools and unidentifiable fragments of microliths, were added to both lists.

In using the two typologies, Valla noted some difficulties. Both typologies focused on the Kebaran and Geometric Kebaran rather than on the Natufian and epi-Natufian (Valla 1984: 22-23). In addition, the two typologies differed with respect to the key variables on which they were based. Bar-Yosef's approach tended to emphasize overall morphology, while Hours's analysis clearly stressed the choice of retouch in identifying tool types. Valla suggested that both dealt poorly with the classification of notched pieces, blades with fine retouch or use wear, simple retouched flakes and blades, and fragments.

Olszewski's (1986) analysis of the late Epipaleolithic chipped stone tools from Abu Hureyra, Syria, depended primarily on Tixier's (1963) North African typology. Recent modifications of that typology (Inizan and Tixier 1980) were also taken into account. Her list of tools contained 74 types, subdivided into 12 categories: scrapers, borers/perforators, burins, sickle blades, lunates, other geometric microliths, nongeometric microliths, notches and/or denticulates, massive scrapers, picks, chisels, and various tools.

In Goring-Morris' research on the Epipaleolithic of the Negev and Sinai, the typology, in which 15 tool classes and 115 tool types were distinguished, is based, with some differences, on Bar-Yosef's study (Goring-Morris 1987: 50-55). The typology does place more emphasis on morphology, yet types such as Helwan bladelets and lunates are still utilized. In addition, attribute analysis was conducted of the scrapers and microliths in an attempt to identify stylistic variation between groups of sites.

In comparing how different scholars have classified Natufian chipped stone tools, discrepancies are readily apparent, and this forces comparisons of published Natufian assemblages to be restricted to the level of tool class (e.g. Henry 1973b; Olszewski 1986). It is on this level that studies of functional variation between assemblages is most appropriate, while studies of variability at the sub-class level appear to be more affected by stylistic parameters (Goring-Morris 1987: 50; Close 1978). Classificatory variability between the different typologies includes: variation in emphasis of morphological and retouch features in distinguishing tool types; whether or not debitage blank type (flake, blade, bladelet) is a criterion in distinguishing tool types; and the use of categories for fragments, particularly of microliths, which are typically the most numerically frequent microlithic group. All of these differences hamper rigorous comparisons between assemblages.

Study of the Beidha chipped stone tools concentrates on two aspects: their typological classification and the ways in which they were manufactured.

Initially, in an effort to formulate a replicable classification for the retouched tools, the typologies of Bar-Yosef, Henry, and Hours were examined, and an attempt was made to integrate them. This was difficult, since it was sometimes impossible to determine exactly how particular terms were defined and, for Henry and Hours, no definitions or illustrations were provided to assist in clarifying obscure aspects (although Hours states extensive reliance on Tixier's definitions). After development of an initial classification, a trial analysis was conducted on a sample of the Beidha tools assemblage, and

then this was subsequently revised in light of the problems encountered. This included drawing a distinction between bilateral and unilateral retouched end scrapers, a revision of the notch and denticulate tool group in an attempt to better characterize patterns in the variation of small notches and simple retouch, and the addition of the tool type of asymmetrical lunates (Appendix G).

One area where this study differs from previous ones concerns the use of blank type in the classification of tool type. Typically, blank type was only recorded later in the detailed attribute analysis phase. For example, separate tool types are not distinguished for retouched blades, bladelets, and flakes (as in Hours 1974). Nor were backed blades and bladelets distinguished as separate tool types. Only in the category of end scrapers were some flake tools identified. This was done because for many Natufian tools the original category of blank could not be definitively identified due to extensive retouch.

A second area of obvious difference between this typology and those used previously is that the initial classification of the backed pieces was based on an explicitly morphological approach. The shape of the backed edge and of the ends was emphasized, rather than the type of backing or retouch. For example, there are not separate types for Helwan lunates and lunates manufactured by other forms of retouch. Variation in retouch was, nevertheless, examined in detail during the attribute analysis.

A third area of difference concerns the treatment of fragments. The lack of categories for fragments seems to be a major drawback of most previous studies (yet see Valla 1984), as researchers, presumably, had to classify fragments as particular tool types on the basis of incomplete information. When the majority of a tool is still present the tool can be classified accurately with considerable confidence, while in other situations the classification will be less accurate. In this study, fragments of nonmicrolithic tools whose tool type cannot be accurately determined were placed in the tool type of indeterminate retouched fragment. With respect to backed pieces, most fragments were assigned to one of several backed fragment categories. The major exception to this prescription concerned lunates where if over half of a lunate was present, it was so classified.

The working typology had 94 types divided into 11 classes. The tool classes included: scrapers, multiple tools, burins, notches and denticulates, truncations, drills, retouched pieces, geometric microliths, nongeometric microliths, backed microlithic fragments, and various (Appendix G, figures 40-42).

In addition to the examination of variation in the frequency of different tool types, analysis of the complete sample of tools also entailed examination of morphological and retouch characteristics within a tool class. These included: length, width, thickness, completeness, retouch location, percentage retouched, type of retouch, shape of the backed edge, shape of the retouched ends, retouch on the ends themselves, edge damage on the cutting edge of microliths, and presence of sickle polish (Appendix F).

The analysis was concerned with variation within and between each of these tool groups. Emphasis was placed on the microliths, particularly with respect to the nature of the backing retouch, and size dimensions, since these have been shown to vary significantly through time (Bar-Yosef and Valla 1979).

Intrasite spatial and temporal variability

Analysis of site structure, the internal variability in the distribution of artifacts and cultural features, involves a number of assumptions regarding the nature of the distribution of artifacts. These assumptions include spatial segregation of activities, and subsequent spatial relationships between the artifacts that provide evidence of these tasks (see O'Connell 1987; Carr 1984). This research has shown that there is considerable variability in the amount of spatial segregation of activities and the distribution of the residue which those behaviors create (Yellen 1977; Gould 1967; O'Connell 1977, 1987; Binford 1980). Ethnographic research has also demonstrated that small artifacts, such as chipping debris, are more likely to remain in primary context, while larger artifacts are often moved and redeposited as secondary refuse (Binford 1978; O'Connell 1977; Schiffer 1972).

O'Connell has argued, based on his research with the Alyawara of central Australia, that the primary factors which affect the appearance of prehistoric hunter-gatherer archaeological assemblages are the degree of food storage, seasonal variation in the weather, household population size, and the length of time that activity areas are used (O'Connell 1987). Length and intensity of occupation are particularly important factors that affect the nature of the chipped stone artifact assemblage (Hayden 1978; Binford 1978; Sullivan 1987) and, hence, variation in chipped stone artifacts have the potential to yield information on the nature of settlement intensity.

The Beidha analysis examined spatial variability in the distribution of chipped stone artifacts between excavation areas to determine whether inferences can be made regarding spatial distribution in stages of chipped stone manufacturing or in the processing of other material for which stone tools were used. The analysis entails an examination of variation in the frequencies of flakes versus blades, small blades and flakes, microburins, and tool groups. Statistical measures of association serve to evaluate the significance of the variation. Finally, these same variables are examined to determine whether there are changes over time in their frequencies in the occupation horizons of the Natufian.

5. Analysis of the chipped-stone assemblage

This chapter presents a detailed analysis of the chipped stone assemblage from the Natufian horizon at Beidha. The major components of the discussion include the nature of the reduction technology, tool typological variability, tool manufacturing techniques, and spatial and temporal variability in artifact distribution.

Reduction strategy

In examining the steps in the reduction process discussion concentrates on the raw material used, the nature of the cores and the initial reduction pieces, the major debitage categories of the industry, the selection of blanks for tool manufacture, and spatial and temporal variability with respect to the reduction technology.

Raw material

The raw material exploited, as evidenced by the core and the debitage samples, is almost entirely (over 99%) a fine-grained flint. The patina on the flint ranges in color from white to gray to blue-gray, and the surface has also been altered by wind polishing to produce a somewhat shiny and in places quite glossy appearance. Fresh breaks reveal a dull grayish interior which is probably the original color of the flint prior to weathering and chemical alteration. Less than 1% of the cores are a coarse chert: either light brown or cream color with darker inclusions.

The relative frequency of chert as a raw material is slightly higher among retouched tools than among either the cores or the unretouched debitage sample (table 2). In addition, the use of chert varies significantly between different tool groups. Chi-square test results show that chert is represented in significantly higher frequencies in the end scraper and various tool groups than for other tools (table 3).[5] Similar results were obtained when these two tool groups, end scrapers and various tools, are compared with the cores or the debitage sample. When the other

tool groups are contrasted with the cores and the debitage sample the results indicate that there are no significant differences between the two.

There are two possible explanations for the difference in raw material frequencies between the end scraper and various tools, and the debitage and cores: either, the coarser grained tools were not manufactured on the site (or not in the areas excavated), but at the source of the raw material, or the coarser grained material represents an outer "skin" of the finer raw material. While on a few artifacts both coarse and fine grained material are present in a layered structure, the absence of chert debitage suggests that the first explanation is more likely. Undoubtedly the fine quality flint was worth bringing back to the site as blocks of raw material, but only already completed tools of chert were worth transporting. Furthermore, the coarser chert is not well suited for the production of microliths and other finely manufactured tools, hence, it is not surprising that the two tool classes with the largest average dimensions have higher frequencies of chert.

The cortex still remaining on the cores was examined in order to gain insight into the source of the flint. In the majority of cases, the cortex had been totally removed (81.2%, N=452). However, approximately one fifth of the cores still had some cortex remaining; it was generally battered in appearance (11.7%) and occasionally simply rounded in shape (6.4%). Only rarely was the exterior surface flat, suggesting the use of tabular flint. Thus, the source of most of the flint appears to have been cobbles which had been eroded out from the flint deposits in the limestone hills to the east of the site. Today, such cobbles are not uncommon in the wadis of the Beidha area (Kirkbride 1985: 122). The tabular flint sources in the nearby hills of Jebel Shara appear not to have been directly exploited.

[5]A similar pattern has been observed at the early Natufian site of Wadi Hammeh 27, where coarse-grained chert was used more often for the larger tools (Edwards 1987: 144).

	Flint	Lt. brown chert	Speckled chert	Other chert	Total%	N
Scrapers	83.4	8.7	3.9	3.9	99.9	332
Burins	98.2	0.0	0.0	1.8	100.0	111
Notches & denticulates	99.4	0.3	0.0	0.2	99.9	870
Drills & borers	100.0	0.0	0.0	0.0	100.0	32
Retouched pieces	97.1	1.4	0.4	1.1	100.0	277
Multiple tools	98.8	0.0	1.2	0.0	100.0	85
Truncations	100.0	0.0	0.0	0.0	100.0	186
Lunates	99.5	0.3	0.0	0.3	100.1	367
Triangles	100.0	0.0	0.0	0.0	100.0	7
Nongeometrics	100.0	0.0	0.0	0.0	100.0	158
Backed fragments	100.0	0.0	0.0	0.0	100.0	370
Various	92.9	5.7	0.0	1.4	100.0	70
Total	97.3	1.4	0.5	0.8	100.0	2866

Table 2. Relative frequency of raw material types by tool group.

	N	Chi-square	D.F.	P
Scraper & various tools versus remaining tools	2866	257.6	1	<.001
Scraper & various tools versus debitage	1022	105.6	1	<.001
Scraper & various tools versus cores	860	76.8	1	<.001
Other tools versus debitage	3084	0.004	1	.946
Other tools versus cores	2922	0.7	1	.795

D.F.: Degrees of Freedom
P: Significance

Table 3. Chi-square results of variability in the frequency of raw material between tool groups, cores and debitage.

Cores and initial core reduction pieces

Over 400 cores were recovered, and their frequency varies between provenience units from 1% to 4% of the assemblage (table 4). Blade cores, defined by having a predominance of flake scars that are of blade dimensions, dominate the assemblage (table 5). Most are single platform blade cores of which the subtypes subpyramidal (fig. 11:a,b,e), single face (fig. 11:d, fig. 12:c), and pyramidal (fig. 11:c) are present in decreasing frequencies. Multiplatform blade cores, both opposed platform and 90 degree platforms, occur in lower frequencies (fig. 12:a,b,d). Flake cores represent only 3% of the assemblage.

Intensive reduction of cores was commonplace. The ratio of total debitage to cores is quite high, averaging 50:1. In general, cores are small and fully exhausted; hinge fractures and crushed platforms are frequent. Blade core size averages 37 mm by 32 mm by 26 mm – and bladelet sized flake scars predominate. The average size of the

small number of flake cores was only slightly larger, averaging 44 mm by 42 mm by 28 mm.

When the ratio of flake and blade debitage to cores is examined, considerable variability is apparent between excavation units (table 6). In general, all levels in area K-2 and level 3 of area F-1 are characterized by higher values, ranging between 80:1 and 117:1. The remainder of the provenience units have considerably lower debitage-core ratios, ranging from 22:1 to 56:1. The higher debitage/core ratios of the former provenience units suggests either that more intensive reduction was occurring in these areas, creating more debitage, or that fewer cores were discarded there.

Debitage that characterizes initial steps in the reduction sequence are scarce, as primary elements range in frequency between 2% and 7% of the assemblage (table 4). The ratio of primary elements to cores, 2:1, is quite low – similar to that at Rosh Horesha and Rosh Zin (Henry 1976: 325; Marks and Larson 1977:

Area	Level	Blades	Flakes	CTE	CT	BS	MbP	PE	Cores	(Tools)	Subtotal%	N	Debris	ID	Total
K-2	1	48.0	42.8	0.2	0.2	0.4	3.4	3.8	1.1	(11.0)	99.9	5270	1008	1117	7395
	2	46.8	43.9	0.1	0.3	0.3	2.7	4.7	1.1	(9.5)	99.9	2809	364	346	3519
	3	51.2	40.5	0.0	0.3	0.3	1.8	5.0	0.8	(10.6)	99.9	1059	154	82	1295
Subtotal		48.0	42.9	0.2	0.2	0.3	3.0	4.2	1.1	(10.5)	99.9	9138	1526	1545	12209
F-1	1	47.4	44.5	0.1	0.1	0.3	1.4	4.2	1.9	(9.2)	99.9	718	103	62	883
	2	50.0	25.0	0.0	0.0	0.0	0.0	25.0	0.0	(0.0)	100.0	4	0	0	4
	3	52.8	40.9	0.0	0.4	0.8	1.3	2.5	1.3	(12.1)	100.0	240	59	26	325
	4	51.8	40.2	0.0	0.6	0.0	1.2	3.1	3.1	(9.3)	100.0	162	27	25	214
Subtotal		49.2	43.0	0.1	0.3	0.4	1.3	3.7	1.9	(9.8)	99.9	1124	189	113	1426
J-2	1	50.9	37.7	0.7	0.3	0.2	1.9	4.7	3.6	(21.4)	100.0	2917	366	405	3688
	2	49.6	41.9	0.5	0.2	0.3	1.4	3.9	2.1	(12.6)	99.9	5684	870	583	7137
	3	47.2	45.7	0.4	0.5	0.3	1.4	2.7	1.8	(10.1)	100.0	959	141	85	1185
Subtotal		49.8	40.9	0.5	0.3	0.3	1.5	4.1	2.5	(15.1)	99.9	9560	1377	1073	12010
F-1	1 (1964)	48.6	42.0	0.1	0.6	0.5	0.5	3.0	4.6	(14.9)	99.9	801	67	91	959
H-4	55	46.9	40.9	0.4	0.4	0.9	4.8	2.2	3.5	(22.1)	100.0	231	29	32	292
C-01	2	41.8	46.7	0.7	0.2	0.7	1.8	4.7	3.5	(12.0)	100.1	450	91	101	642
	3	45.1	36.4	0.0	1.7	0.0	7.6	5.0	4.2	(4.2)	100.0	119	27	28	174
	4	44.6	37.6	0.1	0.9	0.0	8.1	7.0	1.8	(8.4)	100.1	1498	146	256	1900
Subtotal		43.9	39.5	0.2	0.8	0.2	6.7	6.4	2.3	(8.9)	100.0	2067	264	385	2716
Total		48.5	41.8	0.3	0.3	0.3	2.6	4.3	2.0	(12.5)	100.1	22921	3452	3239	29612

CTE: Core trimming element
CT: Core tablet
BS: Burin spall
MbP: Microburin product
PE: Primary element
ID: Indeterminate debitage

Table 4. Frequency distribution of debitage classes by provenience unit.

202).[6] The ratio of primary elements to flake and blade debitage is shown in table 6. The lowest ratios, less than 26:1, characterize the majority of the provenience units, including K-2 levels 1-3, F-1 level 1, J-2 levels 1 and 2, and area C-01 levels 2 and 4. Slightly higher ratios, greater than 32:1, are seen in F-1 levels 3 and 4, J-2 level 3, F-1 level 1 (1964), and H-4 level 55. The provenience units with higher ratios of primary elements to flake and blade debitage may have been locations where slightly more initial reduction took place. The general overall low frequency of primary elements, however, indicates that

initial core shaping, prior to extensive reduction, occurred primarily off-site or in areas of the site that were not excavated.

Core trimming elements, created during the initial formation of the blade core, are quite rare (table 4). The ratio of core trimming elements to cores is 1:6. Their scarcity corresponds with the rarity of primary elements, further supporting the argument that initial core shaping and preparation took place elsewhere – as observed at some other Natufian sites – e.g., Hatoula (Lechevallier and Ronen 1985: 20). It is possible, however, that the technique of core preparation which yields core trimming elements as a by-product was rarely used in the reduction process. These elements, although rarely discussed in any detail, occur in low frequencies at most Natufian sites (e.g. Edwards 1987: 163; Henry 1976: 325; Goring-Morris 1987: 287; Marks and Larson 1977: 202-203).

[6]Other Natufian chipped stone studies have defined primary elements differently, making comparisons more hazardous. Different approaches include defining primary elements as having more that 20% or 30% cortex, or not distinguishing such a category, preferring to examine cortex variability in the context of separate debitage categories such as flakes and blades (e.g. Goring-Morris 1987: 49; Calley 1986: 13; Olszewski 1986: 200).

a

b

0   cms   3

c

d

e

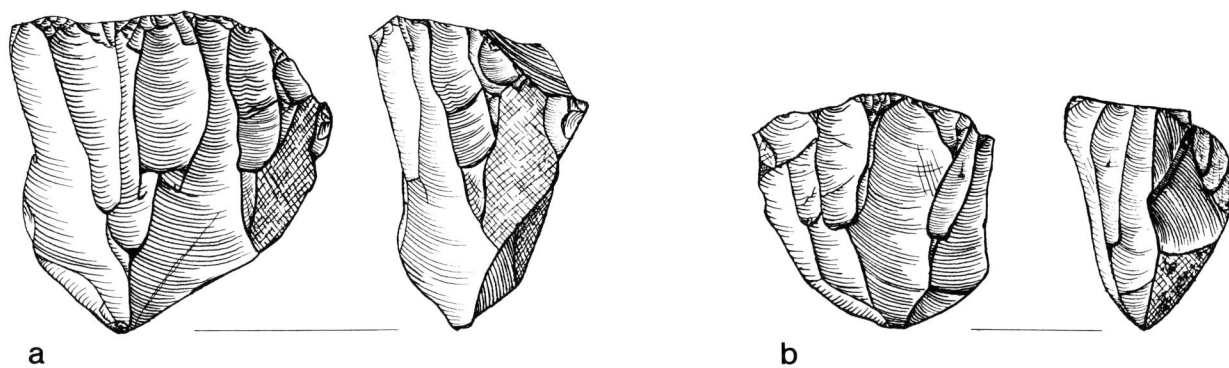

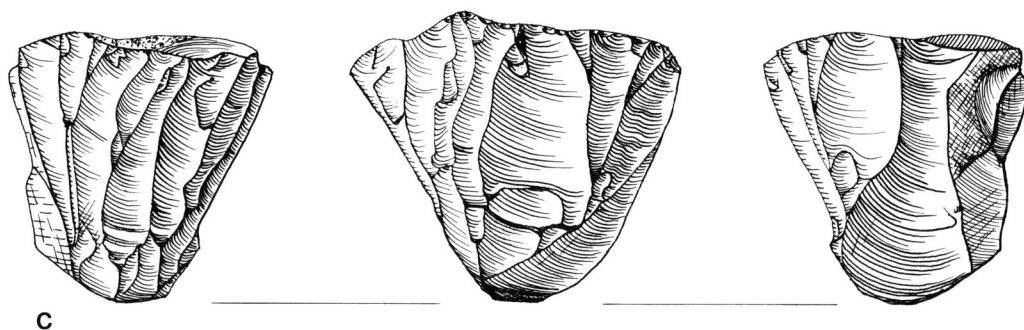

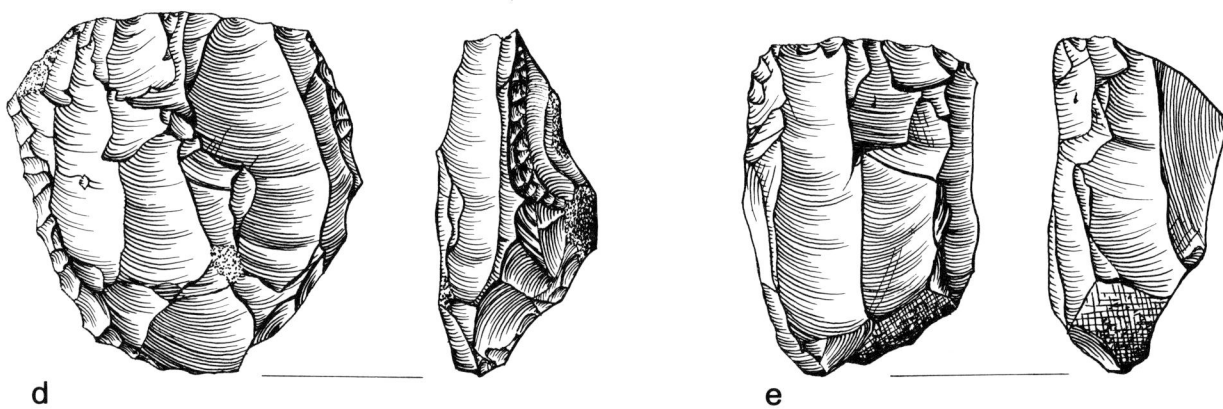

Fig. 11. Blade cores.

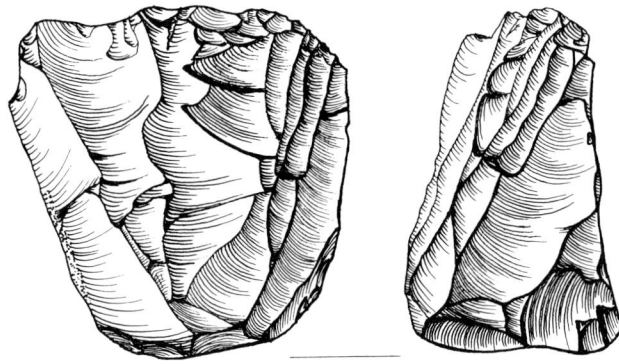

a

b

0   cms   3

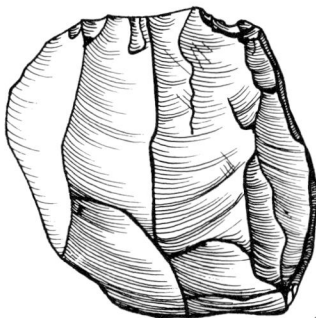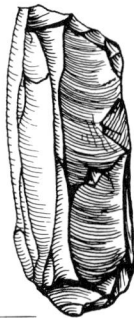

c

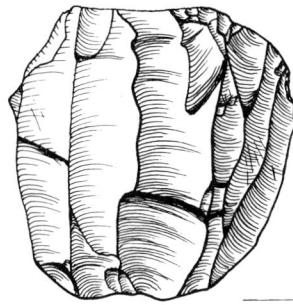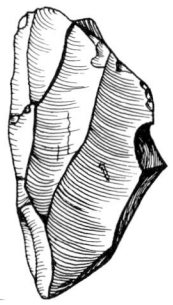

d

Fig. 12. Blade cores.

| Area | Level | Blade cores | | | | Flake | Ind | Total% | N |
		Single	Opposed	Ninety	Fragment				
K-2	1	49.2	8.5	11.9	8.5	5.1	16.9	100.1	59
	2	51.7	13.8	0.0	13.8	6.9	13.8	100.0	29
	3	55.6	0.0	22.2	11.1	0.0	11.1	100.0	9
Subtotal		50.5	9.3	9.3	10.3	5.2	15.5	100.1	97
F-1	1	42.9	14.3	7.1	28.6	0.0	7.1	100.0	14
	3	33.3	0.0	0.0	33.3	0.0	33.3	99.9	3
	4	0.0	0.0	0.0	20.0	0.0	0.0	100.0	5
Subtotal		50.0	9.1	4.6	27.3	0.0	9.1	100.1	22
J-2	1	58.1	9.5	2.9	19.0	3.8	6.7	100.0	105
	2	62.5	7.5	8.3	15.0	0.8	5.8	99.9	120
	3	64.7	5.9	11.8	11.8	0.0	5.9	100.1	17
Subtotal		60.7	8.3	6.2	16.5	2.1	6.2	100.0	242
F-1	1 (1964)	70.3	2.7	2.7	21.6	0.0	2.7	100.0	37
H-4	55	75.0	12.5	0.0	12.5	0.0	0.0	100.0	8
C-01	2	50.0	8.3	0.0	0.0	25.0	16.7	100.0	12
	3	80.0	0.0	0.0	20.0	0.0	0.0	100.0	5
	4	60.0	8.0	4.0	12.0	8.0	8.0	100.0	25
Subtotal		59.5	7.1	2.4	9.5	11.9	9.5	99.9	42
Total		58.9	8.0	6.0	15.4	3.3	8.3	99.9	448

Ind: Indeterminate

Table 5. Relative frequency of core types by provenience unit.

Provenience	D/C	D/PE	B/F	D/T	T/C
K-2:1	87.83	26.09	1.12	9.09	9.67
K-2:2	90.61	21.28	1.07	10.52	8.61
K-2:3	117.67	19.98	1.26	9.46	12.44
F-1:1	51.29	23.93	1.07	10.88	4.71
F-1:3	80.00	40.00	1.30	8.28	9.67
F-1:4	32.40	32.40	1.29	10.80	3.00
J-2:1	27.52	21.29	1.35	4.67	5.90
J-2:2	47.37	25.04	1.19	7.91	5.99
J-2:3	56.41	36.88	1.03	9.89	5.71
F-1:1 (1964)	21.65	33.38	1.15	6.68	3.24
H-4:55	28.88	46.20	1.14	4.53	6.38
C-01:2	28.13	21.43	0.90	8.33	3.38
C-01:4	55.48	14.27	1.18	11.89	4.67

D/C: Debitage (blades & flakes only)-core ratio
D/PE: Debitage-primary element ratio
B/F: Blade-flake ratio
D/T: Debitage-tool ratio
T/C: Tool-core ratio

Table 6. Selected ratios of different artifact classes.

Core tablets, created during the rejuvenation of core platforms are also infrequent at Beidha (table 4).[7] The ratio of core tablets to cores is 1:8, and they appear not to have been important in the reduction process, as has been noted for other Natufian sites (e.g. Calley 1986: 165).

Blade or flake industry?

One important aspect of the study of chipped stone industries has been characterization based on the main debitage class represented. In late Epipaleolithic assemblages this has entailed a consideration of whether an industry should be characterized as a blade, bladelet, or flake industry (Henry 1981; Bar-Yosef 1983; Valla 1984; Olszewski 1986, 1988; Calley 1984). Henry has stated that "... Natufian assemblages are characterized by a microlithic technology based on the production of rather broad bladelets ..." (Henry 1981: 432). This view was reiterated by Bar-Yosef, while noting that both blades and flakes are abundant (Bar-Yosef 1981: 399; 1983: 17).

Recently, Valla's (1984) examination of the chipped stone assemblage from Ain Mallaha, and Olszewski's (1986) study of the lithics from Abu Hureyra, have made a point that flake debitage typifies the assemblages. Naturally, the way in which these terms are defined and artifacts classified is crucial in making these characterizations. Two important aspects of this process, that is generally not discussed, are whether the blanks from which tools were made are considered in computing the frequency of blades and flakes, and the criteria for classifying fragments of debitage as blades or flakes. How these two issues are treated can have considerable effect on the relative frequency of debitage categories.[8] For example, if tools were being made predominantly on one type of blank, and were not included in the debitage totals, the results would be an inaccurate reflection of core reduction.

For the Beidha assemblage, tools were classified by their original debitage category as far as possible, and these totals were added to the appropriate debitage category totals. This provided a more accurate assessment of the overall production frequency of various debitage types. If the tool was extensively retouched, it was often impossible to determine its blank type; this results in a residue of "indeterminate" pieces. Geometric microliths, however, were generally assumed to be made from blades (unless it was obvious they were not and, therefore, were *a priori* placed in the blade category), even though their blank dimensions usually could not be clearly ascertained.

The method of classification of debitage fragments also has a major effect on the characterization of an industry. As already mentioned, for the Beidha assemblage fragments over 1 cm maximum dimension were classified as blades, if the length was greater than twice the width, lateral margins intact and axis of flaking obvious (see Tixier 1963: 38). Fragments with parallel sides and parallel flake scars, but with a length less than twice their width, were initially placed in the subcategory of small fragments in the indeterminate debitage category. After a detailed study of the characteristics of blades and flakes was completed, an estimate of what percentage of these fragments were originally blades or flakes was made. Although the steps in this procedure are discussed elsewhere, 64% of these small fragments were estimated to have been blades and the remainder flakes. These small fragments were then removed from the indeterminate debitage category and added to the flake and blade categories for each occupation level.

Blades are somewhat more numerous than flakes in the Natufian of Beidha. The frequency of blades ranges from 52% to 41% of the assemblage (table 4). The lowest percentages occur in C-01, and the highest in F-1 level 2 and J-2 level 1. Blades are always more frequent than flakes, with the exception of C-01 level 2 where flakes are slightly more common. The ratio of blades to flakes is presented in table 6. In general, there is considerable similarity between provenience units. Significant differences in frequencies between provenience units, based on chi-square test results, occur primarily when area C-01 level 2 is contrasted with the proveni-

---

[7]Some scholars, in reporting core trimming elements, have not made a separate category for core tablets (e.g. Edwards 1987: 161).

[8]Goring-Morris and Bar-Yosef (1987: 108-110), although they did not attempt to add the tools into their respective debitage categories, point out that it has a considerable effect on the relative frequency of blades and flakes. Henry (1974: 390) makes a similar point with respect to how the microburin technique is evaluated.

ence units at the upper end of the values distribution (table 7). In addition, when the deposit with the second lowest ratio of blades to flakes, area J-2 level 3, is contrasted with the area with the highest blade flake ratio, J-2 level 3, there is also a statistically significant difference.

The frequencies of the different blade subcategories appear in table 8 (see Appendix E for classification). Complete blades and large fragments, which occur in roughly equal frequencies, represent about 80% of the blades. Within the category of large fragments, however, proximal and distal pieces are more than twice as common as medial pieces. Small fragments constitute about 17% of the sample. Microblades vary in frequency from none in some excavation areas to over 3% in area C-01.

The accepted definition for the difference between blades *sensu stricto* and bladelets is detailed by Tixier (1963: 35-39). Blades *sensu stricto* are characterized by having the following characteristics; (1) length greater than or equal to two times the width, (2) length greater than or equal to 5.0 cm, and (3) width greater than or equal to 1.2 cm. Bladelets, on the other hand, are characterized by two features; (1) length greater than or equal to twice the width, and (2) width less than or equal to 1.2 cm. Applying this standard definition for the difference between blades *sensu stricto* and bladelets to the debitage sample from Beidha, only a small fraction are blades (6.29%, N=620). A scatter plot of a sample of debitage from area C-01 level 4 indicates that the distinction between blades *sensu stricto* and bladelets is arbitrary and that the blades are merely the upper end of a continuous unimodal distribution (fig. 13).

Blade size varies little between the different occupation levels (table 9). Examination of the mean, median and coefficient of skewness suggests that, although the distribution of blade length is positively skewed (values less than 1.0), there is only minor variation between the mean and median (less than 0.2 cm generally). The mean is, therefore, presented here. Mean blade length varies from 31 mm to 34 mm for all samples except those from C-01 level 2, where the mean length is 27 mm. Mean width averages between 11.5 mm and 13 mm (excepting C-01 level 2), while mean thickness averages around 3.6 mm (with C-01 level 2 somewhat lower). The mean length-width ratio is also quite similar between provenience units, generally ranging from 2.6 to 2.8, with the value from area C-01 level 2 being slightly lower.

A Kruskal-Wallis one way analysis of variance test was conducted to determine whether these differences in value for the length, width, thickness and length-width ratio differed significantly between provenience units. This nonparametric test was selected as it does not require the assumption that the cumulative frequency distribution is uniform, and is more appropriate for a distribution that is somewhat positively skewed. When the three samples from area J-2 were examined for changes in blade length over time, the results of the Kruskal-Wallis test showed no significant differences between samples (N=334, Chi-Square=3.70, P=.157). When all seven blade samples were examined, significant differences between samples were present for mean length (N=620, Chi-Square=17.0, P=.009), width (Chi-Square=14.4, P=.026), and the length-width ratio (Chi-Square=12.8, P=.047). When the sample from C-01 level 2 is excluded from the test, the results indicated that the samples were not significantly different (N=581, length: Chi-Square=10.2, P=.071; width: Chi-

	N	Chi-Square	D.F.	P
C-01:2 versus C-1:4	1628	5.6	1	0.018
C-01:2 versus J-2:1	2980	14.26	1	<0.001
C-01:2 versus F-1:3	623	4.5	1	0.034
C-01:2 versus J-2:2	5601	7.01	1	0.008

D.F.: Degrees of freedom
P: Significance

Table 7. Chi-square results for the difference between the frequency of flakes and blades between provenience units.

Area	Level	Blades								Flakes							
		Large fragments				Micro	Small fragments	Total%	N	Large fragments				Micro	Small fragments	Total%	N
		Complete	Proximal	Medial	Distal					Complete	Proximal	Distal	Lateral				
K-2	1	37.0	20.9	9.3	16.7	0.5	15.4	99.8	2529	55.0	14.5	8.8	3.1	8.9	9.7	100.0	2257
	2	41.7	12.1	8.2	16.6	0.8	20.6	100.0	1316	57.1	10.7	7.1	6.1	6.7	12.3	100.0	1235
	3	46.5	11.6	6.1	15.3	0.0	20.5	100.0	542	61.4	8.6	7.5	3.9	3.9	14.6	99.9	429
Subtotal		39.6	17.2	8.6	16.5	0.5	17.6	100.0	4387	56.4	12.6	8.1	4.1	7.6	11.1	99.9	3921
F-1	1	37.6	14.1	6.2	16.4	0.0	25.7	100.0	341	53.9	8.8	10.0	7.8	4.1	15.4	100.0	319
	2	50.0	50.0	0.0	0.0	0.0	0.0	100.0	2	100.0	0.0	0.0	0.0	0.0	0.0	100.0	5
	3	38.7	21.3	4.7	16.6	0.0	18.7	100.0	127	54.9	10.2	9.2	7.1	5.1	13.6	100.1	98
	4	45.3	10.7	3.6	10.7	0.0	29.7	100.0	84	58.4	7.7	6.2	1.5	4.6	21.6	100.0	65
Subtotal		39.0	15.4	5.4	15.5	0.0	24.6	99.9	553	54.8	8.9	9.3	6.8	4.3	15.8	99.9	484
J-2	1	49.8	14.5	5.3	16.2	0.1	14.2	100.1	1484	58.6	13.7	12.1	3.8	1.0	10.8	100.0	1098
	2	40.2	18.5	6.1	18.9	0.0	16.3	100.0	2822	63.4	11.5	11.0	2.3	0.9	10.9	100.0	2381
	3	45.5	13.5	5.5	17.7	0.0	17.8	100.0	453	62.9	13.0	10.0	2.7	0.9	10.4	99.9	438
Subtotal		43.7	16.8	5.8	17.9	0.0	15.8	100.0	4758	61.9	12.3	11.2	2.8	0.9	10.8	99.9	3918
F-1	1(1964)	46.5	18.5	4.6	18.7	0.0	11.7	100.0	389	66.6	12.5	12.2	1.2	0.0	7.6	100.1	337
H-4	55	52.6	11.1	1.9	13.8	0.0	20.7	100.1	108	49.7	13.7	11.6	4.2	7.4	13.3	99.9	95
C-01	2	36.2	13.8	6.4	14.4	3.7	25.5	100.0	188	51.9	9.0	4.3	2.4	19.5	12.9	100.0	210
	3	35.4	13.1	1.9	14.9	3.7	31.0	100.0	54	46.1	4.6	9.2	0.0	18.5	21.6	100.0	43
	4	50.8	12.9	5.2	13.0	3.8	14.3	100.0	667	41.4	7.1	3.9	1.2	36.8	9.5	99.9	563
Subtotal		46.9	13.1	5.3	13.4	3.7	17.6	100.0	909	44.4	7.5	4.3	1.5	31.4	11.0	100.1	816
Total		42.3	16.6	6.8	16.9	0.5	17.0	100.1	11105	57.9	11.9	9.3	3.4	6.5	11.1	100.1	9570

Table 8. Relative frequency of blade and flake subcategories by provenience unit.

Square=10.2, P=.069; length-width ratio: Chi-Square=7.1, P=.213). This reveals that only the sample from the later Natufian occupation of level 2 in area C-01 is significantly different. The sample size from this level is, however, quite low.

The morphological characteristics of the different blade samples are also very similar. The vast majority of the pieces (90%) have no cortex (fig. 14), and when cortex is present it generally covers between 11% and 50% of the exterior. Punctiform platforms are the predominant platform type (fig. 15). Crushed platforms occur somewhat less commonly, and plain platforms only occasionally; cortical, dihedral and multiple faceted platforms are rare. The flake scar patterns on blade exteriors are generally either parallel or converging (table 10). The remaining flake scar categories are uncommon. Blades generally have an incurving lateral profile (63.9%, N=620), although flat profiles (15.2%) and twisted profiles (15.5%) occur frequently. Rippled and outcurving profiles are uncommon. The distal end is usually blunt (50.0%, N=620), although pointed ends occur consistently (28.9%). Overshot blades (14.4%) and hinge fracture terminated blades (6.1%), the result of unsuccessful detachment of blades, are less common, but still represent almost a fifth of the sample. Their low frequency testifies to the high level of success in blade removal and, undoubtedly, based on examination of the exhausted cores, the majority of the hinge fractures occurred at the end of a core's uselife. Examination of the skew distribution of blades shows little patterning: the highest frequency (34.61%, N=401) is at the central value and the frequency decreases equally on both sides of the center. There appears to be no consistent skewing, positive or negative.

Flakes, although almost always less numerous than blades, still constitute a major portion of

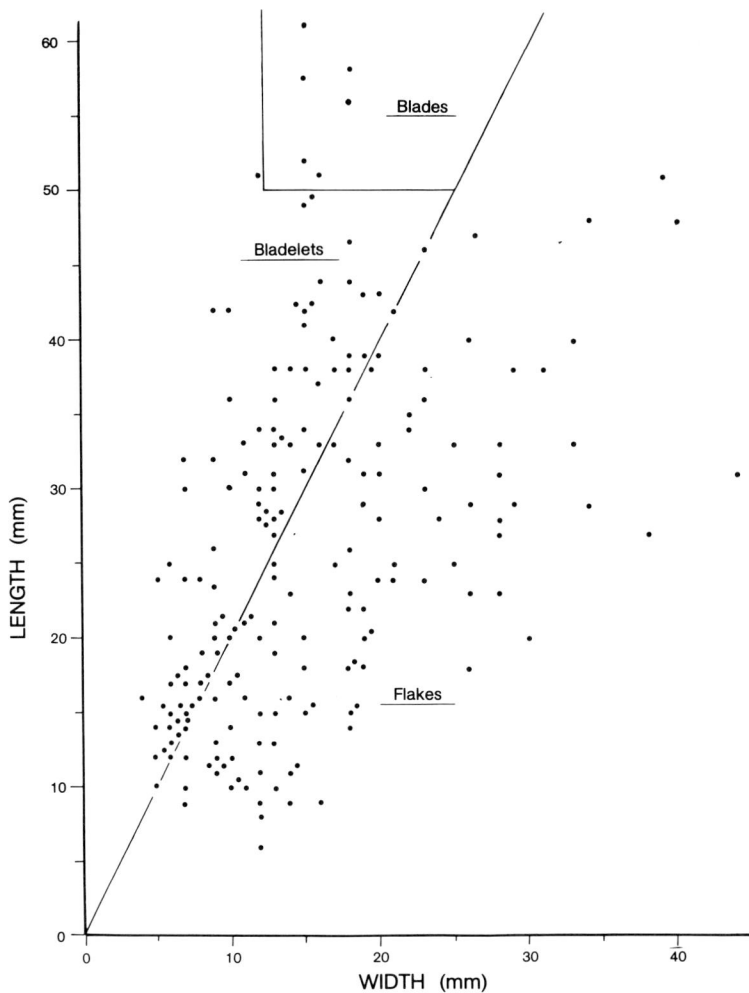

Fig. 13. Length-width scatter plot of complete blades, bladelets and flakes (N=195).

the chipped stone debitage (table 4). About two thirds of the flakes are complete (table 8). Flake fragments represent slightly over 25% of the sample; proximal, distal and lateral pieces occurring in decreasing frequencies (see Appendix E for classification). Microflakes constitute 7% of the assemblage. The percentage of microflakes, however, varies widely between the different excavation areas; from 35% in C-01 to none in some of the other areas.

In order to examine whether the higher frequency of microflakes and microblades in area C-01 versus the other excavation areas is significantly different, a chi-square test was conducted. Microflakes and microblades were combined and contrasted with all other blades and flakes. Initially, a chi-square test was conducted contrasting area C-01 with the samples from all the other areas. The results showed a significant difference between the two samples

(N=20,065, Chi-Square=163.7, D.F. 1, P<.001). A further test was conducted between area C-01 and area K-2, which overall has the second highest frequency of microflakes. The results again indicated that area C-01 has significantly higher frequencies of microflakes and microblades (N=10,003, Chi-Square= 42.92, D.F.=1, P<.001). There are two possible explanations for this variation; either area C-01 was a locale within the site where considerable detailed retouching and manufacturing took place or the difference is due to the more detailed recovery technique employed in area C-01. I suspect that the latter interpretation is the more likely one.

Samples of complete flakes from areas J-2 and C-01 were studied in order to compare morphological features. The results showed considerable similarity between the two samples. Mean flake size is small: 23 mm by 20 mm by

42

4.8 mm (table 9). Cortex is usually absent from the exterior (fig. 14). Plain platforms are the most common platform type, and cortical, multiple faceted and dihedral platforms are uncommon (fig. 15). Punctiform and crushed platforms, generally thought of as typifying blade production, are, surprisingly, quite common and represent over a third of the assemblage. Radiating exterior flake scar patterns are only slightly more frequent than parallel flake scar patterns (table 10). This would also appear unexpected, since flakes are typically characterized as lacking parallel flake

scar patterns (e.g. Calley 1986: 13), and is further evidence for the lack of discrete attributes to distinguish the flake and blade categories.[9]

A considerable number of small broken pieces with parallel sides and parallel flake scars were provisionally placed in the category of indeterminate debitage. Attribute analysis was then conducted of a sample of these pieces, in an attempt to determine what percentage could be estimated as being flakes or blades.

The mean width of the sample of small broken pieces, 13.33 mm, is very similar to the mean for the sample of blades (see table 9). Cortex occurs very rarely on these pieces (fig. 14). Punctiform and crushed platforms are predominant, plain platforms occur infrequently (fig. 15). Given that flake-sized pieces frequently have parallel sides, parallel flake scars, and crushed or punctiform platforms, it was necessary to estimate

[9]Edwards (1987: 144-147) observes of the Wadi Hammeh early Natufian assemblage that bladelets are generally short and wide, and both blades and flakes have a low frequency of cortex and high frequency of punctiform platforms – more similar than perhaps would have been expected.

Area	Level	N	Length	Width	Thickness	LW ratio
Blades						
K-2	1	102	30.42	11.57	3.78	2.7257
F-1	1	86	32.46	12.45	3.73	2.7049
J-2	1	129	32.50	12.93	3.75	2.6142
	2	104	34.18	12.84	3.67	2.7508
	3	101	31.62	12.00	3.62	2.7285
C-01	2	39	27.23	10.97	3.05	2.4983
	4	59	32.32	11.63	3.76	2.8319
Flakes						
J-2	1	118	23.67	20.96	4.70	1.1909
C-01	2&4	101	22.69	19.00	4.91	1.2336

LW ratio: Length-width ratio

Table 9. Mean length, width and thickness of complete blades and flakes.

	Blades		Flakes	
	N	%	N	%
Parallel				
Parallel	264	42.6	50	22.8
Expanding	33	5.3	6	2.7
Coverging	230	37.1	31	14.2
Opposing	16	2.6	3	1.4
Parallel & transverse	29	4.7	9	4.1
Nonparallel				
Radiating	32	5.2	80	36.5
Other	7	1.1	35	16.0
Indeterminate	9	1.5	5	2.3
Total	620	100.0	219	100.0

Table 10. Frequency distribution of exterior flake scar patterns on blades and flakes.

what percentage of these pieces may have been flakes or blades. By contrasting the relative percentages of these attributes that occur in the blade and flake samples, it was estimated that 32% of the small broken pieces with parallel sides and parallel flake scars were probably originally of flake size, and the remainder of blade size. This percentage of small fragments was then added to the respective flake and blade debitage categories. A residue of other indeterminate debitage, often called chips, then remained (see table 4).

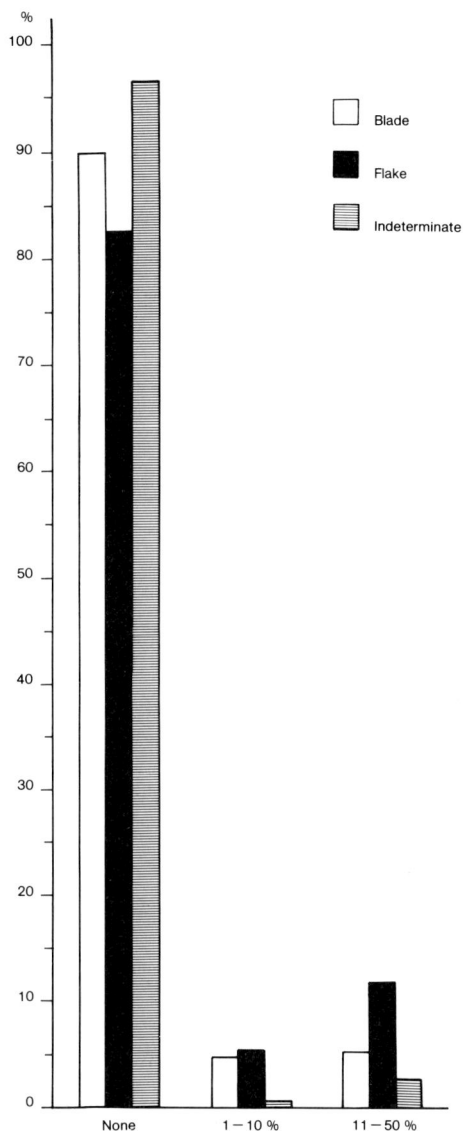

Fig. 14. Bar chart showing the relative frequency of cortex on the exterior of blades (N=620), flakes (N=219), and small fragments of indeterminate debitage (N=100).

The Beidha assemblage can best be understood in the context of a continuous reduction sequence. As core size decreases the pieces removed become shorter, but not always narrower. The distribution of relative dimensions of blades versus flakes is continuous with no break between the two debitage categories (fig. 13). This model of a continuous reduction sequence is further supported by the high frequency of pieces with the dimensions of flakes, but with morphological features similar to those of blades: parallel flake scar patterns, and punctiform and crushed platforms.

The proportional distinction between flakes and blades, and a simple characterization of the assemblage as focused on flakes or blades, is not really adequate for an understanding of how this assemblage was produced. A more useful assessment of the Beidha industry is gained from examination of a wider range of variables including: size distribution of debitage, the nature of the flake scar patterns and platforms, the size of raw material sources, the number of primary elements, and the nature of the cores. With these lines of information, more accurate insight into the phases of reduction that took place at the site is obtained. Only then can comparisons with sites with similar recovery techniques be undertaken, allowing greater insight into variability in settlement pattern and intensity of occupation.

Tool blank analysis

The frequency of debitage which has been retouched into tools varies by level, but is generally between 8% and 15% of the total debitage (table 4). The preferred blank for the manufacture of tools, constituting almost two thirds of the sample, falls in the proportional size category of blades (table 11). Flake-size pieces represent only a small fraction of the sample. This holds true for all the major tool groups except burins and simple retouched pieces, where flakes are more common. Retouched tools were made infrequently on debris, primary elements and cores.

The size of tools that retain their original blade blank dimensions (length and width) is presented in table 12. Most tool groups only have a small number of pieces retaining original dimensions. The notch and denticulate category, however, is well represented. The size of notch

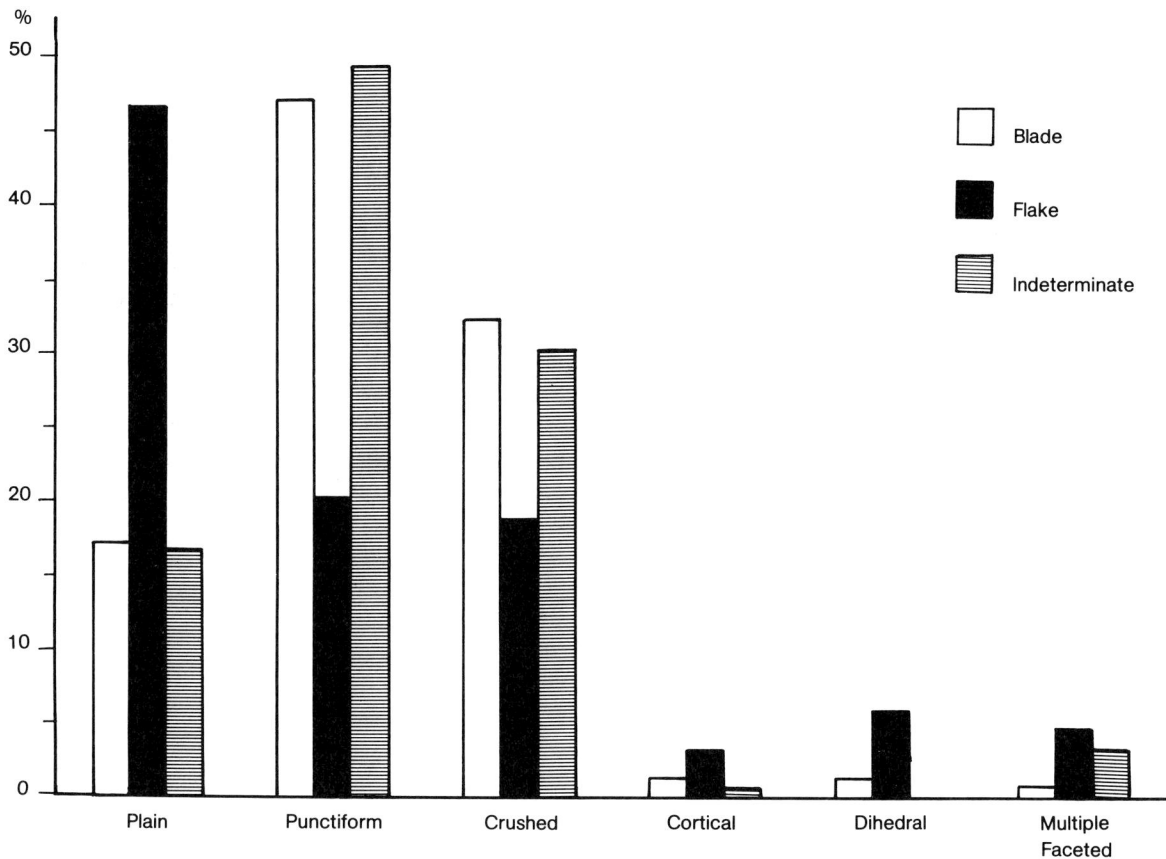

Fig. 15. Bar chart showing the relative frequency of platform types for blades (N=620), flakes (N=219), and small fragments of indeterminate debitage (N=156).

and denticulate tools with complete dimensions averages 41 mm in length and 17 mm in width. Based on Mann-Whitney test results, the mean size of these pieces is significantly larger than that of the sample of unretouched bladelets (table 13). The length-width ratio of 2.5 for the notches and denticulates, however, is similar to that of the unretouched pieces. This is readily apparent when the scatter plot for the sample of unretouched blades (fig. 13) is contrasted with the scatter plot of a sample of notches and denticulates with blank dimensions extant (fig. 16). There are very few notch and denticulate tools with their length less than 30 mm, and the frequency of blades *sensu stricto* is considerably higher.

Tools still retaining the original blade width were also examined. Scrapers have the greatest width, averaging 19.91 mm, while burins, notches and denticulates, multiple tools, and retouched pieces have somewhat narrower widths, averaging near 15 mm (table 12). The

widths of these larger tool groups (scrapers, burins, multiple tools, retouched pieces, and various tools) are significantly larger than the width of unretouched blades (table 13). Smaller tools (truncations, drills, nongeometrics, geometrics and backed fragments) have average widths which are not significantly different from those of unretouched blades (table 13).

The size of tools which have retained their original flake blank dimensions are presented in table 12. Based on a Mann-Whitney test, tools of flake blank size in the notch and denticulate group are significantly larger (mean length 37 mm and mean width 25 mm) than the unretouched flake sample (table 13). In addition, the length-width ratio for these tools is somewhat greater (1.5 versus 1.2).

What these trends in size variation suggest is the differential utilization of pieces removed during the process of core reduction. When the core was relatively new and producing quite large pieces, the blanks (usually blades but

45

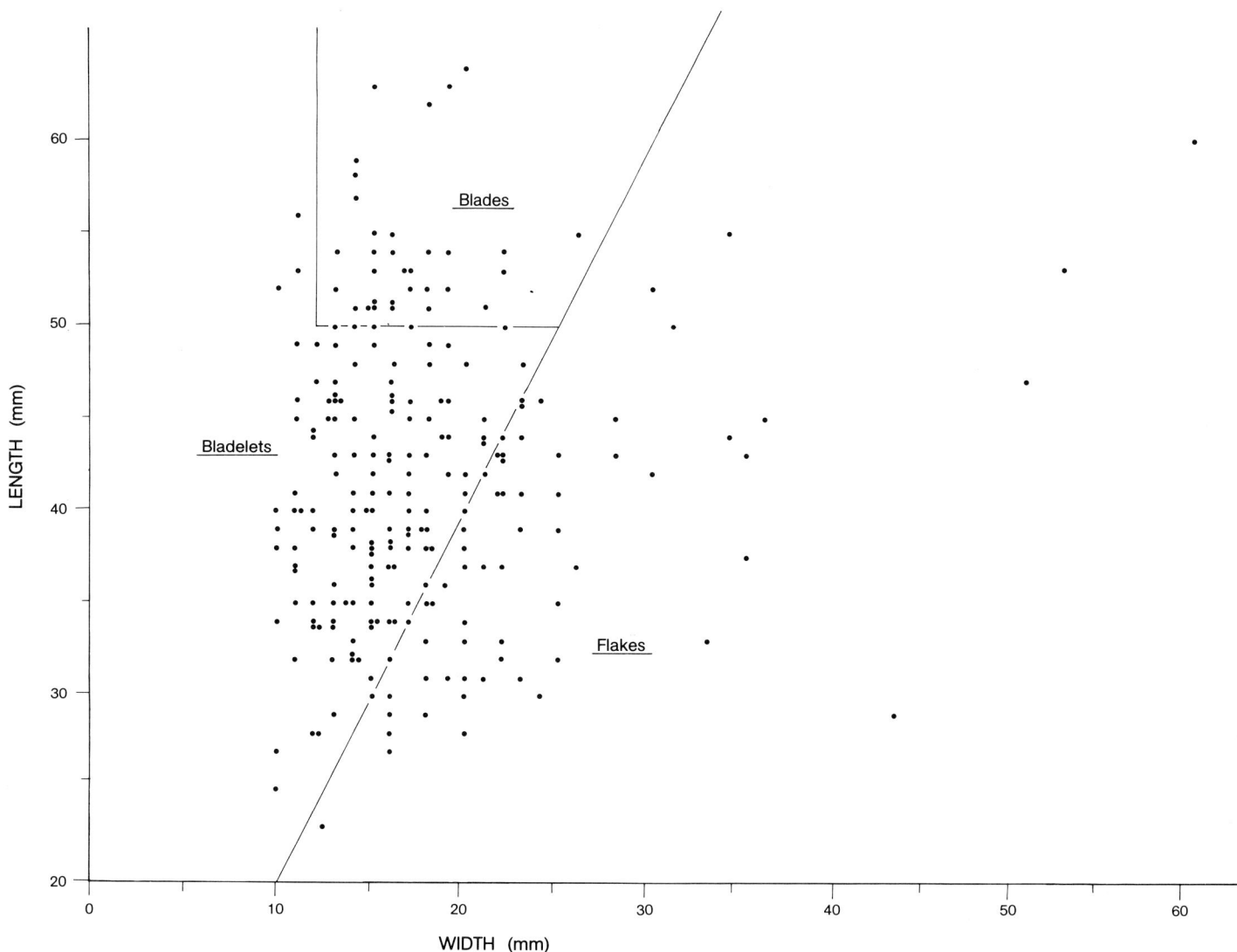

Fig. 16. Length-width scatter plot of notched and denticulated tools with complete blank dimensions extant (N=236).

occasionally flakes) were intensively utilized for the manufacture of scrapers, burins, retouched pieces, multiple tools and notches and denticulates. Later, as the pieces removed become shorter (and generally proportionally narrower) they were less intensively used for retouched tool manufacture, and the tools were almost entirely backed bladelets, truncations and drills.

Although the ratio of tools to debitage varies between provenience units, there is no apparent pattern in their distribution (table 6). Only level 2 from area C-01 and level 4 of F-1 have very low ratios. The remainder of the provenience units have values which vary from 6.6 to 11.9.

The variability in the ratio of tools to cores is more patterned. Levels 1 to 3 of area K-2 and level 3 of area F-1 all have high ratios, ranging from 9.6 to 12.4, while the remaining proveni-

ence units have lower ratios, between 3.0 and 6.4. These four provenience units with high ratios are the same units with high debitage to core ratios. This is consistent with the assertion that these provenience units were either a focus of intensive debitage production and subsequent tool manufacture or that cores were less frequently discarded in these locations.

Microburin products

The microburin technique is often used to truncate bladelets prior to the manufacture of backed bladelets (e.g. Tixier 1963: 137-145; Henry 1974), and this holds true for Beidha. The percentage of microburin products at Beidha, however, varies considerably between provenience units from less than 1% to 8% (table 4). In areas F-1 and J-2, the frequency of

	Blade	Flake	Debris	Ind	PE	Core	Other	Total%	N
Scrapers	31.9	8.4	0.9	47.3	9.0	1.5	0.9	99.9	332
Burins	28.8	32.4	4.5	27.9	3.6	0.0	2.7	99.9	111
Notches & denticulates	61.4	11.6	0.3	24.5	0.9	0.0	1.3	100.0	870
Multiple tools	65.9	7.1	1.2	24.7	1.2	0.0	0.0	100.1	85
Truncations	63.4	2.2	0.0	33.3	0.0	0.0	1.1	100.0	186
Geometrics	99.2	0.5	0.0	0.0	0.0	0.0	0.3	100.0	375
Nongeometrics	89.2	1.3	0.0	9.5	0.0	0.0	0.0	100.0	158
Backed fragments	68.9	0.0	0.0	30.3	0.3	0.0	0.5	100.0	370
Retouched pieces	50.8	22.2	3.2	16.7	6.3	0.0	0.8	100.0	126
Drills	56.3	0.0	0.0	31.3	6.3	0.0	6.3	100.2	32
Various	30.2	5.9	1.4	58.6	0.9	0.5	2.7	100.2	222
Total	61.5	7.7	0.7	26.9	2.0	0.2	1.1	100.1	2867

PE: Primary element
Ind: Indeterminate

Table 11. Relative frequency of blank type by tool class.

	N	Width	WStDev	WMin	WMax	Length	LStDev	LMin	LMax	LWRatio	LWStDev
omplete blade blanks											
Notches & denticulates	149	15.23	3.15	10.00	26.00	42.13	7.59	25.00	63.00	2.85	0.67
Retouched pieces	9	16.22	3.34	11.00	20.00	43.89	9.61	25.00	56.00	2.78	0.68
Various	10	15.70	3.71	9.00	22.00	45.50	10.47	29.00	62.00	2.97	0.65
omplete flake blanks											
Notches & denticulates	52	25.08	8.52	12.00	59.00	37.90	7.60	23.00	60.00	1.58	0.29
lade blank widths											
Scrapers	44	19.91	5.56	9.00	39.00						
Burins	26	15.15	4.35	9.00	24.00						
Notches & denticulates	177	15.15	3.28	9.00	26.00						
Multiple tools	13	14.92	2.43	11.00	19.00						
Truncations	63	11.16	2.55	5.00	21.00						
Retouched pieces	13	14.92	3.68	10.00	20.00						
Drills	10	10.80	3.22	5.00	15.00						
Various	16	15.25	3.44	9.00	22.00						

WStDev: Width standard deviation
WMin: Width minimum value
WMax: Width maximum value
LStDev: Length standard deviation
LMin: Length minimum value
LMax: Length maximum value
LWRatio: Length width ratio

Table 12. Mean size for tools with complete blade dimensions extant (only tool groups with sample sizes of greater than 8).

	Mean rank	Cases	U	W	Z	2-tailed P
Blade length						
Unretouched blades	344.65	620	21449.5	99896.5	-11.9957	.0000
Notches & denticulates	580.79	171				
Blade width						
Unretouched blades	385.74	620	46651.0	174434.0	-11.6785	.0000
Large tools	603.58	289				
Small tools	316.58	84	23023.0	26593.0	-1.7304	.0836
Unretouched blades	357.37	620				
Flake length						
Unretouched flakes	123.40	219	2935.0	24335.0	-10.5665	.0000
Notches & denticulates	240.94	101				
Flake width						
Unretouched flakes	137.90	219	6111.0	21159.0	-6.4396	.0000
Notches & denticulates	209.50	101				

Table 13. Mann-Whitney test results of the difference in length and width between tools with complete blade dimensions and unretouched blades.

47

Area	Level	Mb	TP	KMb	BKMb	Total%	N
K-2	1	93.8	6.2	0.0	0.0	100.0	179
	2	92.2	5.2	2.6	0.0	100.0	77
	3	90.0	10.0	0.0	0.0	100.0	20
Subtotal		93.1	6.2	0.7	0.0	100.0	276
F-1	1	80.0	10.0	10.0	0.0	100.0	10
	3	100.0	0.0	0.0	0.0	100.0	3
	4	100.0	0.0	0.0	0.0	100.0	2
Subtotal		86.7	6.7	6.7	0.0	100.1	15
J-2	1	91.1	8.9	0.0	0.0	100.0	56
	2	94.8	3.9	1.3	0.0	100.0	77
	3	92.3	7.7	0.0	0.0	100.0	13
Subtotal		93.2	6.2	0.7	0.0	100.1	146
F-1	1 (1964)	100.0	0.0	0.0	0.0	100.0	4
H-4	55	90.9	9.1	0.0	0.0	100.0	11
C-01							
	2	50.0	25.0	0.0	25.0	100.0	8
	3	88.9	0.0	0.0	11.1	100.0	9
	4	55.4	2.5	11.6	30.6	100.1	121
Subtotal		57.2	3.6	10.1	28.9	99.8	138
Total		84.6	5.6	3.1	6.8	100.1	590

Mb: Microburins   TP: Trihedral points
KMb: Krukowski microburins   BKMb: Beidha Krukowski microburins

Table 14. Relative frequency of microburin products by provenience unit.

Initial microburin index: $$Imbt = \frac{mb}{tools + mb} \times 100$$

Restricted microburin index: $$rImbt = \frac{mb}{backed\ pieces + mb} \times 100$$

Adjusted microburin index: $$aImbt = \frac{mb}{truncations + mb} \times 100$$

Re-adjusted microburin index: $$raImbt = \frac{mb\text{-}tp}{truncations = (mb\text{-}tp)} \times 100$$

mb= Microburins
tp= Trihedral points

Table 15. Formulas used for calculating microburin indices.

microburin products increases slightly over time, while in area C-01 the frequency decreases over time (although the sample size in area C-01 level 2 is very small). The highest percentage of microburin products occurs in area C-01. Chi-square test results show that there is a significantly higher frequency of microburin products in area C-01 than in other excavation areas (N=590, Chi-Square 91.29, D.F.=1, P<.001). When area C-01 is contrasted with level 55 in area H-4, the deposit with the next highest frequency of microburins, a significant difference is still noted (N=149, Chi-Square 11.93, D.F.=1, P=.003). The higher frequency of

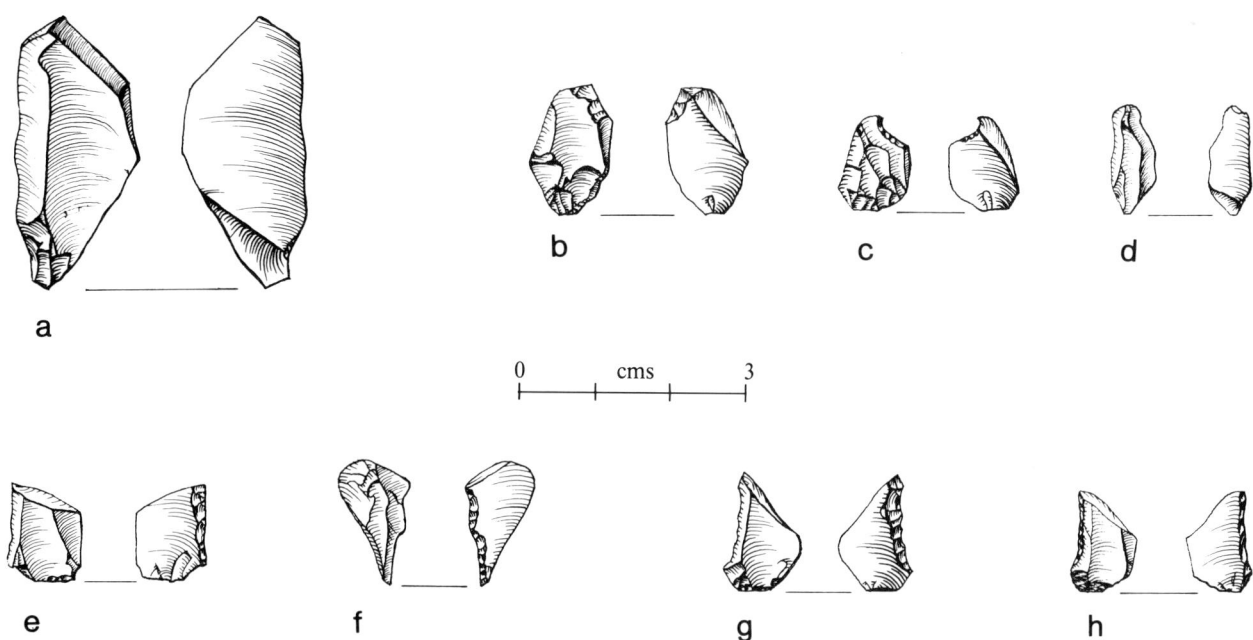

Fig. 17. Microburins (a-d) and Beidha Krukowski microburins (e-h).

microburins in area C-01 may be due to more intensive manufacture of microliths by that technique or, as suggested previously for micro-flakes and microblades, may result from the use of a more intensive recovery technique in area C-01.

Microburins represent the majority of the microburin products recovered (table 14; fig. 17:a-d). Trihedral points are rare, since they were usually retouched into truncations or backed bladelets. Krukowski microburins, generally viewed as the products of accidents in the backing process or occasionally as intentionally produced by-products of breaking backed blades on an anvil (Bordes 1957; Tixier 1963: 142-145; Brezillon 1968: 129-130; Bar-Yosef 1981: 400), are uncommon at Beidha. There is another microburin product which, although undocumented at other sites, occurs at Beidha. I have termed it the Beidha Krukowski micro-burin (fig. 17:e-h), and it occurs only in area C-01 where it comprises over a quarter of the microburin products.

The Beidha Krukowski microburins are typically proximal pieces retouched on the left lateral edge. The retouch is primarily semisteep interior retouch with the *positive* microburin scar always on the interior – microburins typically have the positive microburin scar on the exterior.

Although at first glance these could be viewed as the result of accidents during backing (they lack the notching which Tixier [1963: 142-145] considers evidence for intentional creation), the consistent pattern of features suggests that this was an alternative way of truncating backed bladelets – the truncation executed after the backing had begun.

Several indices have been used to measure the frequency in the use of microburins. The first index, proposed by Tixier (1963) and used by Bar-Yosef (1970) on Levantine assemblages, measured the frequency of microburins in relationship to the total tool assemblage (table 15). Henry (1973a: 78-79) argued that this was a misleading index, as it did not accurately indicate the frequency of microburins in relationship to backed bladelets (tools where truncations were present), and proposed the restricted microburin index to measure this relationship (Henry 1974). Later, Marks and Larson (1977: 204-205) in their report on Rosh Horesha, introduced an alternative formula which would accurately reflect the intensity of microburin use in truncating bladelets. The number of microburins was compared with the total number of truncations on tools. This adjusted microburin index is, in my opinion, a more interesting and relevant measurement.

49

Area	Level	Truncations	aImbt	raImbt	raImbt (with BKMb)
K-2	1	264	38.89	37.29	-
	2	120	37.17	35.83	-
	3	53	25.35	23.19	-
F-1	1	32	20.0	17.95	-
	3	21	12.50	12.50	-
	4	7	22.22	22.22	-
J-2	1	251	16.88	15.49	-
	2	288	20.44	19.55	-
	3	52	17.46	17.46	-
F-1	1 (1964)	33	10.81	10.81	-
H-4	55	30	25.00	23.08	-
C-01	2	29	12.12	6.45	12.12
	3	4	66.67	66.67	69.23
	4	97	40.85	39.75	51.01

aImbt: Adjusted microburin index
BKMb: Beidha Krukowski microburins
raImbt: Re-adjusted microburin index

Table 16. Microburin indices by provenience unit.

Area	Level	ProxLeft	ProxRt	DistLeft	DistRt	Ind	Total%	N
K-2	1	20.2	20.2	29.8	25.6	4.2	100.0	168
	2	25.4	18.3	26.8	29.6	0.0	100.1	71
	3	16.7	33.3	44.4	5.6	0.0	100.0	18
Subtotal		21.4	20.6	29.9	25.3	2.7	99.9	257
F-1	1	37.5	12.5	37.5	0.0	12.5	100.0	8
	3	0.0	33.3	66.7	0.0	0.0	100.0	3
	4	50.0	50.0	0.0	0.0	0.0	100.0	2
Subtotal		30.8	23.1	38.5	0.0	7.7	100.1	13
J-2	1	27.4	23.5	27.4	19.6	1.9	99.8	51
	2	26.4	25.0	30.6	16.7	1.4	100.1	72
	3	27.3	18.2	45.4	9.1	0.0	100.0	11
Subtotal		26.9	23.9	30.6	17.2	1.5	100.1	134
F-1	1 (1964)	25.0	50.0	25.0	0.0	0.0	100.0	4
H-4	55	20.0	40.0	10.0	30.0	0.0	100.0	10
C-01	2	50.0	25.0	25.0	0.0	0.0	100.0	4
	3	12.5	12.5	62.5	0.0	12.5	100.0	8
	4	61.2	6.0	7.5	20.9	4.5	100.1	67
Subtotal		55.7	7.6	13.9	17.7	5.1	100.0	79
Total		28.6	20.1	27.4	21.1	2.8	100.0	497

ProxLeft: Proximal left
ProxRt: Proximal right
DistLeft: Distal left
DistRt: Distal right
Ind: Indeterminate

Table 17. Relative frequency of microburin notch locations by provenience unit.

The adjusted microburin index could be, however, improved slightly by taking into account the number of trihedral points (unused microburin products) present in an assemblage (table 15). This "re-adjusted" index provides a slightly more accurate assessment of the actual use of the microburin technique to shape backed and retouched blades. Table 16 presents the values for both the adjusted microburin index and the "re-adjusted" microburin index at Beidha – they vary only slightly.

The microburin indexes vary between provenience units at Beidha – ranging from 6.45 to 39.75 (table 16). The values are highest in level 4 of area C-01 and level 1 of area K-2. The values in area C-01 are even higher when the Beidha Krukowski microburins, which I view as intentional, are included. The lowest values occur in level 2 of area C-01. In general the technique was used almost half of the time bladelets were truncated and backed – an index of 50 represents an equal number of truncations to microburins.

The location of microburin notches lacks consistent patterning in almost all excavation areas (table 17). The exception is level 4 of area C-01 where microburin notches are typically on the left proximal side (over two thirds of the sample), the microburin facet being on the distal end of the bladelet.

Summary

Analysis of the Beidha Natufian reduction sequence has shown that the inhabitants exploited high quality flint available in the nearby wadis. The low frequencies of primary elements recovered indicate that the cores were partially roughed out prior to being brought to the site or possibly in a restricted area of the site that has not been excavated. Tools made on chert were occasionally carried to the site and discarded there, but only rarely were cores of this material reduced or discarded at the site. Core trimming elements, used for initiating core production, and core tablets, formed by rejuvenating core platforms, are rare. The generally high ratios of debitage to cores and the extremely exhausted nature of the cores themselves testify to the intensive reduction that took place.

Analysis of the flake and blade debitage samples has shown that the two debitage categories overlap considerably with respect to the attributes of size, flake scar patterns, and platform characteristics. Blades, however, are slightly more numerous than flakes, and blades *sensu stricto* occur only rarely.

Blades are the predominant debitage type selected for tool manufacture. The size of the blanks selected varies significantly between tool groups; scrapers, burins, retouched pieces, multiple tools, and notches and denticulates have a significantly larger tool size than the debitage samples and the tool classes of microliths, truncations, and drills. Microburins were commonly used in the truncation of bladelets prior to manufacture into tools.

Analysis of spatial and temporal variability in the reduction strategies reveals considerable homogeneity between provenience units. The size and the morphological characteristics of debitage also appear to change little over the habitation span of the settlement. Variability may partially be obscured, however, by differences in the nature of the recovery technique of the 1983 excavations in area C-01 versus the earlier excavations. Significantly higher frequencies of microflakes, microblades, and possibly microburins in area C-01 appear to be the result of recovery variability.

There are some differences, however, that may not be due to differential recovery technique. The higher ratios of flake and blade debitage to cores and of tools to cores in all three levels in K-2 and level 3 of F-1, imply that either cores were more extensively reduced in these locales or that fewer cores were discarded here. In addition, the upper phase in area C-01 has a slightly higher ratio of flakes to blades than have other excavation units, and perhaps this may be a result of temporal differences (yet the sample size is very small).

Analysis of the chipped stone technology from Beidha raises some broader questions with respect to the Natufian complex. Natufian sites west of the Jordan River have been characterized as sharing a common chipped stone technology, with the production of blades/bladelets from multiplatform blade cores a prominent feature of these descriptions (Henry 1981: 432; Bar-Yosef 1983: 17). If sites in the eastern and extreme southern Levant are to be considered Natufian, then it must be recognized that single platform cores are generally predominant in these areas. This holds true for such Jordanian Natufian sites as Beidha, Ain Rahub (Muheisen *et al*, 1988: 483), Jebel es-Subhi (Betts 1987), Tabaqa (Byrd and Rollefson 1984), and Azraq 18 (Garrard *et al*. 1987: table 2), as well as contemporary sites in northern Syria (Olszewski 1988: 132; Calley 1986: 165), and the Negev and Sinai (Goring-Morris 1987: 284-285; Goring-Morris and Bar-Yosef 1987).[10] Multiplatform blade cores are, however, predominant at the early Natufian site of Wadi Hammeh in northwestern Jordan (Edwards 1987: table 4.3), and it is possible that the higher frequency of multiplatform cores is related to settlement intensity.

In addition, the results of this study suggest that a reliance solely on the normative definitions of the frequencies between blades and flakes is an inadequate criterion for understanding the technology of the industry and for characterizing it. The categories of blade and flake are not necessarily discrete. At Beidha, the uncritical use of these categories results in the imposition of an arbitrary boundary on a continuous reduction sequence. This sequence begins with long narrow pieces (blades), to shorter narrow pieces (bladelets), and to a final stage, characterized by short and wide pieces often of "flake" dimensions (length is less than twice width). Detailed examination of the reduction process is needed, in order to understand the steps used in the reduction sequence, which stages occurred at the site, and the limitations imposed by raw material.

Without clear understanding of the way these two categories, flakes and blades, were defined, how fragments were classified, and whether tools were classified by blank categories and then added to the blank totals, the wide variation in the relative frequency of blades/bladelets versus flakes from various Natufian sites and the characterizations of these industries as blade/bladelet or flake dominant (Henry 1981; Bar-Yosef 1983; Calley 1984, 1986; Valla 1984; Olszewski 1988) is of minimal interpretive value. What is needed is a more comprehensive description of the stages of the reduction sequence that took place at each site. This

requires detailed study of chipped stone morphological features beyond size dimensions, including flake scar patterns, platform types, and the size and nature of available raw material. Calley's research on the technology of the Mureybet Natufian is an example of such research (Calley 1986). Only then will we be able to make strong inferences regarding intersite occupation intensity and functional variability.

Chipped stone tool analysis

This section discusses spatial and temporal variability in the distribution of tool groups, the characteristics of the different tool groups, and the manufacturing techniques used in producing the tools.

Spatial and temporal variability between tool groups

Table 18 presents the distribution of the eleven tool groups by excavation area and provenience unit. Chi-square tests were undertaken to determine whether the frequency of different tool groups varied significantly between excavation units. Initially, areas K-2 and J-2 were analyzed for spatial and temporal differences. Within area K-2, the results of a chi-square test indicate that there is only minimal difference between the three occupation levels (table 19). Similar results were obtained when area J-2 was examined for temporal variation; the levels were not significantly different. Next, variation between areas was examined by comparing each level from area K-2 with the same level from area J-2. Only for level 2 was there a significant difference at less than 0.05 (at 0.39), and with the large sample sizes used in the chi-square test, it is uncertain how significant these differences are in respect to variation in human activity.

In examining the distribution of tool groups between occupation areas, it appeared that area C-01 had more small tools than the other areas. Given the results from the analysis of the reduction technology, which indicated that recovery technique differences provided higher frequencies of small artifacts in area C-01, chi-square tests were conducted to determine whether recovery technique was also influencing the

---

[10]Goring-Morris (1987: 285) notes that the higher frequency of multiplatform cores recorded by Marks and Larson (1977) and Henry (1976) in their studies of the Natufian in the Negev versus his own work may be due to different classificatory criteria.

Area	Level	Scrapers	Burins	N & D	RetP	Drills	MT	Trunc	Geometrics	Nongeo	BkFrags	Various	Total%	N
K-2	1	10.0	4.2	29.2	10.0	1.4	3.4	6.6	13.6	4.3	14.2	3.1	100.0	579
	2	10.1	3.4	29.9	9.4	0.8	3.0	7.1	12.7	3.8	16.5	3.4	100.1	267
	3	9.8	4.5	25.9	12.5	0.0	1.8	3.6	14.3	5.4	17.9	4.5	100.2	112
Subtotal		10.0	3.9	29.0	10.1	1.0	3.1	6.4	13.5	4.3	15.2	3.3	99.8	958
F-1	1	15.2	1.5	28.8	15.2	1.5	1.5	4.6	12.1	6.1	12.1	1.5	100.1	66
	3	3.4	6.9	27.6	13.8	0.0	0.0	6.9	6.9	20.7	13.8	0.0	100.0	29
	4	13.3	0.0	26.7	20.0	0.0	0.0	6.7	0.0	13.3	6.7	13.3	100.0	15
Subtotal		11.8	2.7	28.2	15.4	0.9	0.9	5.4	9.1	10.9	11.8	2.7	99.8	110
J-2	1	11.4	4.9	33.4	8.8	1.4	3.0	5.4	11.7	6.4	10.7	2.7	99.8	625
	2	14.9	1.7	33.7	8.8	1.1	3.6	6.5	11.4	5.9	10.9	1.4	99.9	719
	3	12.4	4.1	28.9	10.3	1.0	2.1	10.3	14.4	7.2	7.2	2.1	100.0	97
Subtotal		13.2	3.3	33.2	8.9	1.2	3.3	6.3	11.7	6.2	10.6	2.0	99.9	1441
F-1	1 (1964)	15.0	6.7	31.7	10.0	0.0	4.2	8.3	5.0	2.5	14.2	2.5	100.1	120
H-4	55	7.8	5.9	31.4	11.8	0.0	0.0	5.9	19.6	3.9	13.7	0.0	100.0	51
C-01	2	12.7	9.1	10.9	14.6	0.0	1.8	3.6	14.6	7.3	21.8	3.6	100.0	55
	3	0.0	20.0	20.0	0.0	0.0	0.0	0.0	40.0	0.0	20.0	0.0	100.0	5
	4	3.2	4.8	16.7	7.1	2.4	0.8	10.3	32.5	4.8	16.7	0.8	100.1	126
Subtotal		5.9	6.4	15.0	9.1	1.6	1.1	8.1	27.4	5.4	18.3	1.6	99.9	186
Total		11.6	3.9	30.4	9.7	1.1	2.9	6.5	13.1	5.5	12.9	2.4	100.0	2866

N & D:	Notches and denticulates	Nongeo:	Nongeometrics
Trunc:	Truncations	MT:	Multiple tools
RetP:	Retouched pieces	BkFrags:	Backed fragments

Table 18. Relative frequency of tool classes by provenience unit.

	Chi-Square	D.F.	P
All tool groups			
Between levels in area K-2	8.85	20	.854
Between levels in area J-2	24.71	20	.212
Between K-2:1 & J-2:1	10.31	10	.413
Between K-2:2 & J-2:2	19.10	10	.039
Between K-2:3 & J-2:3	11.14	10	.346
Large versus small tools			
Area C-01 versus all other areas	39.04	1	<.001
Area C-01 versus H-4:1	17.21	1	<.001

D.F.:	Degrees of freedom
P:	Significance

Table 19. Chi-square test results of the difference in the frequency of tool groups between provenience units.

appearance of the tool group frequencies. The tool groups were classified into large tools (scrapers, burins, notches and denticulates, retouched pieces, and various tools) and small tools (drills, truncations, geometrics, nongeometrics and backed fragments). Initially, area C-01 was contrasted with all other areas and the chi-square results strongly indicated that there were significant differences (table 19). Then area C-01 was compared with area H4 level 55 which appeared to have the next highest frequencies of small tools. The chi-square results also strongly indicated that there are significantly higher frequencies of small tools recovered

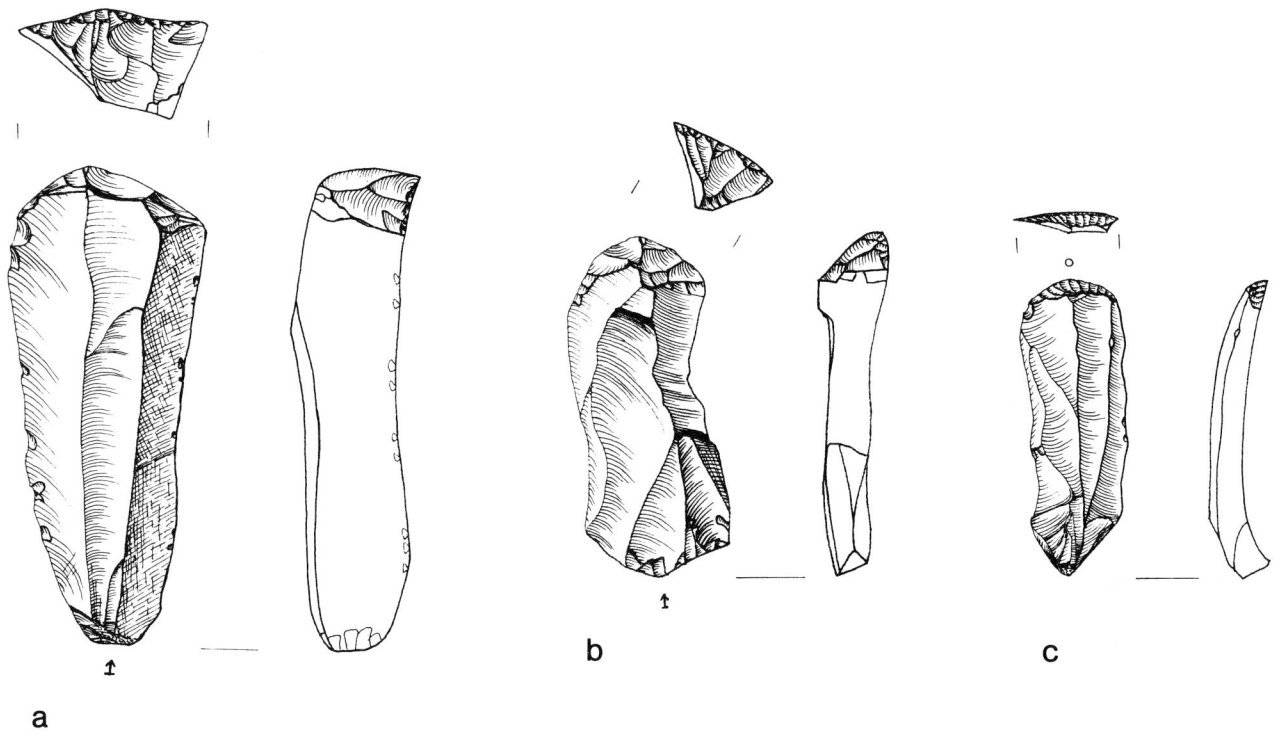

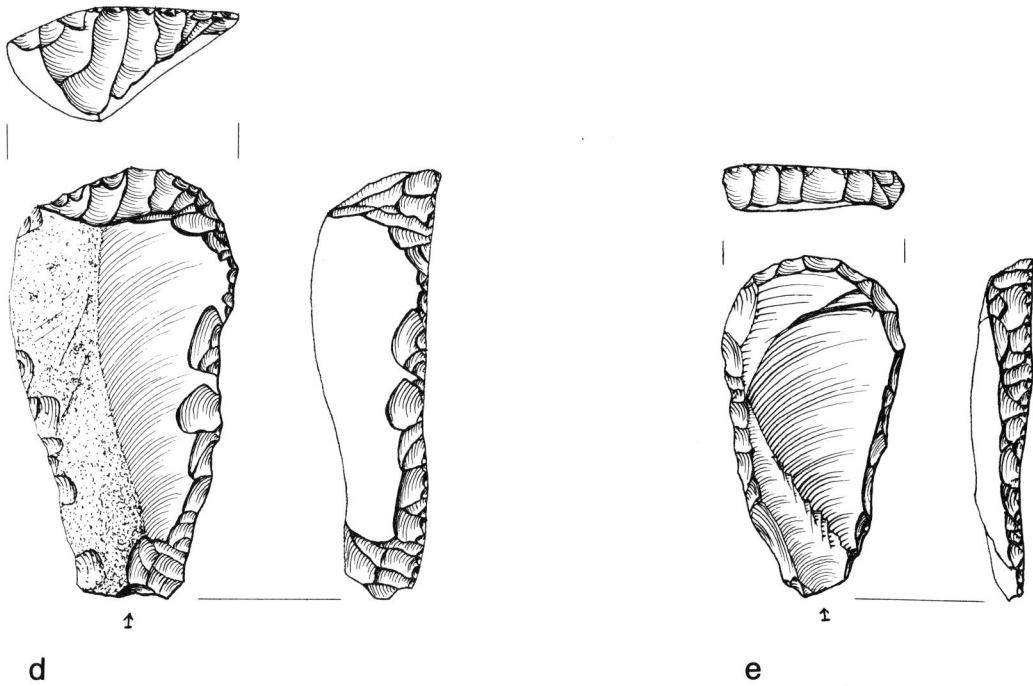

Fig.18. Simple end scrapers (a-c) and bilaterally retouched end scrapers (d-e).

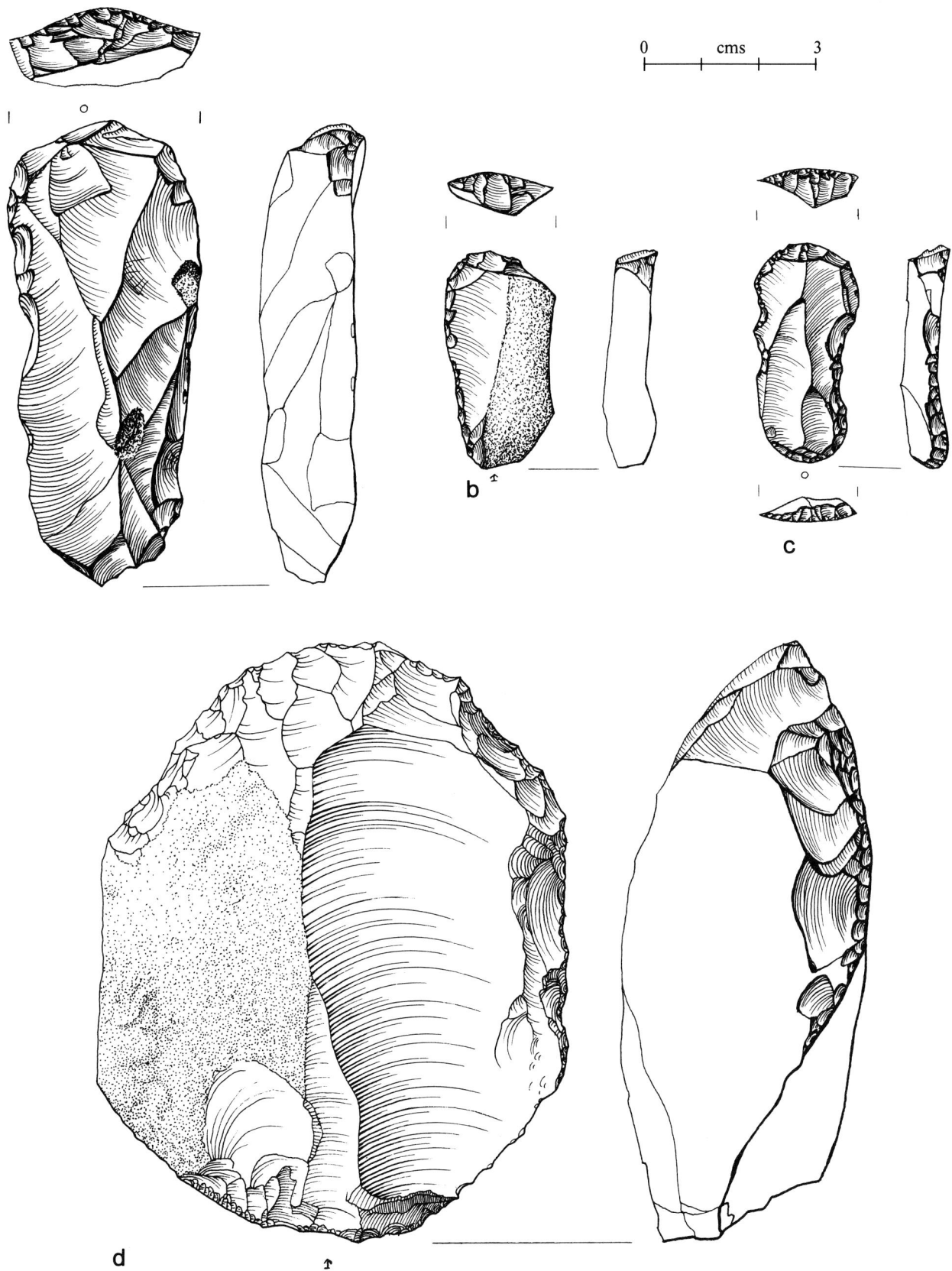

Fig. 19. Unilaterally retouched end scrapers (a-b), double end scraper (c), and rounded end scraper on flake (d).

55

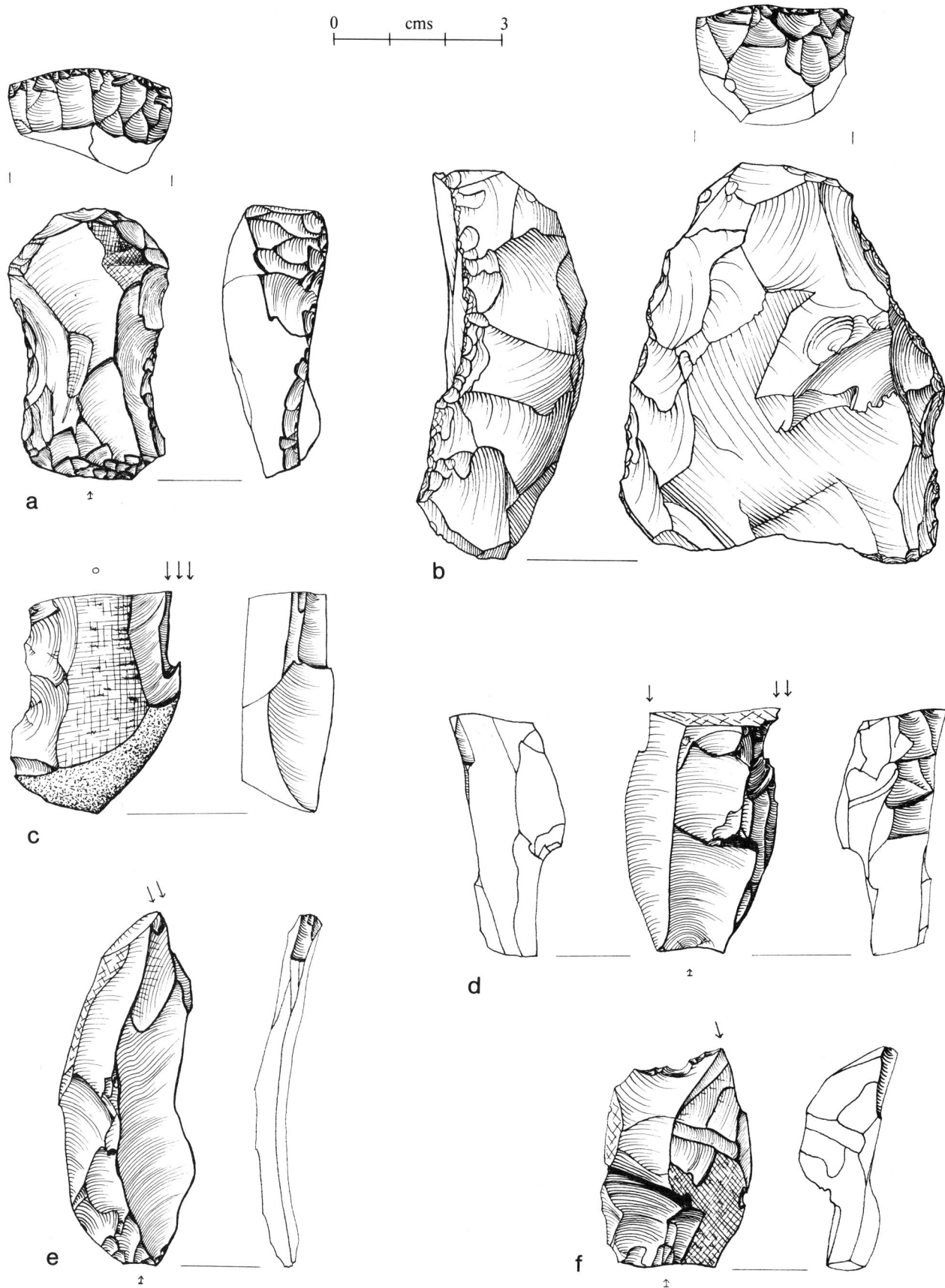

Fig. 20. Bilaterally retouched end scraper with steep retouch (a), nosed end scraper (b), burin on a break (c), burin on natural surface (d-e) and burin on concave truncation (f).

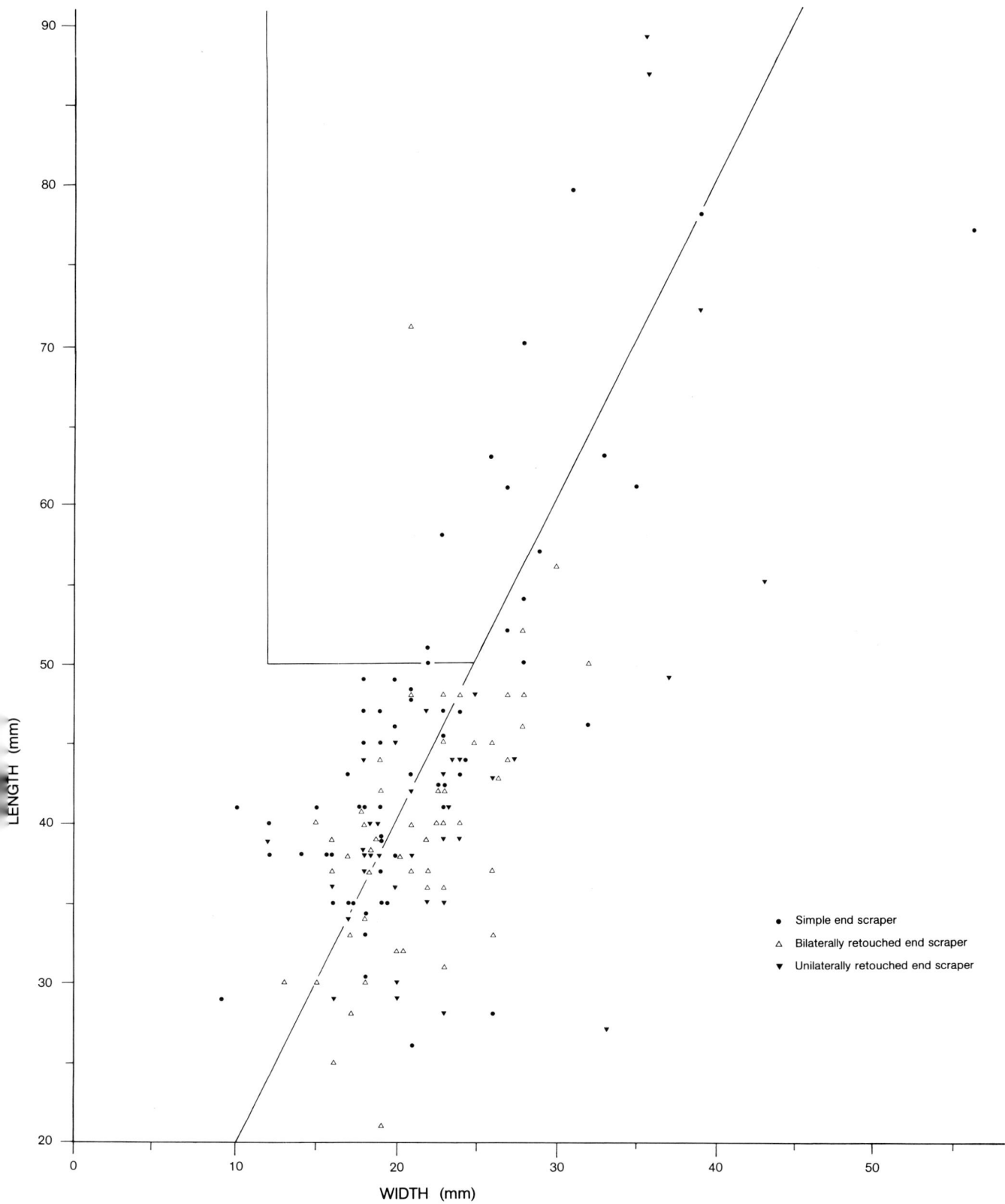

Fig. 21. Length-width scatter plot of complete pieces of the three predominant types of scrapers: simple end scrapers, bilaterally retouched end scrapers and unilaterally retouched end scrapers (N=149).

57

from area C-01. This suggests that the major source of variability between excavation units is due to recovery variability, and where that variable can be controlled and large samples are available, there appears to be little significant difference in the frequency of different tool groups.

Scrapers

Overall, scrapers represent 11% of the tool assemblage (table 18). There is considerable variability in the frequency of the sixteen types of scrapers which occur at Beidha with three types comprising 84% of the assemblage: simple end scrapers, bilaterally retouched end scrapers, and unilaterally retouched end scrapers (table 20). Simple end scrapers are the most frequent, representing 40% of the assemblage (fig. 18:a-c). Bilateral (fig. 18:d-e) and unilateral (fig. 19:a-b) end scrapers occur less frequently. Six types have frequencies between 3% and 1% (fig. 19:c-d, fig. 20:a-b). An additional seven types occur only rarely.

There appears to be little temporal variation in the frequency of scraper types. Between excavation units there is also minimal difference in the frequency variation between types, with level 4 of area C-01 being the most distinctive. The low relative frequency of scrapers recovered in area C-01 is undoubtedly due to the higher frequency of small tools.

The size range of the complete tools from the three most common scraper types is very similar, and quite a number of them are of flake size, despite their nonmetric blade blank characteristics (fig. 21). Scrapers were typically made on blades (table 11). The scraper tool class, however, has a very high frequency of indeterminate blank types, due to the extensive retouch these tools have undergone during their use life. The present dimensions of the tools are undoubtedly significantly smaller than the original size of the blanks.

Generally, the distal end is retouched, and it was chosen for retouching about two thirds of the time. The proximal end of the blank is missing in about one quarter of the sample. Occasionally, there is retouch on the interior of the proximal end, perhaps to facilitate hafting. Lateral retouch on the unilaterally retouched end scrapers occurs with equal frequency on the left and right lateral.

Burins

Burins occur infrequently at Beidha, representing less than 4% of the tool assemblage (table 18). Burins on a natural surface (fig. 20:d-e), and burins on breaks (fig. 20:c) are the most common types (table 20). These types constitute almost two thirds of this tool class, and are generally single-blow burins. Dihedral burins, and those on truncations (fig. 20:f) occur less frequently. The most common dihedral burin is an offset dihedral variety, and the most frequent truncated burin has a concave truncation. The remaining burin types occur very infrequently.

Over 30% of the burins are made on flake blanks (table 11). This is the the highest frequency of flake utilization for any tool class and reflects a more 'casual' selection criteria for suitable burin blanks. Burins on a natural surface are most commonly on flake-sized blanks, while, at the other end of the range, dihedral burins are most commonly on blade-sized blanks. The location of the burin blow is predominantly on the distal end of the piece.

Notches and denticulates

Notches and denticulates are the largest tool class in the Beidha assemblage, accounting for over 30% of the retouched tools (table 18). Two types, multiple small notches (fig. 22:b-c), and multiple small notches with additional retouch (fig. 22:d-e), predominate the assemblage, comprising almost 60% of the tool class (table 20). Small single notched pieces (fig. 22:a), and small single notched pieces with retouch represent another 19% of the tool class. Denticulates (having small notches, with or without additional retouch) represent another 16% of the assemblage (fig. 22:f-i). Small notches on breaks, large notched tools, and denticulates with large notches (fig. 23:b) occur infrequently.

Most of the notched and denticulated tools were made on blanks with blade dimensions, as clearly shown in the scatter plot (fig. 24). The exceptions are generally single large notched tools, and denticulates with large notches. These two types are made primarily on large flakes.

Table 20. Frequency distribution of tool types by tool class. →

	Subtotal N	%	Total N	%
End scrapers			332	11.58
Simple end scraper	133	40.1		
Bilaterally retouched end scraper	80	24.1		
Bilaterally retouched end scraper with steep retouch on laterals	9	2.7		
Unilaterally retouched end scraper	64	19.3		
Unilaterally retouched end scraper with steep retouch on laterals	4	1.2		
Double end scraper	8	2.4		
Ogival end scraper	1	0.3		
Nosed end scraper	8	2.4		
Circular end scraper	1	0.3		
Transverse e.s. on flake	1	0.3		
Rounded e.s. on flake	6	1.8		
Carinated e.s. on flake	2	0.6		
Nucleiform/core scraper	3	0.9		
Double core scraper	3	0.9		
Side scraper	7	2.1		
Denticulated scraper	2	0.6		
Burins			110	3.87
Dihedral	2	1.8		
Dihedral, offset	10	9.1		
Double dihedral	1	0.9		
Single burin on break	23	20.9		
Multiple burin on break	5	4.5		
Single burin on natural surface	30	27.3		
Multiple burin on natural surface	4	3.6		
Transverse burin on n.s.	11	10.0		
Straight truncation burin	4	3.6		
Concave truncation burin	7	6.4		
Convex truncation burin	1	0.9		
Multiple truncation burin	1	0.9		
Multiple burin, mixed	6	5.5		
Nucleiform burin	1	0.9		
Burin on interior surface	4	3.6		
Notches and denticulates			870	30.36
Large single notch	8	0.9		
Denticulate with large notches	22	2.5		
Small single notch	86	9.9		
Small single notch with retouch	80	9.2		
Multiple small notches	245	28.2		
Multiple small notches with retouch	269	30.9		
Denticulate with small notches	70	8.0		
Denticulate with small notches and retouch	65	7.5		
Small notch on break	25	2.9		
Drills			32	1.12
Perforator	21	65.6		
Multiple perforator	2	6.3		
Borer (bilateral retouch)	9	28.1		
Retouched tools			277	9.67
Complete pieces	126	45.5		
Indeterminate fragments	151	54.5		
Multiple tools			85	2.97
Notch & denticulate class with				
Scrapers	19	22.4		
Burins	12	14.1		
Drills	6	7.1		
Retouched pieces	4	4.7		
Truncations	7	8.2		
Backed pieces	11	12.9		
Other	1	1.2		
Burin class with				
Scrapers	8	9.4		
Single truncations	5	5.9		
Backed piece	4	4.7		
Other	3	3.5		
Other multiple tools	5	5.9		
Truncations			186	6.49
Single	127	68.3		
Double	59	31.7		
Geometrics			375	13.08
Lunate	346	92.3		
Asymmetrical lunate	22	5.9		
Triangle	3	0.8		
Asymmetrical triangle	4	1.1		
Nongeometric tools			158	5.51
La mouillah point	1	0.6		
Curved pointed piece, arched backed	7	4.4		
Arched backed with modified base	5	3.2		
Symmetric backed & double truncated	35	22.2		
Asymmetric backed & double truncated	15	9.5		
Backed & one truncation	35	22.2		
Backed, one truncation & modified base	8	5.1		
Backed, modified base & blunt Natural end	5	3.2		
Backed, modified base & pointed Natural end	1	0.6		
Backed, blunt distal end	7	4.4		
Backed, pointed distal end	2	1.3		
Partially backed, no end modification	4	2.5		
Double backed piece	14	8.9		
Various backed pieces	19	12.0		
Backed fragments			370	12.91
Proximal with truncation	74	20.0		
Distal with truncation	87	23.5		
Indeterminate with truncation	6	1.6		
Medial	54	14.6		
Proximal without truncation	48	13.0		
Proximal with base modification	22	5.9		
Distal, blunt end without truncation	14	3.8		
Distal, pointed end without truncation	5	1.4		
Partially backed	40	10.8		
Indeterminate	20	5.4		
Various			70	2.44
Edge damaged piece	58	82.9		
Sickle blades (unmodified)	3	4.3		
Battered piece	3	4.3		
Pick	2	2.9		
Varia	4	5.7		
Total			2866	100.00

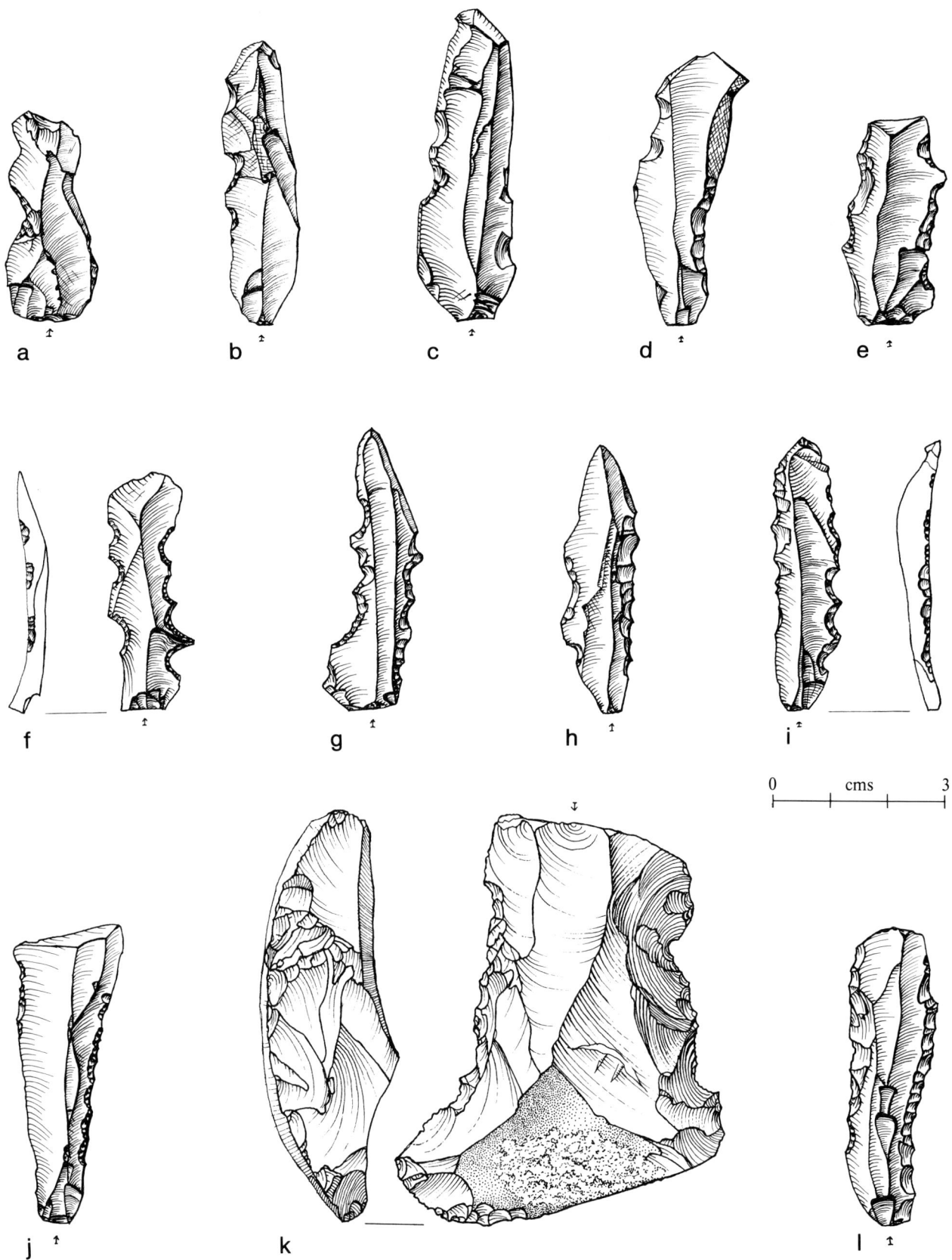

Fig. 22. Small notched and denticulated pieces (a-i), and complete retouched pieces (j-l).

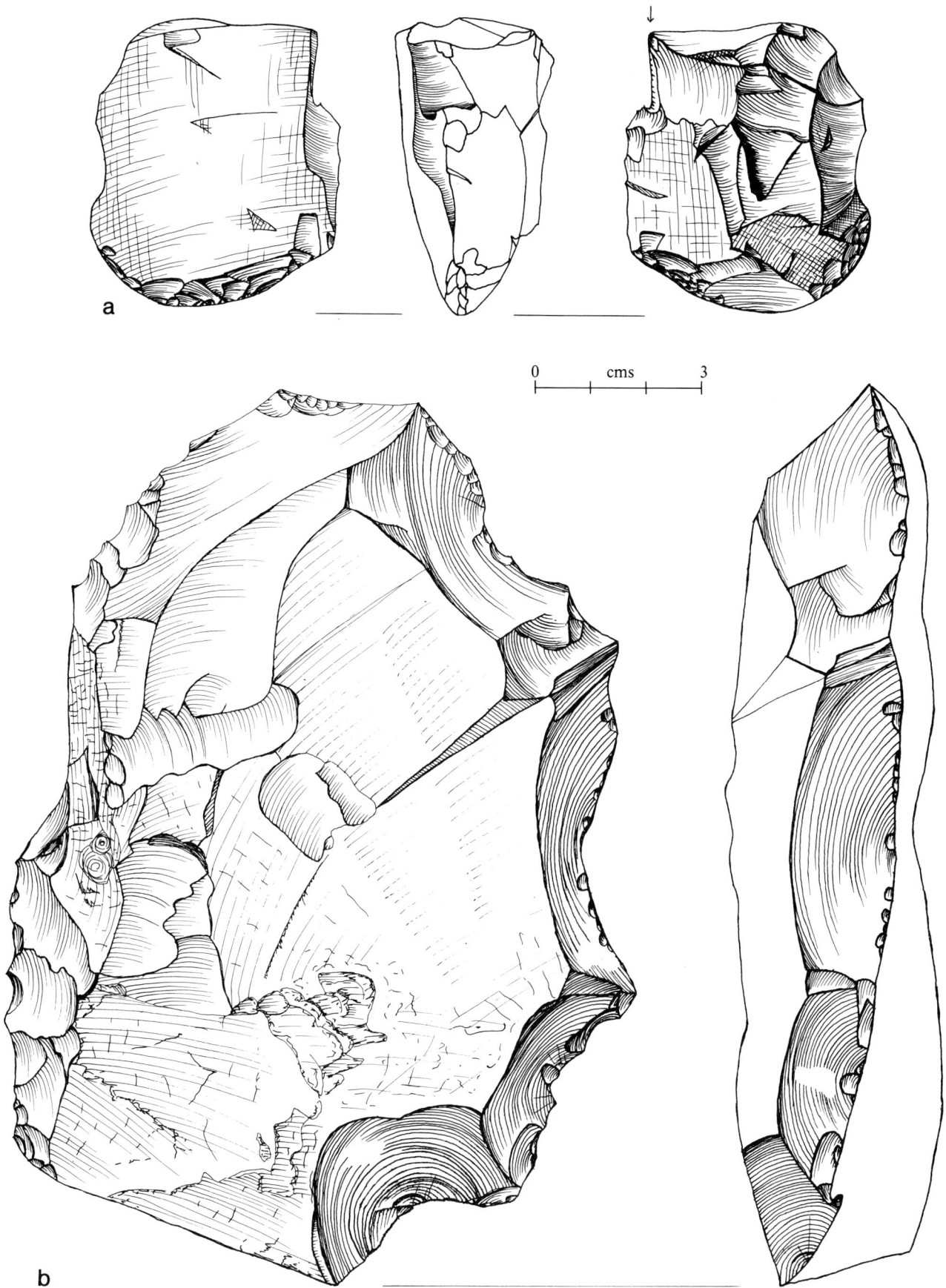

0 cms 3

Fig. 23. Multiple tool (a) and large notched denticulate (b).

61

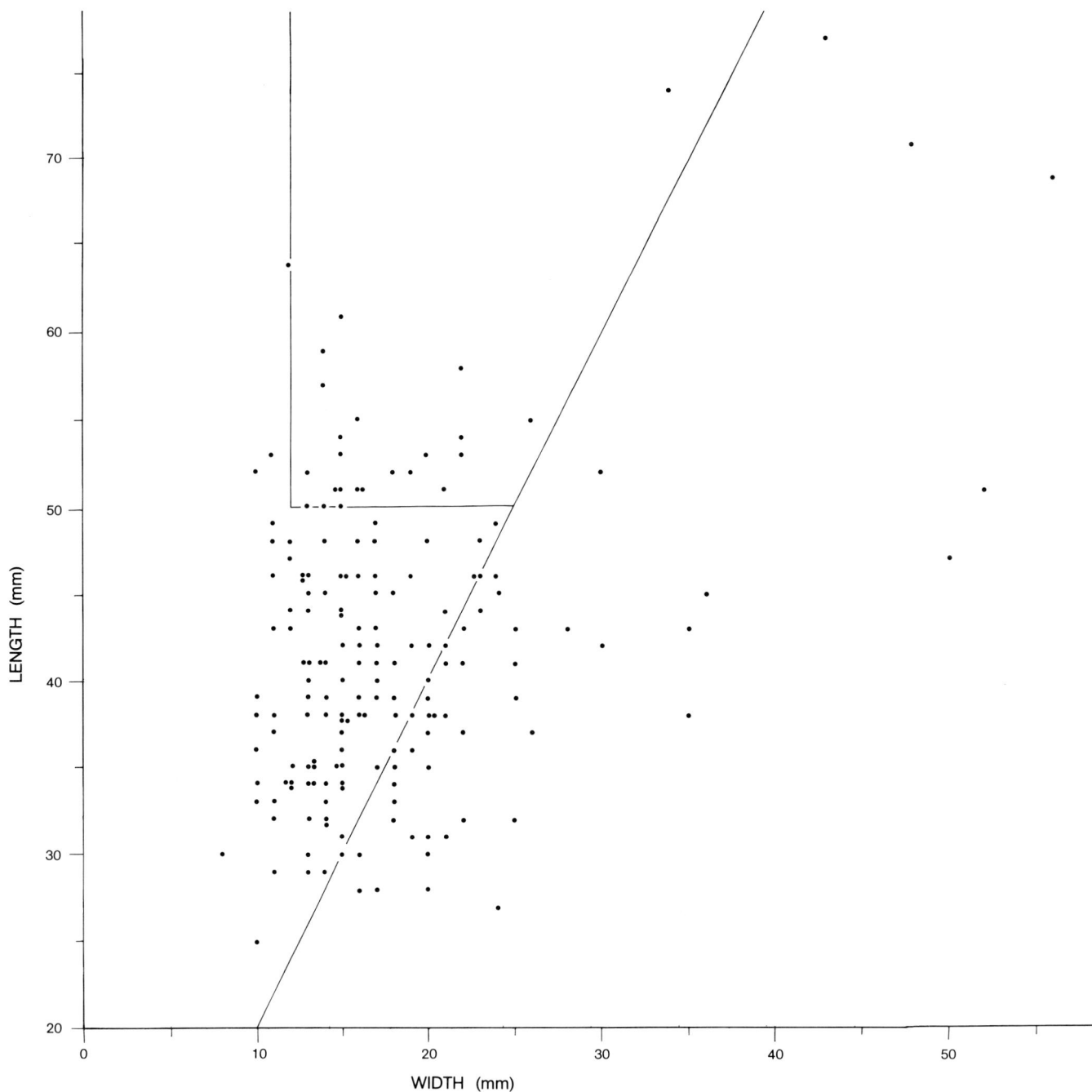

Fig. 24. Length-width scatter plot of complete notched and denticulated tools (N=170).

Retouched pieces

Simple retouched pieces constitute almost 10% of the tool assemblage (table 18). The retouch is generally irregular and semisteep (see Tixier [1963: 45-49] for a definition of the terms to characterize different categories of retouch). Complete retouched pieces represent 45.5% of this tool class (fig. 22:j-l) and retouched frag-

ments constitute the remainder (table 20). It is quite likely that many of the fragments would be classified as other tool types, such as notches and denticulates, or end scrapers, if they were complete. This would, of course, lower the frequency of this tool class.

Blade sized retouched pieces are over twice as common as flake sized retouched pieces (table

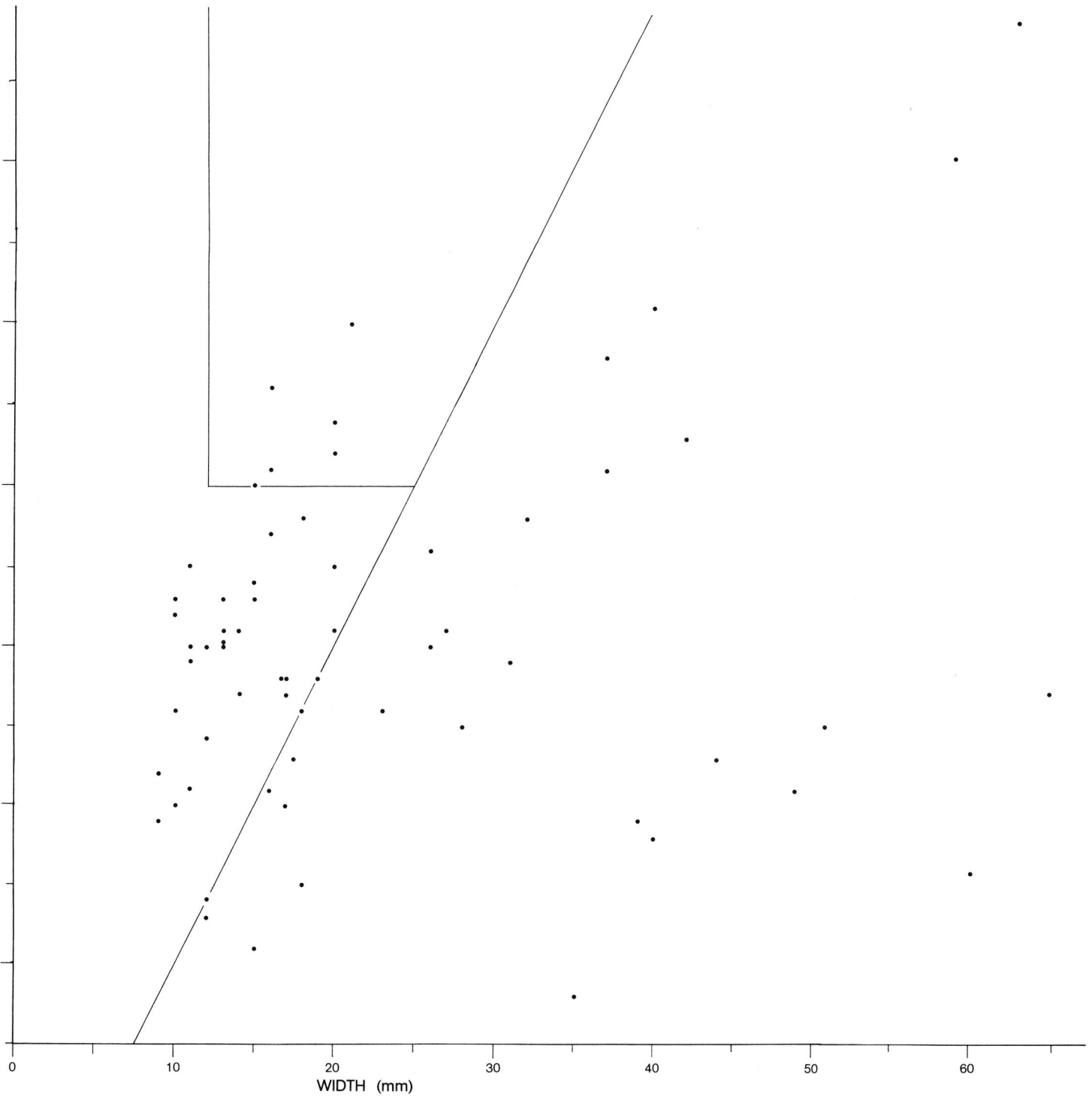

Fig. 25. Length-width scatter plot of complete retouched tools (N=62).

11). Yet the percentage of flake-sized pieces for this tool class is quite high in comparison to other tool classes. The average length for the complete retouched tools is 37 mm, while the width is 20 mm (fig. 25). The retouched pieces generally are retouched by semisteep exterior retouch, although steep exterior retouch occurs with some regularity. Other forms of retouch are uncommon.

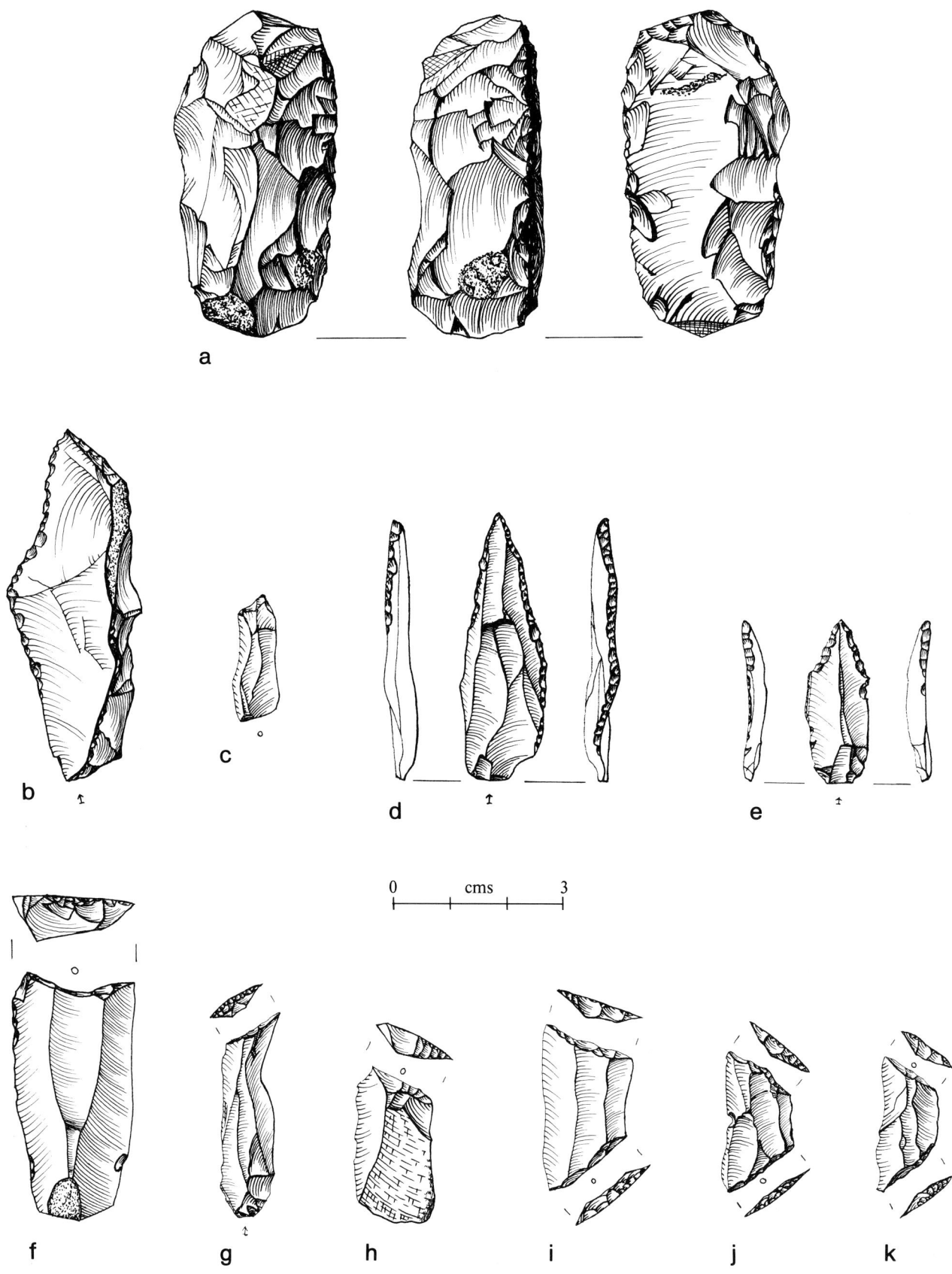

Fig. 26. Pick (a), perforators (b-c), borers (d-e), single truncations (f-h) and double truncations (i-k).

	Truncations				Lunates			
	Single		Double		Proximal end		Distal end	
	N	%	N	%	N	%	N	%
None	0	0.0	0	0.0	42	13.2	27	8.2
Abrupt exterior	114	89.8	50	84.7	185	58.0	194	58.8
Semisteep exterior	4	3.1	2	3.4	7	2.2	7	2.1
Semisteep interior	5	3.9	1	1.7	25	7.8	31	9.4
Bifacial (Helwan)	1	0.8	0	0.0	29	9.1	37	11.2
Alternate series	1	0.8	2	3.4	2	0.6	3	0.9
Minute burin blow	0	0.0	0	0.0	26	8.2	27	8.2
Other	2	1.6	4	6.8	3	0.9	4	1.2
Total	127	100.0	59	100.0	319	100.0	330	100.0

Table 21. Frequency distribution of retouch types on truncations and the ends of lunates.

	None		Light edge damage		Heavy edge damage		Total	
	N	%	N	%	N	%	N	%
Truncations	180	96.8	4	2.2	2	1.1	186	100.1
Geometrics	362	96.5	9	2.4	4	1.1	375	100.0
Nongeometrics	131	82.9	12	7.6	15	9.5	158	100.0

Table 22. Frequency distribution of edge damage categories on truncations, geometric microliths, and nongeometric microliths.

Drills

Drills are uncommon in the Natufian at Beidha, representing only 1% of the assemblage (table 18). They are generally complete tools, with steep retouch typically at the distal end. Simple perforators (fig. 26:b-c) predominate this tool class, and borers with bilaterally converging retouch (fig. 26:d-e) comprise most of the remainder of the tool class (table 20). Multiple perforators are rare.

Multiple tools

Multiple tools occur infrequently, and represent less than 3% of the tool assemblage (table 18). The vast majority of the multiple tools are tools with one or more notches co-occurring with the retouch typical of a second tool type (table 20). Multiple tools which combine burins with other tool classes comprise most of the remainder of the tool class (fig. 23:a). Scrapers with notches from the most common multiple tool type. Burins with notches, and backed pieces with notches also occur frequently. In addition, notches with truncations, drills, or retouched pieces, and burins with scrapers, single truncations, or backed pieces are present.

Truncations

Truncations comprise over 6% of the tool assemblage (table 18). Single truncations represent over two thirds of the truncation tool class (fig. 26:f-h), the remainder are double truncations (fig. 26:i-k, table 20).

Only 41% of the single truncations are complete tools. Incomplete single truncations are divided between pieces missing distal or proximal ends. The distal end is truncated about 56% of the time, while the proximal end is truncated only about 41% of the time. Retouch is generally present over the entire length of the truncation. Incomplete retouch over greater than 50% of the truncation occurs around one quarter of the time. Retouch is primarily steep exterior retouch (over 85%); all other types of retouch are uncommon (table 21).

Single truncation tools typically have straight oblique or convex oblique truncations (fig. 27). The remnant of a microburin scar is visible only about 14% of the time. As these truncations are generally completely retouched, the actual use of the microburin technique to snap the blanks prior to truncation retouch may have been considerably higher. Edge damage occurs only infrequently (table 22).

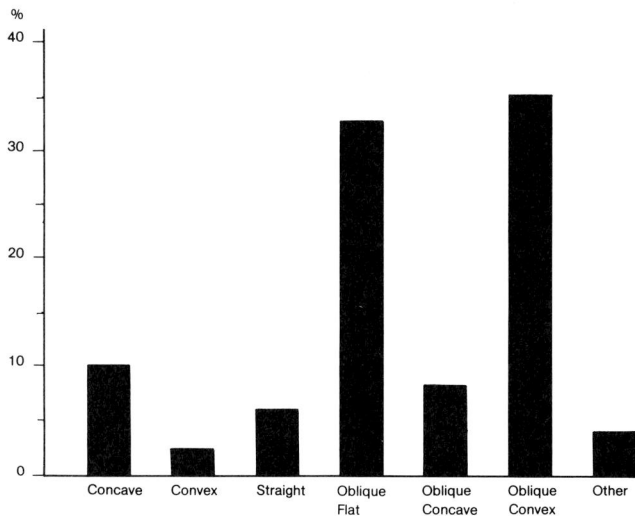

Fig. 27. Bar chart showing the relative frequency of truncation shapes on single truncation tools (N=119).

The manufacturing characteristics of double truncations are similar to those of single truncation tools. On double truncations, there is no preference for which lateral edge (see Tixier 1963: 34 for definition of left and right lateral edges) is the shorter (presumably, this was the hafted edge). The distribution is almost equally divided between the right and left lateral, and this edge is generally either straight or somewhat convex.

For double truncations the percentage of retouch on the truncation is almost evenly divided between complete retouch, and retouch of 51-99% of the edge. The remnant of a microburin scar occurs more often than on single truncations, occurring on over one quarter of the double truncations. This higher frequency of microburin scars on double truncation tools, as opposed to single truncation tools, is undoubtedly only a result of the less intensive retouch.

Geometric microliths

Geometric microliths are an important tool class at Beidha, and constitute over 13% of the assemblage (table 18). Lunates, the "fossil directeur" of the Natufian, represent over 98% of the geometric microliths (fig. 28, table 20). The arch of the backed edge on most of the lunates is symmetrical, and only rarely asymmetrical (fig. 29:a-b). Triangles constitute the remainder of this tool class (fig. 29:c). The

few triangles that occur at Beidha appear to have been manufactured more often by abrupt exterior retouch than by bifacial retouch. Other geometric types are absent.[11]

The length of complete lunates appears to vary minimally between provenience units except between level 4 and level 2 in area C-01 (table 23). In general, mean lunate length varies from 25 mm to 28mm, and this varies little between the different retouch categories. In area C-01, where lunate length is considerably less, it averages between 18 and 23 mm. A Mann-Whitney test indicates that the length difference between level 4 (e.g., fig. 28:o-r) and level 2 in area C-01 (fig. 28:s-v) is significant (N=33, U=17.0, W=32.0, P=0.006).

The shape of the backed edge varies within the lunate tool type. The backed edge is a uniform arch from one end to the other in only about one quarter of the lunates. Typically (over 60% of the time), the shape of the backed edge is convex with a sharper angle at each end (fig. 28:i-n).[12] This is undoubtedly because the backing, truncation and retouching of the ends were separate steps in the manufacturing process. The backing retouch on lunates occurs almost twice as often along the left lateral (63.3%, N=344) than along the right lateral edge (36.7%). In the vast majority of cases, the entire length of the lunate is retouched. Only about 11% of the time is the retouch less than complete.

The type of retouch along the backed edge shows considerable variation. Bifacial (Helwan) retouch is predominant (fig. 28:a-d), occurring over half the time (table 24). Semisteep interior retouch (fig. 28:e-f), and semisteep interior retouch combined with bifacial retouch account for another 23% of the sample. Abrupt exterior

[11]Although Valla (1975) classified some of the microliths at Beidha as trapezes, I have opted to have a slightly broader definition for lunates and, to some extent, for double truncated backed nongeometric microliths. Those tools which were closest to trapezes in classification, typically have a slightly arched backed lateral edge (in contrast, the definitions and illustrations for trapezes emphasize their straight backs) and bifacial retouch. They are few in number, grade into lunates, and most likely represent one end of the range of variation of lunate-like microliths.

[12]Lunates without a smooth curve to the backed edge resemble what Goring-Morris (1987: 456-459) has classified as atypical Helwan lunates (type J10), and double truncated Helwan bladelets (type I28).

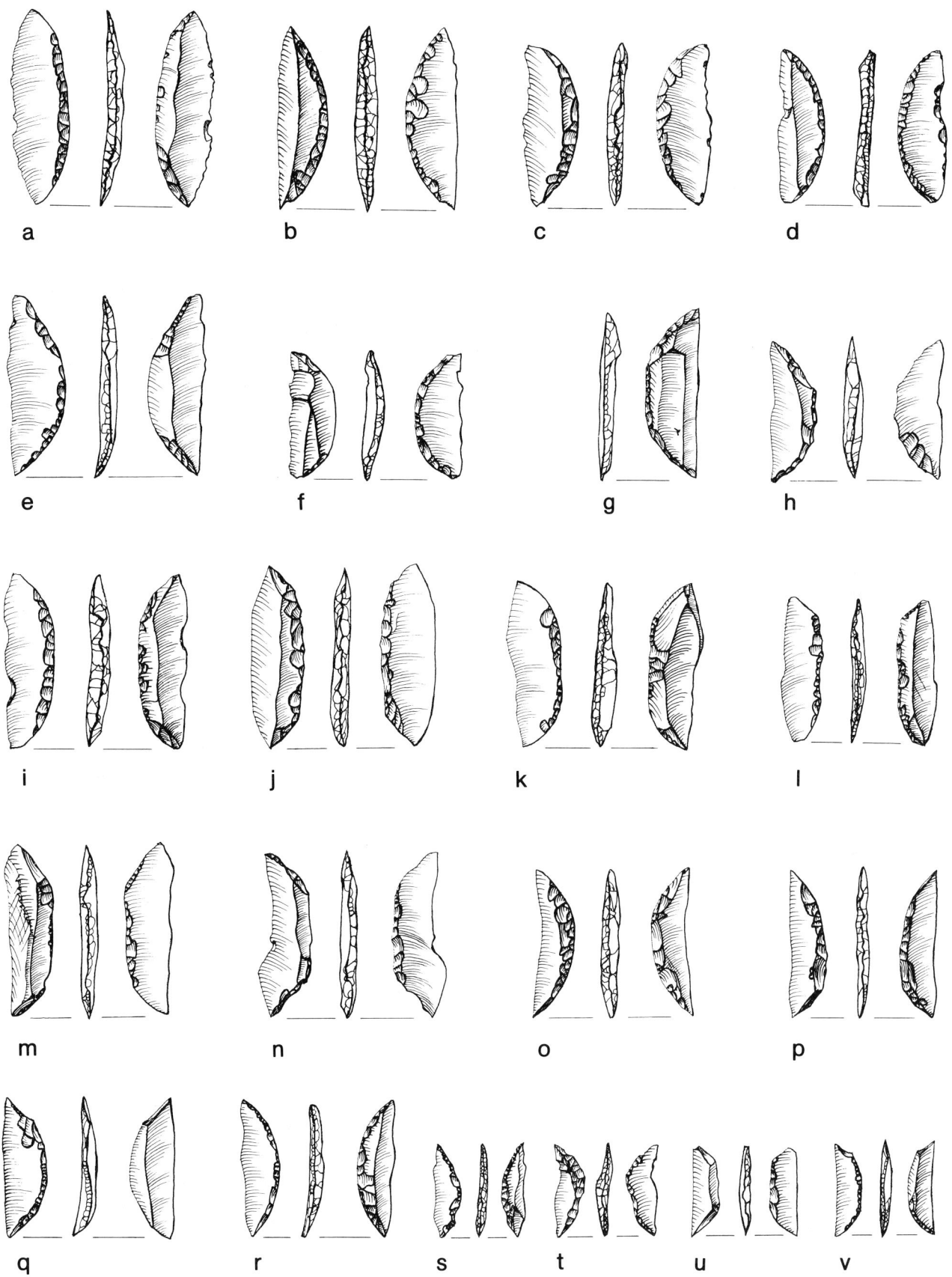

Fig. 28. Symmetric lunates.

0   cms   3

67

Area	Level	N	Length Mean	Length StDev	Width Mean	Width StDev	Length-width ratio Mean	Length-width ratio StDev	Thickness Mean	Thickness StDev
K-2	1	55	26.91	4.58	7.95	1.16	3.40	0.47	2.40	0.53
	2	22	27.50	3.50	8.55	1.53	3.27	0.48	2.50	0.59
	3	11	26.18	3.51	7.82	0.60	3.36	0.44	2.09	0.54
F-1	1	8	27.00	5.18	8.38	1.77	3.28	0.61	2.62	0.52
	3	2	28.50	0.70	7.50	0.71	3.82	0.45	3.00	0.00
J-2	1	62	27.27	3.35	8.60	1.87	3.25	0.48	2.48	0.56
	2	70	28.63	3.62	8.39	1.19	3.46	0.49	2.53	0.50
	3	12	25.75	3.72	7.67	0.89	3.36	0.30	2.50	0.52
F-1	1 (1964)	6	27.33	5.20	7.83	1.47	3.52	0.62	2.50	0.55
H-4	55	9	29.44	3.78	8.78	1.72	3.41	0.48	2.33	0.50
C-01	2	5	18.20	3.27	5.00	1.22	3.70	0.50	1.80	0.84
	3	1	22.00	-	7.00	-	3.14	-	2.00	-
	4	28	23.18	2.39	7.46	2.53	3.34	0.86	2.32	0.48
Total		291	26.95	4.14	8.15	1.63	3.37	0.53	2.44	0.54

StDev: Standard deviation

Table 23. Mean size of lunates by provenience unit.

	SE	SemiI	SI	B	B&I	B&E	O	M	AS	C	Total%	N
Lunates	10.1	1.1	12.8	53.3	10.9	1.1	0.3	0.0	7.6	2.7	99.9	367
All nongeometrics	16.5	0.8	33.9	23.1	13.2	1.7	1.7	2.5	5.8	0.8	100.0	121
Pointed pieces	38.5	7.7	15.4	23.1	0.0	0.0	0.0	7.7	7.7	0.0	100.1	13
Backed, double truncation	14.0	0.0	34.0	38.0	10.0	0.0	0.0	0.0	2.0	2.0	100.0	50
Backed, single truncation	17.1	0.0	31.4	14.3	14.3	5.7	2.9	5.7	8.6	0.0	100.0	35
Backed, single truncation, modified base	12.5	0.0	37.5	0.0	37.5	0.0	0.0	0.0	12.5	0.0	100.0	8
Backed, modified base	0.0	0.0	50.0	0.0	33.3	0.0	0.0	0.0	16.7	0.0	100.0	6
Backed, no end retouch	11.1	0.0	55.6	11.1	11.1	0.0	11.1	0.0	0.0	0.0	100.0	9

SE:	Steep exterior	B&I:	Bifacial & interior	M:	Marginal
SemiE:	Semisteep exterior	B&E:	Bifacial & exterior	AS:	Aternate series
SI:	Semisteep interior	O:	Ochata	C:	Combination
B:	Bifacial (Helwan)				

Table 24. Relative frequency of retouch types for geometric and nongeometric microliths.

	Proximal end N	Proximal end %	Distal end N	Distal end %
None	191	59.9	226	68.5
Positive Krukowski microburin scar interior	3	0.9	1	0.3
Partial positive Krukowski microburin scar interior	19	6.0	5	1.5
Negative microburin scar exterior	4	1.3	5	1.5
Partial negative microburin scar exterior	102	32.0	93	28.2
Total	319	100.0	330	100.0

Table 25. Frequency distribution of microburin scars on the proximal and distal ends of lunates.

68

retouch is present in low numbers (fig. 28:g-h). Edge damage along the unretouched edge rarely occurs (table 22).

The ends of the lunate appear to have been retouched separately from the lateral edge, and they show a number of distinctive characteristics. At a steeper angle than the curve of the backed lateral edge, the shape of the ends are generally obliquely convex. Flat oblique ends occur occasionally, and concave oblique ends occur only rarely. Both the proximal and distal ends are retouched by abrupt exterior retouch the majority of the time, although significantly less than for truncated tools (table 21). Bifacial retouch and semisteep interior retouch are present in much lower frequencies, and this is in notable contrast to the retouch on the backed lateral edge (table 24).

Evidence that the microburin technique was used in the manufacture of lunates is abundant. Negative microburin scars are visible on 32% and 40% of the distal and proximal ends, respectively (table 25). The microburin scars are usually visible on the exterior, and have been partially removed by retouch. A small number of microburin scars, however, are present on the interior. These are positive scars of the Beidha Krukowski microburins, and they occur almost exclusively in area C-01. There is a distinct pattern for the microburin scars on lunates in level 4 of area C-01. The distal ends have higher percentages of microburin scars on the exterior surface, while the proximal ends have higher percentages of positive microburin scars on the interior surface. The interior microburin scars are the result of truncations which generated the Beidha Krukowski microburin by-product.

A model outlining the typical steps in the manufacture of lunates from level 4 in C-01 can be presented by utilizing information on the patterns of the microburin technique and lunate retouch. Initially, the bladelets were truncated at the distal end by the microburin technique. Semisteep interior retouch was then executed on the left lateral edge, generally starting at the proximal end. This end was subsequently truncated, probably by snapping the artifact on an anvil, creating a Beidha Krukowski microburin. Semisteep exterior retouch was then used to produce the final appearance of bifacial backing. The ends were then further modified, if deemed necessary.

Nongeometric microliths

Nongeometric microliths occur infrequently, constituting less than 6% of the tool assemblage (table 18). The Beidha typology, particularly with respect to the microliths, has emphasized artifact shape and retouch location, rather than the retouch type and blank type (particularly blade versus bladelet). Despite this attempt to utilize a more consistent typology that emphasized morphological variability (at the expense of other attributes), there is considerable gradation between nongeometric types and between them and lunates. Furthermore, there is patterned variability within some nongeometric types.

The form of retouch on nongeometric microliths is generally more varied than on the geometric microliths (table 24). In particular, bifacial retouch occurs less than one quarter of the time. Semisteep interior retouch is most prevalent, and abrupt exterior retouch, and a combination of bifacial and interior retouch are common.

Backed and double truncated pieces are the most ubiquitous nongeometric microlith (table 20). Of these, pieces with symmetrical truncations are more than twice as prevalent as asymmetrically truncated pieces. The size range of double truncated pieces is greater than that for the geometric microliths, and mean length is somewhat higher (table 26). The truncated ends are typically fashioned by abrupt exterior retouch, with semisteep interior retouch and bifacial retouch occurring in decreasing frequencies.

Within the tool type of symmetric double truncated pieces, three subtypes are distinguishable. Subtype A, the most frequent (representing two thirds of the sample), is morphologically very similar to the lunate (fig. 29:f-h).[13] The backing along the lateral edge is typically semisteep interior or bifacial retouch. The truncations are generally obliquely flat, with remnants of microburin scars still visible.

Subtype B consists of elongated, narrow pieces with a slightly convex backed lateral edge (fig. 29:i-k).[14] The backing is ordinarily bifacial or semisteep interior retouch. In contrast to

[13]Of the nongeometric microliths, these tools are closest in morphology to trapezes.

[14]These are similar to what Goring-Morris (1987: 458-459) has classified as Helwan bladelets (type I29).

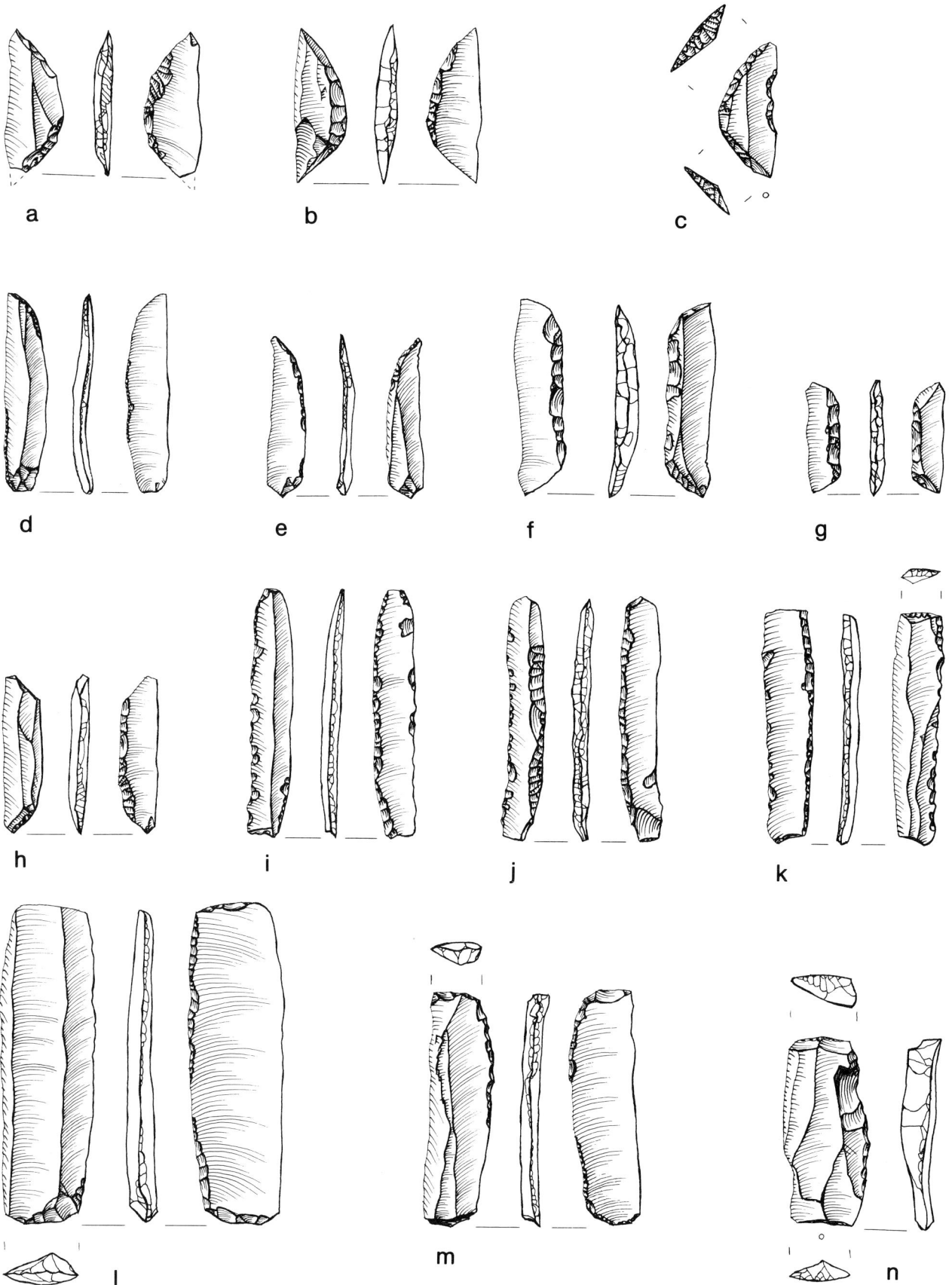

Fig. 29. Asymmetric lunates (a-b), triangle (c), and nongeometric microliths (d-n).

	N	Length		Width		Length-width ratio		Thickness	
		Mean	StDev	Mean	StDev	Mean	StDev	Mean	StDev
Pointed pieces	13	28.30	5.22	9.31	2.25	3.19	0.87	2.38	0.65
Backed, double truncation	50	31.00	9.05	8.74	2.50	3.61	0.81	2.68	0.79
Backed, single truncation	35	37.82	9.16	11.11	3.36	3.57	0.90	3.03	0.78
Backed, single truncation, modified base	8	40.37	8.96	10.25	2.38	3.99	0.60	3.00	0.75
Backed, modified base	6	38.66	4.50	9.50	1.87	4.17	0.77	2.83	0.40
Backed, no end retouch	9	40.11	6.11	10.33	1.80	3.98	0.92	3.11	0.78
Total	121	34.36	9.27	9.74	2.83	3.64	0.86	2.81	0.77

StDev: Standard deviation

Table 26. Mean size dimensions of nongeometric microliths.

subtype A, the truncated edges are varied in shape (primarily convex, straight and concave), and rarely obliquely flat. Microburin scars are absent. These tools appear to have the highest frequency of edge damage along the unretouched lateral edge of any tool group.

In contrast, subtype C (fig. 29:l-n) tools are longer and wider often fitting the conventional (and arbitrary) metric definition for a backed blade *sensu stricto*.[15] The characteristics of the backing and the truncated ends are similar to subtype B, although the small sample (5) makes this observation tentative.

Single truncated pieces are the second most prevalent nongeometric microliths (table 20), and are generally larger in size than the double truncated pieces (table 26, fig. 30). Subtypes B and C, distinguished for double truncated backed pieces, are also recognized within this type (subtype A is not readily recognizable), although a number of tools do not fit into either subtype. The long and narrow tools of subtype B (fig. 31:a-c) have a set of attributes similar to those described for subtype B of the double truncated backed tools. In addition, the truncation is habitually on the distal end, with the bulb of percussion still extant.

Subtype C comprises over two-thirds of the single truncated backed tools (fig. 31:d-f). The backed lateral edge is customarily elongated convex, while straight lateral edges occur less often. The distal end is truncated about three times as frequently as the proximal end. The end shape is typically convex, and microburin scars are rare. Semisteep interior retouch is generally used to truncate these tools, although

[15]Backed blades *sensu stricto* are defined exactly as blades *sensu stricto* except that the width is greater than or equal to 9 mm (Tixier 1963: 39).

abrupt exterior and bifacial retouch also were utilized.

Single truncated pieces with modified bases are infrequent (fig. 31:g-h). The proximal end was normally the end selected for modification and the retouch was typically semisteep interior retouch.

Pointed microliths (types 48-53) are relatively infrequent. The two types of pointed tools that occur most often are curved pointed arched backed pieces (fig. 29:d), and curved pointed pieces with a modified base (fig. 29:e). The shape and size of these tools grades into that of lunates (table 26), and it is quite likely that these tools, particularly those with modified bases, represent one end of distribution of lunate-shaped tools.

Backed pieces without truncations occur in low frequencies. Some have a modified base, while others have unretouched ends (fig. 31:i-j). Partially backed pieces occur occasionally. Double backed pieces, some of which possibly may be broken drills, and various other backed pieces also are present.

Edge damage on the unretouched lateral edge of the nongeometric microliths occurs in considerably higher frequencies than on geometric microliths or truncated tools (table 22). Heavy and moderate edge damage are equally prevalent, heavy edge damage being most prevalent on single truncated nongeometric microliths with modified bases. The higher frequency of edge damage on nongeometric microliths as opposed to geometrics and truncations may be due to the use of these tools in different tasks, specifically cutting as opposed to being used as hunting projectiles. Sickle polish, however, is only identified, tentatively, on one nongeometric microlith.

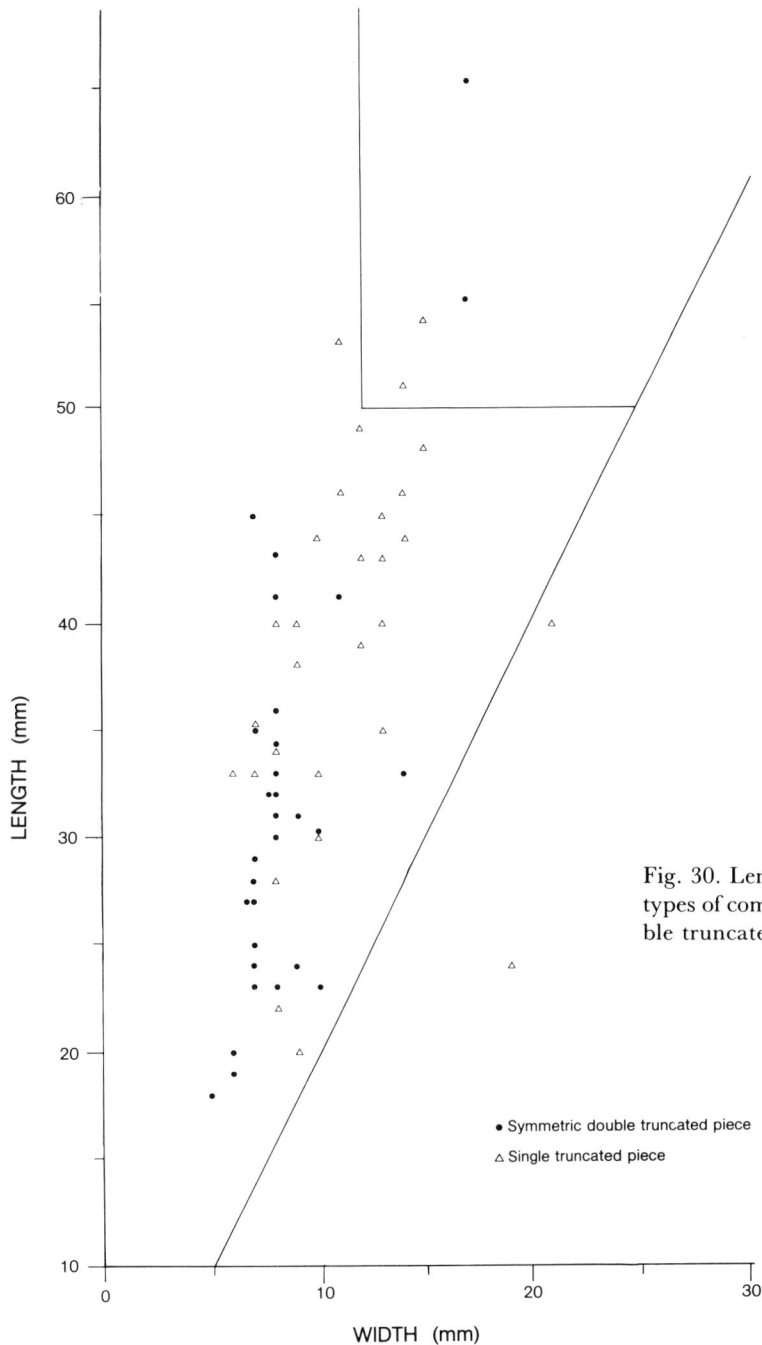

Fig. 30. Length-width scatter plot of the two predominant types of complete nongeometric microliths: symmetric double truncated pieces, and single truncated pieces (N=69).

Backed fragments of microliths

Backed fragments are common, occurring about as frequently as geometric microliths (table 18). Table 20 shows the distribution of the backed fragment types. In general, fragments with truncations and medial fragments are the most common, representing about 58% of the fragments. Proximal fragments without truncations, and indeterminate fragments occur in sizable numbers. These fragments appear to reflect the relative frequency of complete geometric and nongeometric microliths.

Various

This miscellaneous category represents less than 3% of the tools (table 18), and it is primarily pieces exhibiting edge damage (table 20). This may be damage received during use or post-depositional alteration. Picks (fig. 26:a), sickle blades, and battered pieces are uncommon. The assignment of three artifacts to the category of sickle blade must be viewed with caution due to the difficulty in visually separating sickle polish from the post-depositional polishing that is prevalent on most of the Natufian flints at Beidha.

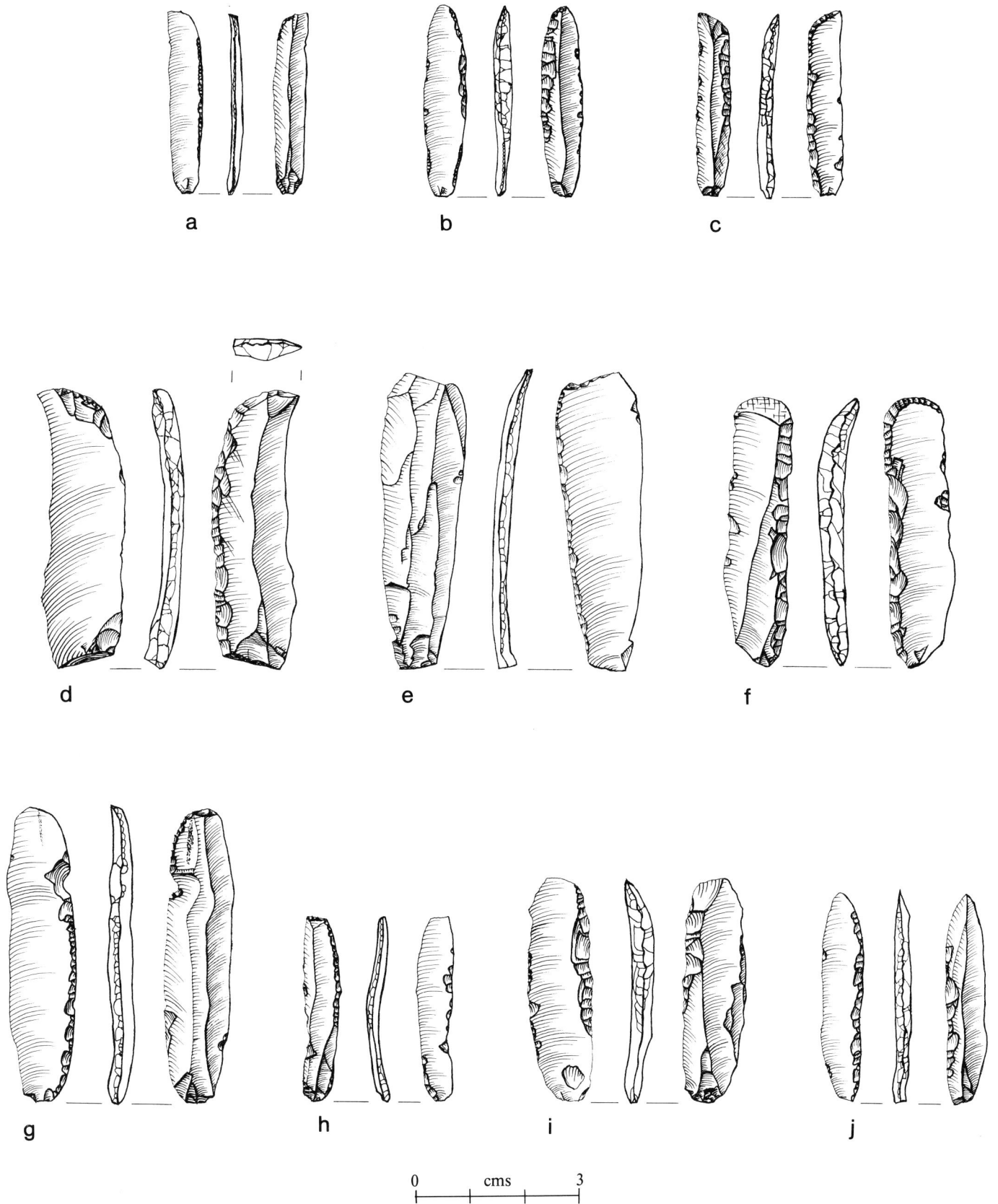

Fig. 31. Nongeometric microliths.

0   cms   3

Summary

There is a formidable degree of homogeneity in the distribution of different tool classes between excavation areas at Beidha. The only exception is the significantly higher frequency of tools with small mean size in area C-01, due undoubtedly to variability in recovery technique. Moreover, temporal variation appears, in general, to be minimal. The major exception appears to be between level 4 and level 2 in area C-01 where the lunate length decreases significantly.

The Beidha chipped stone tool assemblage is dominated by microlithic tools (geometrics, nongeometrics, and their fragments), and notched and denticulated tools, constituting almost two thirds of the sample. Scrapers and retouched pieces (over half of which are fragments) are also common, while truncations and burins infrequent. Drills, pieces with sickle polish, and massive pieces are rare.[16] The frequencies of these different tools classes are congruent with summary characterizations of the composition of the Natufian chipped stone tool assemblage (Bar-Yosef 1983; Henry 1981; Valla 1975), and support the use of the label Natufian to portray the Beidha industry.

Geometric microliths are over twice as frequent as nongeometric microliths, and the former are almost exclusively lunates. Lunate shape varies widely, with the truncated ends often at a different angle than the backed edge — they are comparable to many of the tools from Natufian sites in the Negev and Sinai (Goring-Morris 1987). The large mean length of lunates, and the high frequency of bifacial retouch are congruent with temporal subdivisions proposed for the Natufian based on lunate size and retouch type which would place Beidha in the early phase (Bar-Yosef and Valla 1979: 147; Valla 1987a). The high frequency of semisteep interior retouch on the lunates at Beidha, however, is notable in contrast to earlier characterizations.[17]

Conclusions

The chipped stone assemblage from Beidha is characterized by a considerable degree of intra-site similarity. The major difference in the distribution of artifacts appears to be the result of the greater recovery of smaller artifacts such as microflakes, microblades, microburins, and microliths in the 1983 excavations of area C-01. Within any one area, where recovery technique would not have varied noticeably, there are few observable differences.

Two sets of patterned intrasite variability, however, appear significant with respect to prehistoric behavior. There is significant variability in the relative number of cores, in debitage-core ratios, and in debitage-tool ratios between excavation areas. Whether these differences are related to relative variation in the amount of core reduction or to the discard locations of exhausted raw material is unknown. Furthermore, the later Natufian occupation in layer 2 of area C-01 deviates from other samples in several respects, including the blade-flake ratio and the length of the lunates. The one apparently reliable radiocarbon date available from this occupation episode is considerably later than the three well-clustered dates from level 4, and suggests that the differences between level 2 of area C-01 and other provenience units are temporally related.

Overall the chipped stone assemblage from the Beidha Natufian appears to fit within the range of variation noted for Natufian assemblages. There is, however, patterned variability between groups of Natufian sites with respect to a number of elements. This variability has implications for the range of tasks carried out and the nature of settlement intensity and will be explored in next chapter.

[16]Drills and pieces with sickle polish were previously undocumented at Beidha (Kirkbride: 1966: 47-51; Valla 1975: 84-85).

[17]The discrepancy between these results and Valla's (1975: 75; 1984: 174) characterization of the frequency of retouch types at Beidha may, in part, be due to classificatory criteria. For example, I used a separate category to distinguish pieces that have only partial bifacial retouch (the remainder being another type of retouch).

6. Subsistence patterns and settlement organization

This chapter examines the primary and secondary evidence for subsistence and settlement variability during the Natufian occupation of Beidha; discussion is then expanded to examine the local region and finally to a consideration of Levantine variability in Natufian adaptive strategies.

Beidha

Subsistence base

Hecker reports that caprines are the predominant species exploited during the Natufian at Beidha and that there is no evidence to suggest they were domesticated (Hecker, Appendix C). Two species of caprines, wild goat and Nubian ibex, are identified, and they undoubtedly inhabited different niches in the rugged local setting. Gazelle, probably hunted in the Wadi Araba, is the next most frequent species, while aurochs and onager occur infrequently. Hecker observes that differential procurement strategies are evident: gazelle, typically pursued a considerable distance from Beidha, are generally brought to the site complete, while the very large aurochs, were more often butchered at the kill and the meat-laden portions carried back to Beidha.

Despite flotation in 1964 and 1983, no identifiable botanical material has been recovered from the Natufian of Beidha. This is due in part to the nature of the sandy sediment, resulting in generally poor preservation.

A number of artifact sets have the potential to furnish secondary evidence of subsistence activities. In particular, functional interpretations of chipped stone tool assemblages provide an important line of evidence for examining the range and emphasis of activities at prehistoric settlements. Four sources of functional interpretations can be drawn on: ethnographic analogy, microwear analysis of prehistoric tools, experi-

mental microwear research, and observations based on evidence for prehistoric hafting and use. In the Near East several studies, typically limited in scope, have examined samples from different chipped stone tools classes (e.g. M. Cauvin 1983). Such analysis, and the functional inferences that are required, however, are not without hazards (see Newcomer *et al.* 1986; Odell and Odell-Vereecken 1980; Gendel and Pirnay 1982).

Natufian geometric microliths are typically interpreted as hunting projectiles (Bar-Yosef 1987; Valla 1987b), and they were certainly used as such in Predynastic and Dynastic Egypt (J.D. Clark *et al.* 1974; J.D. Clark 1975-1977). Further support comes from use wear study of lunates and triangles from the Natufian of Abu Hureyra which identified meat polish and hafting techniques (Anderson-Gerfaud 1983: 78-85).

Nongeometric microliths are normally interpreted as plant processing tools, particularly when they exhibit sickle polish. Whether they were used for cutting cereals, reeds or rushes, however, has been debated (see Anderson-Gerfaud 1983: 92-96; Unger-Hamilton 1989).[18] These tools have been found mounted in bone sickles at el Wad (Garrod and Bate 1937) and Wadi Hameh 27 (Edwards 1987), and microwear work suggests they may also have been hafted in wood sickles (Anderson-Gerfaud 1983).

Scrapers have been interpreted as most commonly used for processing of animal skins and hides, although use on bone, wood, and antler has also been claimed (Brink 1978; Gould *et al.* 1971, Evans 1872; Hayden 1977, 1979; Juel Jensen 1983). In the Near East, Unger-Hamilton (1988: 131) has suggested that most of the end scrapers at Neolithic Arjoune in Syria were used for hide working, while Coqueugniot

---

[18]Some of the small and narrow nongeometric microliths may have served the same function as geometric microliths – hunting projectiles – as opposed to the large nongeometric microliths which are typically associated with sickle polish.

(1983: 163) has suggested that end scrapers from Mureybet were used for a variety of tasks: scraping skins, working/cutting of bone and wood, and chopping wood.

Shaving and engraving of wood, antler or bone is the normative functional interpretation for burins (Bordes 1965; Hayden 1977: 185; Newcomer 1974; Keeley 1980). In the Levant this is supported by microwear analysis of burins from Neolithic Abu Hureyra which indicates that the bits were used on hard materials, probably for engraving and boring, and the edges used for working wood or reeds (Moss 1983).[19]

The function of simple retouched pieces, notches and denticulates, and unretouched artifacts is quite difficult to ascertain and generalizations are especially hazardous. This is due in part to the more expedient nature of their construction, that they could be used for a variety of tasks, and that, due to the type and limited intensity of use, traces of use are less evident. Unretouched artifacts and laterally retouched artifacts may have been used for a variety of tasks including cutting and whittling on soft and medium-soft materials, particularly wood (Gould et al. 1971; Hayden 1977; Juel Jensen 1983; Wilmsen 1968; White 1968).

Notches and denticulates may have functioned in a variety of capacities, particularly shaving and woodworking, although hide working and combing of fibrous material may also have occurred (Cahen and Gysels 1983; Morris and Burgh 1954; Moss 1983; Unger-Hamilton 1988). In the Near East, notches at Neolithic Arjoune appear to have been used for wood and bone working (Unger-Hamilton 1988: 153). Büller (1983: 110) has suggested that notches at el Wad were used for cutting sinew, while those at Ain Mallaha were used for a variety of tasks, although this interpretation has been criticized for the lack of documentation (Newcomer et al. 1986: 204). Denticulates at Arjoune may have functioned in a variety of capacities including woodworking, combing of fibrous materials, and perforating or engraving (Unger-Hamilton 1988: 153).

The range and frequency of chipped stone tools represented at Beidha (table 18), suggests that a variety of activities were performed at the site. Undoubtedly re-gearing for hunting and the processing of animal hides were important activities – as indicated by the prevalence of geometric microliths and end scrapers. The production of arrows for hunting is supported by the recovery of two shaft straightener fragments (fig. 32:a-b).[20] The low frequency of nongeometric microliths and the rarity of sickle blades suggest that plant processing activities were less intensive. Drilling or perforating, and engraving and shaving with burins were also infrequent activities. In fact, only one tool that may have been partially manufactured by a burin – a bone point (fig. 32:c) – has been recovered. It is uncertain what the large numbers of denticulated and notched pieces were used for, although wood working and combing of fibrous materials are particularly intriguing possibilities.[21]

Evidence for the processing of cereal or nut resources with ground stone artifacts is minimal. Only two clearly identifiable ground stone artifacts have been recovered; a broken sandstone pestle fragment and a unifacial discoidal handstone (fig. 32:d).[22] The absence of grinding stones, particularly of mortars and pestles, is in marked contrast to many Natufian sites in the western Levant (Bar-Yosef 1983).

In summary, primary and secondary evidence for hunting are abundant, while evidence of plant collecting and consumption is quite limited. The site, however, was certainly not a specialized hunting encampment, as other activities were carried out repeatedly, as indicated by the high frequency of other chipped stone tool classes.

---

[19]The bit may not always have been the business end, rather it may have been an alternative way of blunting prior to mounting in bone or wood shafts (e.g. Mortensen 1970). Interestingly, the ends of lunates at Beidha are occasionally retouched with minute burin blows (table 21).

[20]The shaft straighteners are from area K-2 level 3 (fig. 32:a) and area F-1 (1964) level 1 (fig. 32:b).

[21]The well-preserved early Neolithic assemblage from the dry cave of Nahal Hemar reveals a well-developed fiber and basketry tradition that may have a long history (Bar-Yosef and Alon 1988).

[22]The classificatory terminology is that of K.I. Wright who is currently analyzing the ground stone artifacts from Beidha. The pestle (dimensions: 13 x 7 x 3 cm) was recovered in area K-2 level 2, while the handstone comes from area C01 level 4, hearth 3. In addition, a possible fragment of a handstone was recovered from area C01 level 2.

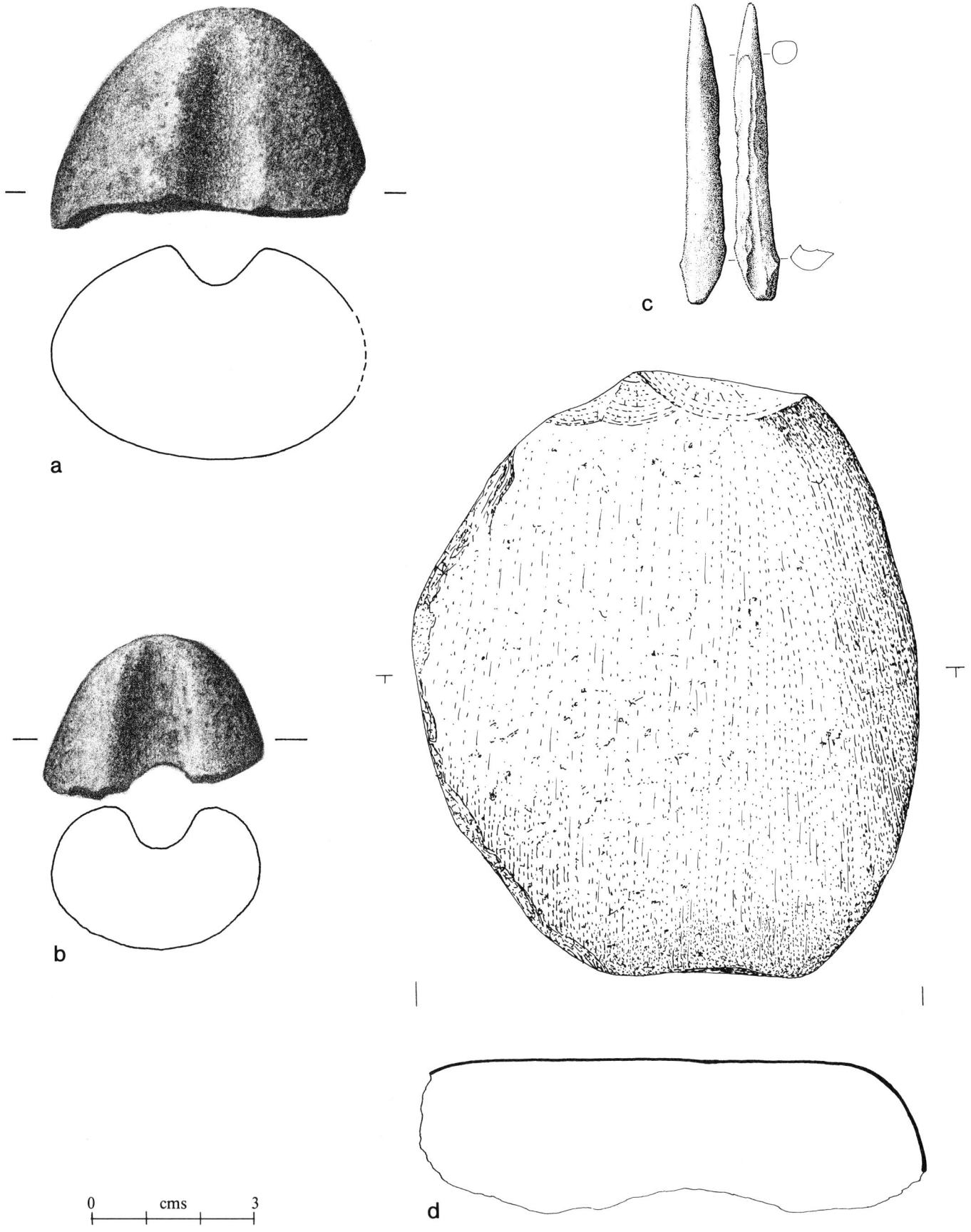

a

b

c

d

0   cms   3

Fig. 32. Shaft straighteners (a-b), bone point (c), and handstone (d).

Settlement characteristics

Two types of features occur in the Natufian of Beidha: hearths and roasting areas. Hearths were found in areas F-1 level 3, F-1 level 1 (1964), C-01 level 2, and C-01 level 4 (two). They are generally oval to round in plan, and range in size from 35 cm to 60 cm in diameter. Relatively shallow, up to 15 cm in depth, the hearths contain very dark gray (10YR 3/1) ashy sand and occasionally small pieces of charcoal. In addition, fire-cracked stones, generally less than 10 cm in diameter, occur within the features. In area C-01 level 4 two hearths are superimposed, one slightly offset from the other, and concentrations of ash in the vicinity suggest episodes of hearth cleaning and reuse.

Roasting areas are defined based on their large size, the presence within them of abundant animal bones and the occurrence of large stones situated around and within the feature. Two have been excavated – the smallest, in area K-2, is approximately 1.5 m in diameter and the dark ashy area is ringed by large stones (fig. 33).

Slightly further to the north in area J-2 is a much larger roasting area, about 2.5 m in diameter (fig. 34). Dense quantities of animal bones, especially fragments of long bone shafts, occurred amongst the dark ashy matrix of the shallow roasting area and several large sandstone slabs (up to 0.6 m in length) are situated around the edge of the area (figures 35, 36).

Despite the extent of the excavations, no other features such as walls, structures, storage facilities or stone pavements were identified in the Natufian of Beidha.[23] In addition, no burials were recovered. The absence of these types of features is in contrast to many Natufian sites in the western Levant (Bar-Yosef 1983).

The extent of the Natufian encampment at Beidha can be estimated based on the distribution of soundings with and without *in situ* occupational debris (fig. 4). It appears that the area of *in situ* material is approximately 60 by 40

[23] As stated in Chapter 3, the earlier assertions of mud brick architecture and a pit dwelling in the Natufian of Beidha are no longer viewed as viable.

Fig. 33. Roasting area in area K-2 viewed from the west.

Fig. 34. Large roasting area in area J-2.

meters in size: 2,400 square meters. This, however, only includes the portions of the settlement that remain today. As the Seyl Aqlat has eroded the western portion of the settlement, how far the site extended in that direction is uncertain, although it may have been a considerable distance (see Field, Appendix A). A projection of 4,000 square meters may not be unreasonable. It is unlikely, however, that the extent of *in situ* material is an accurate reflection of the number of inhabitants encamped at Beidha at any one time. Rather, the locale was undoubtedly reoccupied numerous times, in a series of overlapping settlement areas creating a palimpsest. In fact, a central settlement area can be discerned which has the thickest occupation deposits, while peripheral areas have less cultural build-up, for example to the north in area C-01.

Site type

The most prevalent model of the Natufian annual cycle entails the presence of sedentary base camp with transitory camps situated around it

Fig. 35. Closeup of a portion of the roasting area in area J-2.

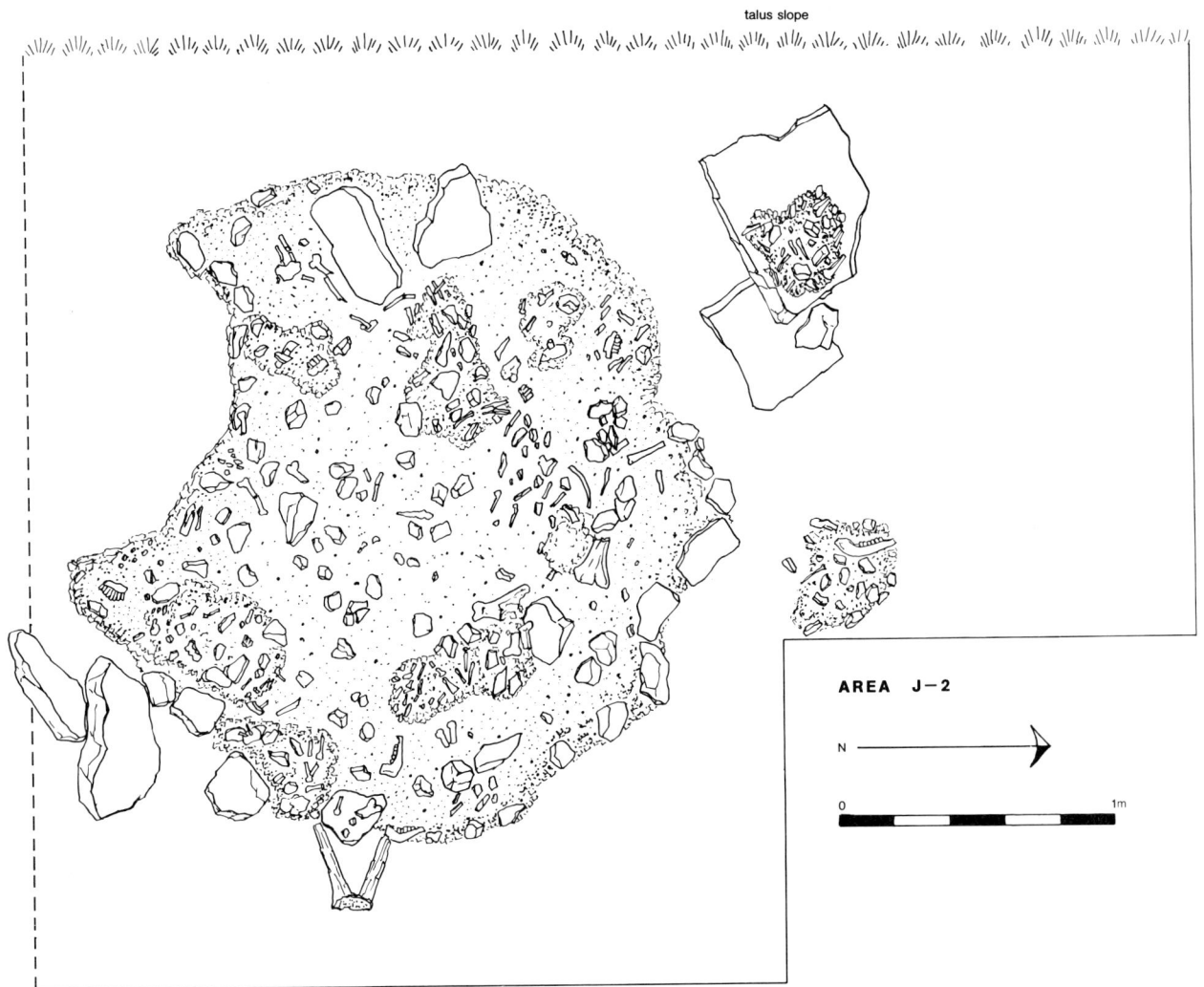

AREA J−2

N

0   1m

Fig. 36. Plan of large roasting area in area J-2.

in a radiating manner (Henry 1985; Bar-Yosef 1983).[24] Although the precise characteristics enumerated for base camps and transitory camps, and the criteria for distinguishing between them have varied somewhat (see Henry 1983: 138, 1985: 371-372; Bar-Yosef 1981: 399; 1983: 24-25), base camp elements included large size, considerable depth of cultural deposits, diversity of material culture (including grinding stones and bone tools), architectural features (such as buildings, storage facilities, and stone pavements) and burials. Transitory sites were characterized by thin cultural deposits, a more limited cultural assemblage (often specialized tool kits), and cluster near the base camps.

In terms of settlement characteristics, Beidha, and many other Natufian sites particularly in the eastern Levant, share features enumerated for both settlement types distinguished for the Natufian. Specifically, Beidha is characterized by the following base camp elements: relatively thick occupation deposits, large site size, and a wide range of chipped stone tools. Furthermore, there is no evidence to suggest that Beidha was a sedentary settlement,[25] although determination of whether a site was a sedentary locale is difficult, as there are no absolute indicators and a variety of lines of evidence must be considered (Bailey *et al.* 1983; Rafferty 1985; Edwards 1987: 329). Unfortunately one particularly useful approach – the use of seasonally available

[24]The have been a number of other models proposed for the Natufian. See Byrd (1989: 173-175) for a more detailed discussion and criticism of these models.

[25]In using the term, I follow Rice's definition of sedentism: "Sedentary settlement systems are those in which at least part of the population remains at the same location throughout the entire year." (1975, p. 97).

resources (plants and animals) – is not applicable at Beidha due to their absence. On the other hand, the site has many characteristics of transitory camps including the absence of architectural features and burials, and a paucity of ground stone and bone assemblages. Hence, the distinction between base camp and transitory camp, as it is presently formulated, is not a useful model for understanding adaptive strategies in the Petra area.

I would suggest that the Natufian at Beidha is best characterized as a short-term or seasonal camp site that was occupied repeatedly over a considerable period of time. The minimal evidence of spatial variability between provenience units in the chipped stone artifact samples (Yellen 1977; O'Connell 1987), the range of activities implied by the chipped stone assemblage, the presence of small hearths and large roasting pits, and the absence of elements typically associated with more permanent occupations (whether or not they were sedentary) – large ground stone implements, and features such as houses, storage facilities and burials – support this interpretation. It was neither a sedentary settlement nor a highly specialized field camp or station (Binford 1980), but rather witnessed occupation by a diverse group of individuals either once or a number of times for a portion of each year.

During which period of the year the site was occupied is uncertain. In an area rich in plant resources, the dearth of evidence for such activities at Beidha implies the site was not occupied during periods when these resources were abundant – spring and early summer, and the autumn (Hillman *et al.* 1989). Winter and mid-summer are periods of limited availability of plant resources and times when procurement strategies may have emphasize hunting. The presence of water in the immediate vicinity of Beidha would be important determinant particularly during the arid summer. On the other hand, this locale would have been an attractive winter camp as it is more sheltered and warmer than the highlands.

Petra area: regional interplay

Resource procurement
The predominance of caprines in the faunal assemblage of Beidha (Hecker, Appendix C) indicates that the immediate rugged area of the sandstone was the primary catchment area for hunting. The steppe and desert of the Wadi Araba was also consistently exploited for the procurement of gazelle. In addition, the woodlands and open areas of the highlands may have been occasionally utilized for onager and aurochs.

Artifacts and raw material that were procured outside the local area of Beidha are limited in their diversity. Several small pieces of malachite, presumably from sources in the Wadi Araba, were recovered from the occupation deposits. No finished products, beads, or other objects, however, occur to indicate whether the malachite was being used to manufacture jewelry or as a source of pigment.

Over 70 marine shells were recovered from the Natufian (Reese, Appendix D). The majority of the shells are Dentalium, although seven other species, along with fragments of coral, also occur. These marine resources were procured primarily from the Red Sea – a distance of 100 km – and were probably used as ornaments on various types of clothing, based on burial context evidence from other Natufian sites Valla 1988). Whether they were obtained through expeditions to coastal areas or through down-the-line trading is not known.

The two shaft straightener fragments recovered from the Beidha Natufian are made of a fine-grained basalt which is not found locally. The nearest source is the volcanic fields in the eastern steppic region. No other imported material, such as obsidian, was recovered from the Natufian levels. Furthermore, all the flint appears to have been locally obtained.

Natufian settlements in the Petra area
Three surveys, of varied purpose and extent, have been conducted in the Petra area. The first was Kirkbride's three week reconnaissance survey in 1965 along the sandstone shelf north and south of Beidha and immediately west in the Wadi Araba (Kirkbride 1966: 54). Although a number of Neolithic sites were identified, no Natufian settlements were noted. In 1984, an

ethnoarchaeological survey was conducted in the area directly around Beidha (Banning and Köhler-Rollefson 1987). The survey covered an area approximately 3 km by 4 km in size, and although research focused on modern Bedouin settlements, all archaeological sites encountered (over 50) were recorded. No evidence of Natufian occupation was found.

Recently, Tübingen University conducted survey and test excavations in the Petra region (Gebel 1986; Gebel and Starck 1985). A number of Epipaleolithic and early Neolithic sites were recorded, two of which, Sunah 1 and Sabra 1, contain evidence of Natufian occupation.

Sunah 1 is late Natufian surface scatter located along the Wadi al-Wayit, at the southwest base of the sandstone massif of Al-Barra (Gebel and Starck 1985). A scatter of artifacts extends for 12,000 square meters, but there appears to be no *in situ* material. The chipped stone assemblage includes abruptly retouched lunates as well as other geometrics. No groundstone artifacts or evidence of architectural features were observed.

The second site, Sabra 1, is located farther to the south near the Nabatean caravansarai of Sabra (Gebel and Starck 1985). A small sounding uncovered a temporally mixed assemblage of nongeometrics, trapeze-rectangles, Helwan retouched lunates, and Khiamian points. No architectural features or groundstone artifacts were recovered. Based on the different diagnostic lithics recovered, the excavators suggested that the site contained evidence of Geometric Kebaran, early Natufian, early Neolithic, and possibly late Natufian occupation.

Annual settlement cycle

Certainly our knowledge of Natufian adaptation in this portion of the southern Levant is very limited and hampers modeling the annual settlement system. Several factors contribute to this situation. First, survey work has emphasized the sandstone shelf; there has been no survey in the forested uplands immediately to the east, and only reconnaissance work in the Wadi Araba system. Furthermore, if alluviation was occurring in other valleys in the sandstone shelf – as it was in the Wadi el Ghurab (Field, Appendix A) – then many Natufian sites are buried and their discovery will be difficult.

As mentioned previously, the base camp – transitory camp model of Henry (1985) and Bar-Yosef (1983) is not applicable to many areas of the Levant. In fact, there is growing recognition that adaptive strategies were quite diverse during the Natufian (Goring-Morris 1987: 434-442; Henry 1987b; Fish and Fish 1988). Any model of the annual settlement system in the Petra area must take into account the rapid altitudinal zonation and consequent diversity of resources. There is also considerable seasonal variation in the availability of plant resources. Annuals such as cereals and legumes ripen in the late spring and early summer, and mature seeds are available for only a brief interval before the seeds disperse themselves. This necessitates close attention to their ripening, and collection must be relatively rapid. Perennials, mostly nut, oil and fruit plants, generally have a more varied seasonal distribution ranging from summer through autumn, and nuts can be harvested into winter (Flannery 1969, 1973: 274). Certainly the time of plant ripening will vary with altitude, and the period of gathering could be extended by moving up the altitudinal gradient (see Flannery 1973). Although it has been asserted that the availability of herd animals fluctuated considerably during the year, particularly in respect to long distance seasonal migrations (Legge & Rowley-Conwy 1987), timing and seasonal changes in calving and the composition of herds certainly made particular times of the year more favorable for hunting than others (Davis 1983).

Natufian adaptation in the Petra area may have been characterized by a point to point collector's strategy, where only certain locations were suitable camp sites, often a considerable distance from one another (Binford 1982). The annual system could have been manifested in a variety of expressions of which seasonal aggregation and dispersal, creating both large and smaller encampments, is but one example (Byrd 1989; Crabtree *et al.* 1987; Goring-Morris 1987: 437; Henry 1987b). Furthermore, yearly fluctuations in resource availability and rainfall would have considerable effect on decision making. The duration of stays at particular locales and movement of camps would have occurred more frequently in concert with local resource availability, particularly given the extensive altitudinal zonation. Aggregation would have been most likely during periods of high resource availability, including the spring to early summer when cereals, legumes and young animals were plentiful, and the autumn when nut resources were abundant. Aggregation sites are most likely to be located in the upland forested area. In addition, field camps of task groups out hunting game were no doubt present (Binford 1980), particularly in the Wadi Araba, where gazelles were procured.

Levantine variability[26]

The primary subsistence evidence recovered from Natufian settlements in the Levant suggests that exploitation strategies were quite varied. This is well documented with respect to hunting strategies where, although gazelle are overall the most common species exploited, hunting of locally available game herds constituted a major subsistence activity (Byrd 1989: table II). With respect to plant gathering and consumption, unfortunately information is limited due to the rarity of preserved archaeobotanical remains.

Patterned variation in intersettlement chipped stone tool assemblages, based on statistical cluster analysis, provides insights into broad differences in subsistence endeavors during the Natufian (Byrd 1989: 179-181).[27] Cluster 1 is characterized by significantly higher percentages of nongeometric backed tools (and a higher sickle-tool ratio), while cluster 2 has significantly higher percentages of notches and denticulates, scrapers, and the various tool group (which is primarily composed of simple retouched pieces). Significantly higher frequencies of geometrics, and lower percentages of burins, differentiate cluster 3. Most of the occupation deposits at Beidha, exemplified by area K-2 levels 1 and 3, fall in cluster 2, while level 4 of area C-01 clusters in group 3.

These clusters of Natufian occupational horizons correlate strongly with particular regions of the Levant: sites in the forest and coastal areas cluster together (1), and the steppe and desert area sites typically cluster into two groups. One steppe and desert area cluster (2) appears to be characterized by a broader range of activities

than the other steppe and desert cluster (3), which appears to represent a greater emphasis on hunting.

Variation in ground stone artifacts also varies between these clusters. Mortars and pestles are more common at sites of cluster 1, while querns and handstones are more prevalent in sites of cluster 2. Many sites in the steppe and desert areas have very few ground stone artifacts.

Patterned variability in settlement characteristics, particularly with respect to duration and intensity of occupation, are also apparent. Sites of cluster 1 are characterized by greater intensity and permanence of occupation. This is manifested by elements of site structure including significantly greater thickness of occupation deposits, and more numerous architectural features, burials, and storage features.[28] In addition, core reduction (lower density of cores per cubic meter) and formal tool manufacture (greater ratio of retouched tools per core) were most intensive at cluster 1 sites. Steppe and desert area sites of cluster 2 are characterized by moderate settlement permanence and activity intensity, and a broad range of activities are represented in the artifact assemblages. Less permanent occupation and more specialized activities focused primarily on hunting typify the other set of steppe and desert sites, cluster 3.

In conclusion, with recent research on the Natufian in the eastern and southern Levant, it is apparent that adaptive strategies were more varied than were thought only a few years ago. In light of this, more flexible models of the annual settlement system taking into account yearly variation in strategies need to be developed. Furthermore, future research must include two elements. First, intensive survey of the full range of ecological settings in a local area with the goal of identifying low visibility and short term encampments. Second, excavation design must include rigorous collection of information on season and duration of occupation.

[26]For a more detailed and documented discussion of the arguments and assertions made in this section, see Byrd (1987: 278-309; 1989: 175-188)

[27]The cluster analysis of 38 Natufian occupation horizons used the Ward Method and the squared Euclidean method.

[28]There is a significantly greater area excavated at sites of cluster 1 and that may be biasing some of the more qualitative distinctions between clusters.

7. Conclusion

When Diana Kirkbride began her excavations at Beidha in 1958, the Petra region of southern Jordan was *terra incognita* with respect to early prehistoric settlement. Today, over thirty years later, our understanding of changing adaptive strategies at the end of the Pleistocene remains limited. In fact, Beidha is the only definite Natufian site that has been excavated in the region, and only exploratory research has been conducted at sites from the millennium immediately preceding and following the Natufian.

A number of remarks, however, can be made with respect to the results of the Beidha Natufian fieldwork. The preliminary paleo-environmental research in the Beidha region, exemplified by the studies of Field and Fish, tend to confirm the assertions that during the Natufian the climate was colder than at present and effective moisture was greater (Valla 1987a). Aggradation of the Wadi el Ghurab during the Natufian suggests that ground cover was more extensive in the alluvial valleys of the sandstone shelf, and that the open forest and transition zone may have been more extensive than today. A permanent or seasonal water source situated in the immediate Beidha vicinity was certainly an important element in site location. Given such a climatic regime and the marked altitudinal zonation of the plant communities there was undoubtedly a diversity of resources, including edible wild plants and a wide range of herd animals, particularly ungulates, in the region.

The Beidha excavations exposed 54 square meters of the Natufian, the second most extensive area of any contemporaneous Jordanian site (Wadi Hammeh being the first). In the central portion of the site, occupation thickness averaged between 0.4 and 0.6 meters and three depositional phases were distinguished within a continuous sequence. On the northern edge of the site, however, a different stratigraphic sequence was apparent: two occupation horizons separated by noncultural deposition. The lower occupation phase in this area, 0.15 m thick, contained an artifact assemblage similar to that recovered from the other excavations at the site. This is an early Natufian settlement and the new radiocarbon dates place occupation prior to 12,000 B.P. The upper occupation phase in the northern portion of the site, despite the small sample recovered, appears to be dated considerably later – at the juncture between the early and late Natufian.

Due to the limited range and diversity of artifact types recovered, analytical emphasis has been placed on the ubiquitous chipped stone assemblage. In particular, the reduction sequence technology and the nature of the retouched tools were examined in detail. Cobbles of high quality local flint were exploited and the predominantly single platform cores were initially prepared elsewhere. Chert was occasionally exploited and almost exclusively represented by tools which were brought to the site and discarded there. Little formal core preparation or rejuvenation occurred but, nonetheless, intensive reduction of cores took place.

Attribute analysis revealed a reduction sequence initiated by the production of rather long, narrow pieces (blades), to shorter, narrow pieces (bladelets), and to a final stage, characterized by short and wide pieces often of "flake" dimensions. The debitage categories of blade and flake, however, overlap considerably with respect to the attributes of size, flake scar patterns, and platform characteristics. Nonetheless, blades are slightly more numerous than flakes, and blades *sensu stricto* in contrast to bladelets are uncommon. Blades were the predominant debitage type that was selected for tool manufacture, their size varying significantly between tool groups.

Two sets of patterned intrasite artifact variability appear meaningful with respect to prehistoric behavior. There is significant variation in the relative number of cores, in debitage-core ratios, and in debitage-tool ratios between some excavation areas. Whether these differences are related to variation in the relative amount of core reduction or to the discard locations of the exhausted raw material is unclear. In addition, the assemblage from the later Natufian occupation in area C-01 differs from other samples in several respects, including the blade-flake ratio and the length of the lunates. These differences appear to be temporally related.

The range and frequency of chipped stone tools represented at Beidha suggest that a variety of activities were performed at the site with considerable emphasis on re-gearing for hunting and the processing of animal hides (based on the frequency of geometric microliths and end scrapers). Evidence for the collection and processing of cereal or nut resources (based on the low frequency of nongeometric microliths, the rarity of sickle blades, and the dearth of ground stone artifacts) is minimal.

The Natufian at Beidha is best characterized as a short-term or seasonal camp site that was occupied repeatedly over a considerable period of time. The limited evidence of spatial variability between provenience units in the chipped stone artifact samples, the range of activities implied by the chipped stone assemblage (primarily hunting related activities), the presence of small hearths and large roasting areas, and the absence of elements typically associated with more permanent occupations – large ground stone implements, and features such as houses, storage facilities and burials – support this interpretation.

Based on the dearth of evidence for plant gathering and consumption activities in a region which was rich in plant resources, I suggest that Beidha was not occupied during periods when these resources were abundant – the spring and early summer (for cereals and legumes), and the autumn (for nut resources). Rather, it may have been occupied during the winter or summer – which are periods of limited availability of plant resources and times when procurement strategies may have emphasized hunting.

Although our knowledge of Natufian adaptation in the Petra area is minimal, settlement may have been characterized by a strategy where encampments were situated at a considerable distance apart. An annual settlement system of seasonal aggregation and dispersal, creating both large and smaller encampments,

may have prevailed. The duration of stays at particular locales and the movement of camps would have occurred in concert with local resource availability, particularly given the extensive altitudinal zonation. Aggregation may have occurred during periods of high resource availability, including the spring to early summer and the autumn. These sites, as yet undiscovered, may be situated in the upland forested area. In addition, field camps of task groups out hunting game are no doubt present in the sandstone shelf and the Wadi Araba.

The limited subsistence evidence available from Beidha reveals no indications as to whether plant cultivation or the domestication of herd animals (based on Hecker's research) was underway. Hence, the role of this area in the early steps toward food production remains obscure.

In designing further research in this region, emphasis on two elements would be particularly beneficial. First, intensive survey, with an emphasis on identifying low visibility and short-term encampments, of the full range of ecological settings, particularly in the upland forested environs and the Wadi Araba system, is needed. Second, excavation (using detailed data recovery techniques) should focus on sites which have the potential to reveal information on season and duration of occupation and subsistence strategies, thereby facilitating our understanding of shifting human adaptation at the end of the Pleistocene.

Appendix A.
Geological setting at Beidha

by John Field

A brief geological reconnaissance of Beidha and its immediate environs was undertaken in August, 1987. Detailed sediment descriptions were made and soil samples were collected for laboratory analysis. Despite the short duration of the study, three major observations were made which contribute to an understanding of site preservation and environmental conditions during occupation:

1. The Natufian occupation occurred during aggradation of the Wadi el Ghurab.

2. The culturally sterile sediments between the Natufian and Pre-Pottery Neolithic B (PPNB) occupations were deposited by ephemeral streams and not by aeolian deposition as suggested earlier (Raikes 1966:71; Kirkbride 1966:47).

3. The early Neolithic occupation occurred during or after erosion and formation of alluvial terraces along the Wadi Ghurab.

Sedimentological sampling was designed to provide a sequence from prior to the Natufian occupation, through the non-cultural deposition directly above the Natufian, into the early Neolithic occupation layers. The samples were collected from the north and east sections of the 1983 excavations of the Natufian in area C-01 (Byrd 1988), and from the west section of a 1967 deep sounding in area F-4 which cut through a large Neolithic building into the earlier Neolithic deposits, and ultimately into the upper portions of the sterile deposits that separate the Neolithic from the Natufian (Kirkbride 1968b: 92, Plate XXIVA).

A schematic, composite stratigraphic column of the site is presented in fig. 37 to help facilitate the following discussion. Sediments throughout the section are over 75% sand (table 27). This results from the nearly pure Cambrian Nubian Sandstone source of the local environs. The large amount of calcium found in the sediment may be supplied by the Cretaceous limestone at the upper portion of the drainage system. Cultural horizons, especially the PPNB Neolithic levels, have a significant amount of silt which was introduced during the occupation, while pedogenic processes may have added silt to both cultural and sterile horizons.

The Natufian horizons and surrounding sediments are grayish brown throughout with a gray band rich in charcoal. The overall grayish color of the sediment results from bioturbation of ash in the charcoal-rich zone. The sediment was largely deposited by streams with limited cultural input. A gravel lens is found near the base of the section (fig. 37). Low phosphorus (P), nitrogen (N), and organic matter (OM) contents in sample 4 also reflect a limited human influence on the sediment in area C-01 level 4, the lower of two Natufian occupation horizons (table 28). This supports the suggestion that Natufian occupation at Beidha was not very intense – only seasonally or even less frequently. Sedimentation during the occupational phases diffused the cultural deposits, so that values for P, N, and OM are lower than expected if no sedimentation occurred.

Sterile sediments between the Natufian and Neolithic components were deposited by ephemeral streams (fig. 37). Several fining upwards sequences of gravely sands are preserved (fig. 38). Fining upward sequences are formed in single stream flow events or by successive flows with decreasing flow strength (Reineck and Singh 1980). The top of each sequence is siltier (table 27) and displays a slight carbonate build-up formed during short periods of nondeposition. The weak soil development is consistent with the almost 4000 years of sterile sedimentation between the two phases.

The sterile sediments at Beidha have a substantial gravel component (table 27). Trough cross bedded sands are visible near the base of the sterile zone. Thin gravel beds and

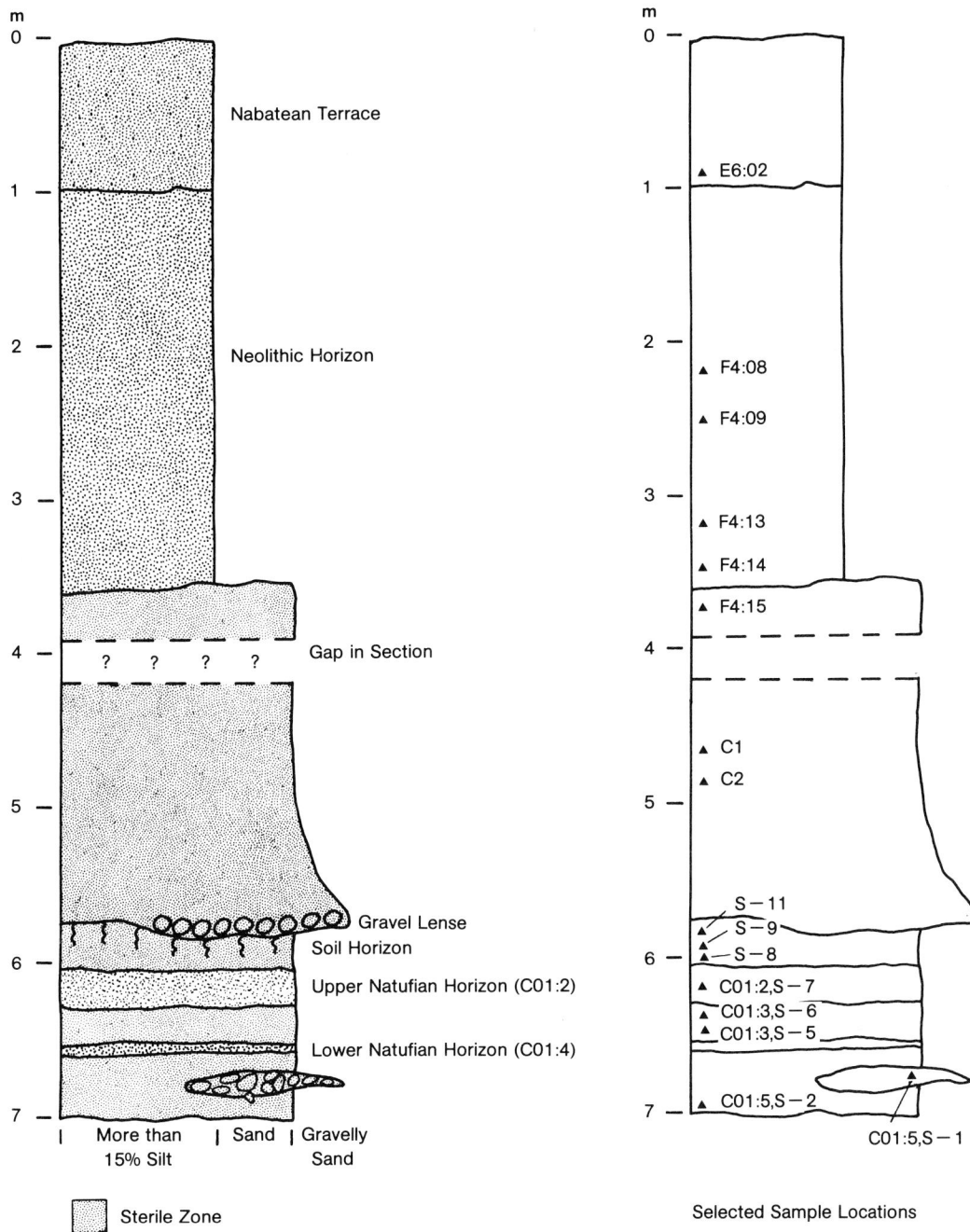

Fig. 37. Composite geomorphological stratigraphic column of Beidha showing sediment and pollen sample locations. Nabatean terrace: terrace wall and yellowish-brown sand terrace fill. Neolithic horizon: yellowish to grayish brown silty sand with cultural stones common. Rare water laid cross bedded sands throughout. Ash filled pits, plastered floors and stone buildings common. Sterile zone: yellowish brown gravely sand to silty sand. Weak carbonate soil development in several horizons (see blowup in Figure 38). Natufian horizons: grayish brown sand with charcoal. Gravel lens in level 5 below.

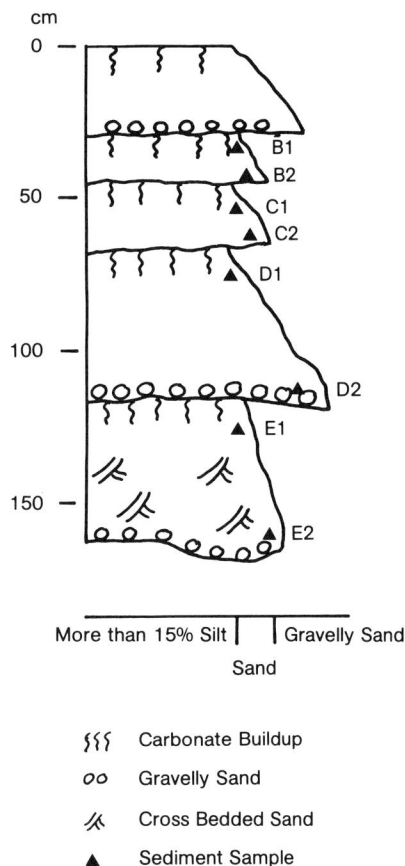

cm

0 —

50 —

100 —

150 —

More than 15% Silt | | Gravelly Sand

Sand

ʃʃʃ   Carbonate Buildup

oo   Gravelly Sand

𝄪   Cross Bedded Sand

▲   Sediment Sample

Fig. 38. Stratigraphic section near base of sterile sediments between Natufian and PPNB Neolithic horizons from east section of area C-01 level 1 showing fining upward stream deposits (see Table 27 for grain size analysis).

cross bedded sand are characteristic of ephemeral stream deposits, while aeolian sediments are typically well sorted and do not contain gravel too large to be moved by the wind (Reineck and Singh 1980). The base of the sterile zone contains abundant pebbles mixed in a matrix of sand.

The earliest Neolithic occupation at the site rests on or close to the present land surface. This land surface is a terrace left isolated after the erosion of sediments deposited in Natufian times. It is unclear whether this erosion occurred before or during the Neolithic occupation. However, the presence along the southern edge of the site of a "retaining" wall with flat footing stones at its base and with steps leading up to the Neolithic settlement (Kirkbride 1968b: 92-93) seems to suggest that this terrace remnant was already stranded by erosion before Neolithic occupation. Aggradation had ceased before Neolithic occupation because these layers

are not buried by natural deposits. Very thin cross bedded sands are found in a few places. These are probably stream deposits from minor tributaries emanating from the cliffs behind the site. The absence of natural sedimentation results in a greater concentration of cultural material. This is reflected in the higher P, N, and OM levels in samples F4:09 and F4:13 (table 28). A higher degree of occupation duration and intensity may also be inferred from these higher levels.

Detailed environmental reconstructions are not possible from sedimentological analyses alone. However, when the above information is considered within the geomorphological context, basic environmental conditions can be inferred. Beidha is on a remnant of an alluvial fill terrace formed during aggradation of the Wadi el Ghurab (fig. 39). Other remnant terraces downstream from the site appear to be at the same level indicating that the entire valley floor was once at a higher level. Canyons cut into the sandstone cliffs have smooth rounded bedrock terraces at the same level. Deep narrow slots have since been carved in the bedrock during erosion of the valley fill before or during Neolithic occupation.

The formation of these terraces occurred during a period of greater sediment supply to the wadi. Such condition would occur during times of less intense rainfall. If rainfall fell in brief torrential bursts, as it does today, sediment would be carried away with the run-off (Raikes 1966). Less intense rains would soak into the ground, increase vegetation, and decrease run-off. As a result sediment would accumulate in the wadi and result in a higher valley floor (fig. 39). Rainfall during this time was not necessarily greater. Weak soil carbonate development indicates at least a semi-arid climate. Soil carbonates are not found in sub-humid to humid soils where carbonate is leached from the soil entirely. Although rainfall may have been the same as today, differences in rainfall patterns were probably sufficient to create a more amicable environment during Natufian times.

The onset of erosion in the Wadi el Ghurab may have coincided with an increase in rainfall intensity and "flashiness". The greater run-off which would result would be sufficient to remove the accumulated sediment and create the high isolated terraces. The Neolithic occupation

	Clay	Silt	Sand	Sediment*	Gravel**
Neolithic					
F4:09	4	16	80	88	12
F4:13	2	22	76	98	2
Sterile horizon					
F4:15	1	13	86	100	0
C01:1-unit B1	2	15	83	95	5
C01:1-unit B2	1	9	91	96	4
C01:1-unit D1	4	20	76	92	8
C01:1-unit D2	4	6	90	98	2
C01:1-unit E1	5	14	81	75	25
C01:1-unit E2	4	3	93	85	15
C01:1-sample 11	6	10	84	100	0
C01:1-sample 9	2	10	88	99	1
Upper Natufian horizon					
C01:2-sample 7	5	18	77	98	2
Sterile horizon between Natufian occupations					
C01:3-sample 5	4	15	81	99	1
Sterile horizon below earliest Natufian horizon (C01:4)					
C01:5-sample 2	5	4	91	97	3

*Sediment includes sand, silt, and clay. Sand, silt and clay percentages are given after gravel removed
**Uncrushed silty carbonate nodules are included in gravel component – especially in sterile horizon

Table 27. Grain size analysis of Beidha sediments showing relative frequency.

	pH	Phosphorus*	Available Nitrogen**	Organic matter
Neolithic				
F4:09	7.9	30	116	1.6
F4:13	8.1	21	370	0.4
Sterile horizon				
C01:1-unit C1	8.6	10	29	0.4
C01:1-unit C2	8.7	3	34	0.5
C01:1-unit D1	7.9	10	33	0.3
Lower Natufian horizon				
C01:4-sample 4	8.0	4	30	0.4

*Parts per million (ppm)
**Pounds per acre (lbs/A)

Table 28. Chemical analysis of selected samples from Beidha.

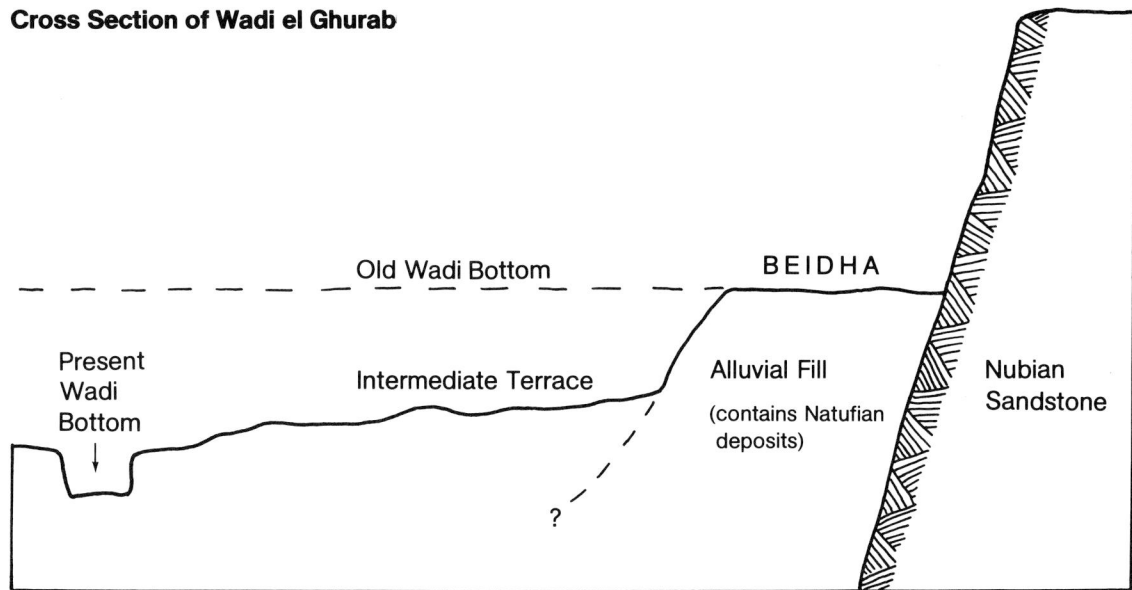

Fig. 39. Geomorphic setting of Beidha looking west (not to scale).

appears to have occurred during this climatic regime and settlements on the high terrace would be free of flash floods probably common in the wadi bottom.

The degree of areal preservation of the two site components is likely very different. The Natufian component is eroding out of the steep bank of the Seyl Aqlat, a minor tributary drainage along the western edge of Beidha. The Natufian horizon, as soundings have indicated, is also buried beneath the Neolithic horizon. To the west, much of the Natufian component may have been destroyed during erosion of the fill sediments by the Seyl Aqlat drainage. The remaining fill sediments where the Natufian site is now found are most likely only a small portion of the once extensive higher level of the Wadi el Ghurab.

Preservation of the Neolithic component is probably much greater. The site rests near the surface and is buried only by other cultural deposits – the culturally introduced sedimentation of the Nabatean terrace system. Since erosion began before occupation of the site, the site area was most likely confined to the present terrace. Lateral retreat of the steep bank on the west side of the site has probably eroded a portion of the site, perhaps as much as one half.

Three tentative conclusions are drawn from this geological study. First, Natufian occupation occurred during a period of less intense rainfall when vegetative cover was probably greater than today. Second, sterile sediments between the Natufian and Neolithic components were not deposited by aeolian deposition as previously thought but by ephemeral streams. Third, areal site preservation of the Natufian component is likely very poor while Neolithic site preservation is probably more complete. Further geological studies should try and reconstruct the extent of the higher valley floor present during Natufian times. Also the timing of erosion and formation of lower terraces in the wadi should be correlated to Neolithic and later occupations. Such information will further our understanding of environmental changes and site preservation at Beidha.

Appendix B.
The Beidha pollen record

by Suzanne K. Fish

Several profiles were sampled at the site of Beidha in order to compile a sequence encompassing Natufian, Neolithic, and Nabatean occupations, as well as intervening periods of noncultural deposition. Preliminary results consist of nine samples, spanning a period preceding the first Natufian occupation to a time of Nabatean agricultural landuse (see fig. 37 for sample locations). The samples were collected primarily from the north and east sections of the 1983 excavations in area C-01 (Byrd 1988) and from the west section of a 1967 deep sounding in area F-4 which cut through the large Neolithic Building 9 into the earliest Neolithic deposits, and ultimately into the upper portions of the sterile deposits that separate the Neolithic from the Natufian (Kirkbride 1968b: 92; Plate XXIVA). The samples reported herein are ones from each of the major cultural divisions that yielded relatively plentiful and well-preserved pollen; a potential remains for greater temporal detail and more comprehensive chronological coverage in future expanded study.

Like other recent investigations of pollen from archaeological sites in southern Levant (e.g. Emery-Barbier 1988; Leroi-Gourhan 1984; Darmon 1984), analysis at Beidha adds to a record of open steppe-like vegetation in the region over much of late Quaternary time. Arboreal pollen (AP) in Beidha samples is always less than 20 percent of total pollen and is generally composed of pine, oak, and juniper or other Cupressaceae. Therefore, vegetational change is primarily expressed through changing proportions of nonarboreal pollen types (NAP), often with broad taxonomic amplitudes.

The palynology of semi-arid and arid environments offers unique interpretive challenges. It is difficult to discriminate the effects of climate, geomorphology, culture and other factors in the pollen record, which is itself a quantitatively biased reflection of source vegetation. Vegetationally important species that are not wind pollinated may disperse minimal amounts of pollen which is highly localized and seldom detected (see, for example, Bottema and Barkoudah 1979). With even the arboreal taxa of restricted height, pollen tends to be released nearer the ground than in mesic forested environments and may produce less homogenized regional assemblages. In addition, vegetational communities are often highly differentiated and localized on the basis of edaphic conditions within a single climatic regime. Widely dispersed, wind-pollinated types characterize large-scale vegetation associations, but abrupt, edaphically controlled boundaries also occur between dominant species and associated pollen spectra in such situation as wadis, slopes, or saline soils.

At Beidha, some variation in pollen percentages over time may reflect changes in local geomorphological conditions (Field, Appendix A). Natufian times were marked by aggradation of the Wadi el Ghurab. An episode of erosion occurred after the Natufian occupations, either before or during the Neolithic period. Lowered water table during intervals of stream incision could decrease available moisture to vegetation of the wadi bottom in a manner only indirectly correlated with climate. Pollen spectra in the Beidha sequence are also potentially influenced by the vegetational impacts of gathering, herding and cropping during and after transition to a Neolithic economy.

Analytical methods

Sixty cubic centimeters of sediment were deflocculated with dilute hydrochloric acid after the addition of Lycopodium tracers. Separation of the heaviest sample fraction was accomplished by a timed swirl-and-settling procedure described by Mehringer (1967: 136-137). Heavy liquid flotation with zinc bromide of 2.0 density further reduced the sample matrix. Silicates were then removed with hydrofluoric acid. Chemical treatments to remove organic residues were made in order to avoid damage to fragile pollen from the coarse, unconsolidated Beidha sediments. Extraction was performed at the Palynology Laboratory, Department of Geosciences, University of Arizona.

A standard sum of 200 pollen grains was tabulated and serves as the basis for calculation of the percentages of individual types in table 29. This sum was not exceeded due to low pollen yields and lengthy tabulations. Indeterminate grains, whether poorly preserved or of unknown taxonomic affiliation, are included in the standard sum. A single aquatic type, *Typha/Sparganium*, was so frequent that it was not excluded. In some instances, taxonomic discrimination was limited by the condition of the pollen grains and by the lack of reference specimens specific to the region. Patricia Fall generously shared taxonomic expertise gained through recent investigations of well-preserved hyrax middens at Petra (Fall *et al.*, in press).

Sterile horizon prior to the Natufian

The earliest sample in the Beidha sequence comes from the sand and gravel lense in level 5 of area C-01, near the bottom of the C-00/C-01 north face. This waterlaid sediment predates the earlier of two Natufian occupations. Two pollen types are strongly predominant. Liguliflorae, a subdivision of the Compositae Family typified by dandelion, accounts for about one quarter of total pollen and, Umbelliferae or the Parsley Family accounts for more than half. Three percent arboreal pollen includes only Cupressaceae, probably juniper, and a single instance of *Pistacia* or pistachio.

It is difficult to characterize the vegetation producing this spectrum, which is likely a highly local record. A modern study of 85 samples from the vegetation zones of Lebanon and Syria reveals a tendency for Umbelliferae pollen to be no more than a few percent of total pollen, with

maxima in the Oro-Mediterranean vegetation zone between 1000 and 1500 meters (Bottema and Barkoudah 1979). Some process of enriched deposition of this type in the lowermost Beidha sample is apparent. The coarseness of the sediment is commensurate with flood deposition, in which case rapid deposition may have encapsulated a seasonal bias. Alternatively, a disproportionate contribution by riparian herbs may be represented by the unusual amounts of this typically less prominent type.

A similar bias may be operative in the abundance of Liguliflorae pollen. However, this pollen occurs occasionally today in values greater than 10 percent. Average values for all modern vegetation zones of Syria and Lebanon are lower, but maxima occur in Oro-Mediterranean, Upper Mediterranean (300-1000 m) and in mixed forest and steppe (500-2000 m) vegetation types. The propensity of various Liguliflorae species for disturbed soils is a further complication in interpreting the significance of this type. Source plants might have grown in naturally disturbed floodplain habitats. Natufian and Kebaran strata at the elevationally lower sites of Mallaha (Leroi-Gourhan 1984) and Hayonim Terrace (Henry *et al.* 1981) in Palestine produced equal or greater proportions of Liguliflorae pollen, although other details of spectra from these sites are not duplicated in the earliest sample from Beidha.

The Natufian period

Level 4 in area C-01, dated prior to 12,000 B.P. (table 1), represents the earlier of two Natufian occupation horizons. The pollen content of these sediments is predominantly Tubuliflorae, another broad subdivision of the Compositae. Arboreal pollen consists of Cupressaceae, *Pinus* (pine), *Quercus* (oak) and *Olea* (olive) for a total of 7 percent. Interpretation of the significance of AP differences between this sample and the preceding one illustrates the ambiguity of contrasts between small percentages in samples of the present size. Pistachio and Cupressaceae are registered in area C-01 level 5, while Cupressaceae, oak and olive appear in area C-01 level 4. However, for types occurring as less than 2 percent in sample sizes of 200, sampling error

Table 29. Percentage of pollen types in the Beidha samples.

Sample	Liguliflorae	Ambrosia – type	Artemisia	Tubuliflorae	Cheno-am	Gramineae	Cerealia – type	Umbelliferae	Plantago	Daphne/Thymelaea	Thalictrum	Ephedra	Capparidaceae	cf. Papilionoideae	Rhamnaceae	Ostrya/Carpinus	Pinus	Quercus	Cupressaceae	Pistacia	Olea	Typha	Indeterminate	Other
Nabatean terrace																								
E6:2, sample 12	11.5	2.0	9.5	14.5	10.5	5.5	1.0	0.0	1.5	4.5	0.0	5.0	5.0	5.5	0.5	0.5	0.5	6.5	4.0	1.5	1.5	0.0	7.5	0.5 Caryophyllaceae, 0.5 *Ficus*, 0.5 Malvaceae
Neolithic																								
F4:8, sample 9	5.5	0.5	24.5	11.0	4.0	7.5	0.0	0.0	3.5	7.5	0.0	1.0	4.0	3.5	0.5	0.5	2.5	4.5	4.5	0.0	1.0	1.0	8.5	1.5 *Scabiosa*, 1.0 *Boerhaavia*, 0.5 *Salix*, 0.5 *Humulus/Cannabis*, 0.5 *Tamarix*, 0.5 Liliaceae
F4:14, sample 3	44.5	0.0	2.5	24.5	5.0	3.5	0.0	0.0	0.0	2.0	0.0	1.5	0.0	1.5	0.0	0.0	0.5	3.5	0.5	0.0	0.0	1.5	7.0	1.0 Boraginaceae, 0.5 *Ficus*, 0.5 *Salix*
Sterile horizons																								
F4:15, sample 2	0.0	2.5	25.5	19.5	2.5	11.5	0.0	0.5	6.5	8.5	1.0	0.5	0.0	2.5	0.5	0.0	7.5	1.0	4.0	0.0	0.0	0.0	4.5	1.0 Cruciferae, 0.5 Malvaceae
C01:1, sample 9	0.0	8.5	6.5	2.0	29.0	6.5	0.0	0.0	10.5	12.5	0.5	0.0	0.0	4.0	1.0	3.0	0.5	7.0	1.0	0.0	1.0	0.0	2.5	2.0 Cruciferae, 1.0 *Boerhaavia*, 0.5 *Salix*, 0.5 *Tamarix*
C01:1, sample 8	0.0	4.0	12.0	8.5	34.5	6.5	1.5	0.0	0.5	4.0	0.0	0.0	0.0	7.0	0.0	0.5	0.0	4.0	5.5	0.0	1.0	1.5	6.5	1.0 Cyperaceae, 1.0 Labiatae, 0.5 *Salix*, 0.5 Rosaceae, 0.5 Myrtaceae
C01:3, sample 6	3.5	10.0	7.5	6.0	19.5	3.0	0.0	0.0	0.0	6.5	1.0	0.0	1.5	4.5	0.0	3.0	9.0	3.5	1.5	0.0	0.0	0.0	5.0	8.5 Labiatae, 4.0 Liliaceae, 2.0 Cyperaceae, 0.5 Malvaceae
Lower Natufian horizon																								
C01:4, sample 4	1.0	4.5	1.5	64.5	4.0	3.5	0.0	0.0	1.0	1.5	0.5	0.0	1.0	2.5	0.5	0.0	0.5	1.5	4.5	0.0	0.5	0.0	6.0	0.5 Rosaceae, 0.5 Boraginaceae
Sterile horizon below Natufian																								
C01:5, sample 1	26.5	0.0	2.5	1.5	3.5	1.0	0.0	59.5	0.0	0.0	0.0	0.0	0.0	0.0	0.0	0.0	0.0	0.0	2.5	0.5	0.0	0.0	2.0	0.5 Liliaceae

93

might account for differential detection among samples. Overlapping confidence intervals around 3 and 7 percent values (Maher 1972) cast similar doubt on a meaningful contrast between levels 5 and 4 in total amounts of AP. In any event, both samples support reconstructions of steppe-like vegetation in the site environs, with at most widely scattered trees.

Tubuliflorae pollen is most abundant in modern samples from steppe or mixed forest and steppe vegetation types with a secondary presence in areas of Mediterranean vegetation that have been heavily degraded by agriculture and grazing (Bottema and Barkoudah 1979). Nevertheless, modern maxima approach only half the percentage in the area C-01 level 4 Natufian deposit. The correlation of exceptionally high Tubuliflorae frequencies with an occupational level raises the possibility of cultural bias. Weedy species of Tubuliflorae may have responded to disturbance and soil enrichment occasioned by activities that produced hearths and ashy areas.

Pollen spectra of three culturally sterile strata in area C-01 postdate the earliest Natufian occupation of area C-01 level 4. Area C-01 level 3 is intermediate between the level 4 occupation and a second Natufian occupation (C-01:2) tentatively dated near 10,900 B.P., or over 1000 years later (table 1). Area C-01 level 1 occurs above the second Natufian occupation but prior to Neolithic times, and the two samples come from near the base of this sterile horizon.

These three samples contain the highest frequencies of chenopod and amaranth (Cheno-am) pollen in the Beidha sequence, with highest frequencies in area C-01 level 1. Although hexagonal grains with large pores (*Noaea*-type) are present, round grains with more numerous pores (*Atriplex*-type) strongly predominate in each sample. Cheno-am pollen is elevated in the earlier part of the Natufian occupations at Mallaha (Leroi-Gourhan 1984) and in the late Kebaran and early Natufian at Hayonim Terrace (Henry *et al*. 1981). The predominance of *Atriplex*-type in earlier Natufian levels in the Judayid Basin of southern Jordan contrasts with later Natufian spectra exhibiting more warm and mesic taxa (Emery-Barbier 1988). The widespread detection of a cool, dry Natufian interval marked by Cheno-am pollen and particularly *Atriplex*-type appears to be further

evidenced in levels 1 and 3 at Beidha, although with lower frequency ranges for those types.

Artemisia pollen, probably produced by *Artemisia herba-alba*, is somewhat higher in levels 1 and 3 than in the earlier samples. Liguliflorae and Tubuliflorae occur in much decreased quantities compared to previous maxima. Pollen attributable to *Daphne* or *Thymelaea* is a consistent component of the pollen assemblage and may mark an earlier prominence of Thymelaea hirsuta or Daphne linearifolia, both of which are shrubs of the Beidha vicinity today (Helbæk 1966). Maximum values for both Thymelaeaceae and *Plantago* among all Beidha samples suggest a very open and xeric vegetation resembling modern overgrazed steppes.

Arboreal pollen other than that of riparian taxa ranges between 3 and 17 percent in the area C-01 samples bracketing Natufian occupation. The high value of 17 percent is due to greater amounts of windblown pine in area C-01 level 3. Oak and juniper are consistently present in low frequencies and likely represent common taxa among scattered trees in regional vegetation surrounding the Wadi el Ghurab. Pistachio pollen was not tabulated, but may also have been occasional among regional trees. Comparatively low dispersal characterizes this genus (Bottema and Barkoudah 1979: 463, 467).

Small amounts of olive pollen may represent occasional trees outside the wadi, but equally probably sources for this type and for *Ostrya* or *Carpinus* are trees growing in more mesic niches of the main wadi and tributary drainages, or near localized spring discharge. Riparian edge trees of the drainages include *Salix*, willow, and *Tamarix*, tamarisk. Permanently damp habitats are evidenced by trace amounts of cattail or bur-read, *Typha* or *Sparganium*, in area C-01 level 1.

The lower sample (#8) from area C-01 level 1 yielded grass pollen of a size and morphology compatible with Cerealia. In the absence of evidence for site occupation at this level, a wild species in indicated. During a dry, cool period, wild cereal grasses may have grown in more mesic wadi soils.

The west section of the sounding in area F-4 furnishes three samples from immediately prior to and during Neolithic occupation. Pollen content from area F-4 level 15, at the top of the culturally sterile stratum which precedes the

Neolithic occupation and separates the Neolithic from the Natufian, does not resemble that of samples from area C-01 level 1 which lie in the lower portion of this same sterile horizon. Cheno-am types are not abundant. *Artemisia* constitutes one fourth of all pollen with Tubuliflorae as a second plentiful category. Zohary (1940: 75) characterizes *Artemisia herba-alba* as an early invader of Mediterranean arboreal communities upon clearing, and its prominence may denote depletion of more favored locales supporting trees. The highest grass values of the sequence suggest a relatively mesic facies of steppe vegetation.

The Neolithic period

Samples from the two Neolithic occupational levels in area F-4 produced dissimilar spectra. Elevated frequencies of Liguliflorae pollen in an earlier sample are not duplicated in a later one. It is possible that weedy Liguliflorae species in area F-4 level 14 (the basal Neolithic deposit in this area) are proliferating locally in response to cultural activity of a different nature or intensity than that of the later Neolithic phase. Although Liguliflorae persists in the later sample in level 8 (situated 1.05 m higher in the Neolithic sequence) of area F-4 in reduced quantities, the proportion of *Artemisia* and overall distribution of pollen types is again similar to that of the level immediately predating Neolithic settlement.

In both Neolithic levels, pollen of *Typha* or *Sparganium* is present. Permanent water sources in the form of springs or pools exist in the area. An additional type in area F-4 level 14, *Ficus* or fig, may be an indigenous species of mesic wadi habitats or a cultivated tree.

The Nabatean period

The latest pollen record at Beidha comes from the buried surface of a Nabatean agricultural terrace in the northern profile in area E-6 level 2 (Kirkbride 1966: Plate IXB). The various categories of Compositae pollen predominate. An increased prominence of *Ephedra* and Capparidaceae is commensurate with persistent shrubs in a regional vegetation being degraded by the effects of clearing, herding, and fuel collection. Oak and Cupressaceae pollen fall within the range of earlier samples.

Fig is again present. Although still in low frequencies, olive and pistachio pollen are highest among Beidha samples. Because other arboreal types show no significant increase, it is likely that cultivated trees contribute at least some of this pollen. A hyrax midden dating between A.D. 160 and 390 at Nabatean Petra, approximately 8 km to the south of Beidha, yielded similar percentages of these pollen types as well as fig seeds (Fall *et al.*, in press).

The second Beidha occurrence of grass pollen exhibiting attributes of Cerealia is in the Nabatean terrace. A terrace crop may be indicated. Alternatively, weedy grasses related to cultivated ones may have grown among other crop plants in the terraces.

Conclusions

A potentially major factor in the configuration of Beidha pollen spectra is the impact of cultural activity. Maximal change in human landuse is intercepted by the stratigraphic sequence. The timespan witnesses incipient agriculture and herding in the region and culminates with intensified food production. Botanical remains from even the earliest agricultural sites in both Old and New Worlds have been found to strongly reflect anthropogenic plant communities shaped by intentional and unintentional manipulation (e.g. Fish 1985; Hillman *et al.* 1989). Trees and even shrubs such as *Artemisia* may be depleted beyond agricultural and residential zones in the quest for fuel (Bottema and Barkoudah 1979). Grazing pressure in the Neolithic is of unknown magnitude (see Hecker 1982). During later parts of the sequence, domesticated animals might have been grazed near the site in the intervals between occupation levels. In addition to reduction of vegetational elements, other species may have been culturally enhanced during occupational episodes in ruderal communities or other anthropogenic habitats such as those created by water storage devices.

Throughout the Beidha sequence, pollen spectra of both cultural and noncultural levels reveal the existence of an open, steppe-like regional vegetation. Denser arboreal communities may have occurred in particularly favorable locales, but no more than widely scattered trees are indicated for the general landscape surrounding Beidha. These results parallel findings in archaeological sediments of similar date in Palestine and Jordan, which counter reconstructions of more forested vegetation based on lacustrine sequences with high waterborne inputs of upland arboreal pollen types (Leroi-Gourhan 1984). Riparian trees and aquatic species emphasize the contribution of wadi or localized spring taxa to overall plant diversity and resource availability. Permanently damp habitats are attested in both Natufian and Nabatean times.

Palynological change over time at Beidha and other sites of the region is expressed in varying proportions of nonarboreal types. Detection of a geographically widespread rise in Cheno-am pollen during a segment of Natufian time at Beidha and elsewhere suggests a horizon of dry, cool climate. Other pronounced abundances of NAP types in the Beidha sequence suggest localized bias, such as the elevated amounts of Tubuliflorae in the Natufian occupation and of Liguliflorae in the older Neolithic level.

Variation in pollen distributions across modern vegetation, as documented by Bottema and Barkoudah (1979), serves as an interpretive guide to prehistoric AP and NAP, but only for the most general parameters. Earlier archaeological spectra may underestimate arboreal components of regional vegetation relative to modern analogs; diminished pollen production today from overgrazed, impoverished understory taxa enhances the proportional representation of wind pollinated arboreal types. Interactions among current climatic factors may diverge from those of early post-Pleistocene time; more importantly, millennia of intensive food production have engendered cumulative vegetational consequences. Although an open structure is inferred on the basis of modern pollen configurations, the plant communities of Natufian and later occupation should not be envisioned in present degraded form (cf. Zohary 1940, 1973; Eig 1946). A vegetationally more productive and resource-rich steppe undoubtedly existed in the past.

At Beidha and chronologically similar regional sites, pollen analysis has been applied primarily as a stratigraphic technique. The variation within single levels and occupations remains unassessed. Distributional bias resulting from resource use, as expressed by differential frequencies of economic species among individual features or between contemporary sites, has not been investigated. Such palynological approaches should be explored as additional means to an understanding of resource availability and utilization during the Neolithic transition.

Appendix C.
Beidha Natufian: faunal report

by Howard M. Hecker

The faunal material recovered from the Natufian occupation horizon is presented in table 30.[29] The material comes from the 1958 and 1959 excavations in areas F-1, K-2 and J-2, the densest concentration occurring in the large roasting area of J-2 (see fig. 34). Although the sample size is small and cannot with confidence be said to be representative of the Natufian occupation as a whole, it still is large enough to give a reasonably good impression of the range and predominance of exploited animal species.

A brief description of the mammalian species identified from the Natufian excavations follows; they will be presented in the order of their frequency starting with the remains of the most abundant form at the site (see table 31 for faunal sample measurements).[30]

Capra species

Two caprine species were identified at Beidha on the basis of their distinctive horn cores; i.e. *Capra ibex nubiana* Cuvier 1825 and *Capra hircus aegagrus* Erxleben 1777.[31] The Nubian Ibex (referred to locally as Beden) has a scimitar-shaped horn core in which the anterior surface is either flat (males) or slightly convex (females). In contrast, the anterior surface of the scimitar-shaped horn core of the Wild Goat (locally referred to as Bezoar) has a pronounced anterior keel in males and a more sharply convex anterior in females. While the horn cores reliably distinguish between these two very closely related forms, their post-cranial skeletons are virtually indistinguishable. As a consequence, the bulk of the caprine sample was identified simply as capra/ibex.

The presence of both species of Capra at Beidha is not at all surprising since this was a region of potential overlap of both forms. In the past this area was near the southern limit of the wild goat and the northern limit of the Nubian Ibex. For example, ibex material has been identified from Pleistocene age deposits in Syria and Lebanon (Fritsch 1893: 22; Hooijer 1961: 52-53) as well as from Palestine (Vaufrey 1951: 202, 212).[32] The palaeodistribution of wild goat, particularly this far south in late Pleistocene and early Holocene times, is, however, somewhat in dispute, though I believe it ought not be (see Hecker 1975: 266-269, for a more thorough discussion of the question). Wild goat has been identified on the basis of horn core remains from Ksar 'Akil (western Lebanon), Madamagh Rockshelter (southern Jordan), Ain Mallaha, el-Khiam and Jericho (east-central Palestine) (Bouchud 1987; Clutton-Brock 1971; Hooijer 1961; Perkins 1966; Vaufrey 1951).

One thing certain is that the immediate environs (i.e. rugged and mountainous) around Beidha are the preferred terrain of these goat forms. Therefore that they were found here in significant numbers should not be surprising particularly if there was increased effective moisture in the region to support the vegetation

[29]In addition to the four primary mammalian species (*Capra*, *Gazella*, *Bos* and *Equus*) one bone each of a canid (*Canis aureus*) and a hare (*Lepus* sp.) were also identified.

[30]The Beidha Natufian sample (N=129) was originally examined by Dexter Perkins (N=102) and briefly reported on (1966: 66-67). Another six specimens (4 *Capra* and 2 *Gazella* are noted in Perkins' notes without further elaboration) were included in the author's 1982 paper but are excluded now because it is felt that it was a mistake to do so). An additional 27 bones were identified by myself (see Hecker 1975: table 11 and Appendix 1). Concerning the sample examined by Perkins only a small portion was available to me for re-examination. Thus the analysis of the total sample is based mainly on his notes.

[31]Perkins identified three horn core specimens as coming from Ibex (2 male and 1 female) and one from a male Wild Goat.

[32]Today there are protected colonies of Nubian Ibex along the Wadi Musa and at Ain Gedi near the northwest shore of the Dead Sea.

	Capra (69.8%)		Gazella (21.7%)	Bos (6.2%)	Equus (2.3%)	
	Perkins	Hecker	Perkins	Hecker	Perkins	Hecker
Humerus	20	0	9	0	0	0
Ulna	4*	0	0	0	0	0
Radius	2	0	0	0	0	0
Metacarpal	5 (2DUF)	0	0	0	0	0
Femur	3	3 (1PF, 2D-1F 1UF)	0	0	0	1 (PUF)
Tibia	7 (1P 6D-2F)	1 (RDF)	2	0	0	0
Metatarsal	1 (DF)	1 (DF)	0	0	0	0
Metapodial	12 (D-1F 10UF)	0	7 (D-2F 5UF)	0	0	0
Calcaneus	1	1 (UF tuber calcis)	0	3 (3f-1 UF tuber calcis)	0	1 (cF)
Astragalus	1	0	0	1 (L)	0	0
Maxilla	1	0	0	0	0	0
Mandible	2	0	0	0	0	0
Scapula	3 (1R 1L)	0	6	0	0	0
Pelvic frags.	5	6 (2R 1L 2UF)	0	0	0	0
Sacral frags.	0	1	0	0	0	0
Phalange I	0	2 (1D 1CF)	2 (F)	0	0	0
Phalange II	2 (F)	0	0	1 (Fc)	1 (cF)	0
Cranial frags.	0	2	1	0	0	0
Horn core	4**	0	1	0	0	0
Naviscular cuboid	0	0	0	1	0	0
Tarsal	0	0	0	2	0	0
Total	73	17	28	8	1	2

*Excludes one ulna in articulation with a radius
**Horn cores (1 aegagrus male, 3 ibex – 2 male, 1 female)
F: fused UF: unfused D: distal P: proximal R: right L: left, c: complete, f: fragment

Table 30. Sample of identifiable fauna (N=129).

they relied upon. This is believed to have been the case (Henry and Turnbull 1985: 61; Neev and Emery 1967: 28; Perrot 1968: 366; Bar-Yosef 1983: 14), and was probably one of the main reasons hunters were attracted to Beidha during the early Natufian.

Gazella cf. dorcas Linnaeus 1758

This small sample was identified almost entirely by Perkins and is based on his notes.[33] Specific identification of gazelle forms is often quite difficult (there is some overlap in the range of identifying characteristics) and without a large sample it is often better to keep the identification at the genus level. In any case we are dealing with either Gazella dorcas (the Red or Dorcas Gazelle), a somewhat larger form Gazella gazella Pallas 1766 (the Arabian gazelle), or both. Based on the distribution of Gazella subgutturosa Guldenstaedt 1790 (Harrison 1968: 364, fig. 165) one should also consider the Persian or Goitered Gazelle as well.

In the G. subgutturosa form, the horns "originate close together, the gap between them is generally much less than half an inch" and "usually widely divergent at their tips" (Harrison 1968: 360). These traits do not appear to be present in the gazelle material from the later Neolithic levels. In G. dorcas, by contrast, the gap between them is a half inch or more, i.e., greater than in G. subgutturosa but less than in G. gazella. In this regard most of the gazelle material from Neolithic layers appears to be closer to the dorcas variety particularly with respect to the breadth across the bases of the horns.

Whether the presence of G. dorcas in the Neolithic levels means they were also present in the Natufian deposits is difficult to determine. However, based on terrain preferences (Bodenheimer 1958: 178; Simmons and Ilany

[33]Perkins examined 28 specimens which he identified as gazelle, only one of which was a horn core fragment. Two additional skeletal elements, unfortunately unspecified, were also noted as coming from gazelle.

1975/1975; Garrard 1984) and the fact that the *G. dorcas* variety has been identified in the later prepottery Neolithic levels at Beidha, it seems likely that it is the species we are dealing with in the Natufian deposits. In this context it may be important to note that the dorcas form was also identified at Jericho (Clutton-Brock 1971: 46-48), el-Khiam (Vaufrey 1951: 210-211), and possibly at Wadi Judayid 2 (Henry and Turnbull 1985: 54-55).

However, the identification of *G. Dorcas* at el-Khiam, and perhaps some of the Jericho material as well, may be incorrect (Tchernov *et al.* 1986: 55). Tchernov and others (1986) assert that this species did not arrive in southern Palestine until after prepottery Neolithic B times. If this assessment is correct, then the assignment of this material to *G. dorcas* would be very much weakened. Therefore, given these uncertainties, it is perhaps best to consider the specific *dorcas* identification provisional at this time.

Bos primigenius Bojanus 1927

This very small sample consists entirely of post-cranial remains and has been identified by myself as coming from *Bos primigenius*. The aurochs, as it is commonly referred to, is know to have been in the region around this time (Clutton-Brock 1971: 44-46; Henry and Turn-bull 1985: 54). The only other large artiodactyl it could be is *Cervus elaphus*, but this form is believed to have retreated further north by Natufian times (Tchernov 1966: 137).

Equus cf. *hemionus* Pallas 1775

Three post-cranial equid remains were identified. This is too small a sample to make a very certain species identification. However, if one takes into account the very similar remains from the subsequent prepottery Neolithic levels (to the extent they can be compared[34]) it would seem that we are dealing with the Syrian Onager, *Equus hemionus*; though this identification must be considered tentative. In this context it may be important to note that the onager and the Dorcas Gazelle are steppe-dwelling forms. The presence of both species in the areas to the east and west of Beidha would have made the steppe that much more attractive to hunters. While they may have been more attracted to these areas by the large herds of gazelle, they apparently were not loath to take down an occasional onager.

[34]None of the three Natufian bones was measurable.

Observations

The Natufian sample is much too small to make anything more than some tentative observations and they are as follows:

1. There is no hard evidence that any of the species recovered from the Beidha Natufian was in any way being culturally manipulated. Rather, it would seem more reasonable to suggest that we are still dealing with a hunting (and gathering) economy. The only forms for which we have a large enough sample to assess this are

Species	Bone msmt*		N	Range	Mean	Var.	StDev	Coef.var.
Capra	Humerus	Bd	19	26.2-40.0	31.8	9.5	3.1	9.7
	Phal I	GL**	2	44.3-45.8	45.1			
		SD	1	13.2				
Gazella	Humerus	Bd	9	23.3-26.3	25.1			

*Using the system for measurements as outlined by von den Driesch (1976)
**The smaller of these two specimens was measured by the author using a different syste (see Hecker 1975: 197 for an explanation) which tends to give slightly smaller overall lengths (at most by 1.5 mm.)

Table 31. Selected measurements (in millimeters) of faunal samples.

99

Species	Usable meat/ Individual	MNI approach – usable meat			OBOI approach – usable meat		
		N	Total	%	N	Total	%
Capra	55 lbs.	15	825	25.4	90	4,950	33.7
Gazella	55 lbs.	5	275	8.5	28	1,540	10.5
Bos	880 lbs.	2	1,760	54.2	8	7,040	47.9
Equus	385 lbs.	1	385	11.9	3	1,155	7.9
Total		23	3,245	100.0	129	14,685	100.0

MNI: Minimum number of individuals
OBOI: One bone (equals) one individual

Table 32. Meat contribution by species.

Capra and Gazelle and here the measurements and the Capra horn morphology indicate that we are dealing with wild forms.

2. While the Beidha inhabitants exploited the relatively flat steppe environments to the west and east, and at some distance from the site, they seemed to have preferred to hunt in the more rugged mountainous terrain of their immediate environs. However, the fact that the steppe was exploited for Gazella and Equus (and possibly for Bos) clearly suggests that sufficient game was abundant there as well. This indicates that climatic conditions in the area then were more favorable than today. I interpret this to mean that the abundance of caprine remains at Beidha most likely reflects hunter preference rather than constraints on choices imposed by the overall distribution of vegetation.

3. I think it is significant that the raw bone counts and the ratio of limb to non-limb skeletal elements of just these four primary food species reflect not only proximity to Beidha but also the differential likelihood that the entire carcass would have been carried back to the site by the hunters, i.e., the schlep effect (Perkins and Daly 1968). According to this model, the size of the animal and the proximity of the kill site to the habitation site will be reflected in the faunal remains discarded at the latter site. If the animal was very large and brought down some distance from the site, then it is likely that only the limb elements, which have the most meat on them, would be carried back to the habitation site, while a smaller animal would more likely be brought back intact. Were the kill to take place close to the habitation site then the hunters would be more likely to bring back the entire carcass regardless of its size.

By this logic, the small to moderate sized caprines, dwelling closest to the site, would be expected to be the most abundant in the sample and they are (70%). Their moderate size would also have permitted the hunters to return with the entire carcass (as evidenced by the 26.7% of the sample which consisted of non-limb skeletal elements). In contrast, the smaller gazelle would have been more likely and more frequently brought back to Beidha in its entirety even though it was hunted at some distance (over 4 km to the west). Again relative frequencies of body parts support these observations in that gazelle remains are the second most abundant form representing 22% of the faunal collection – 40% of which are non-limb skeletal elements. On the other hand the much larger onager was probably hunted at some distance from Beidha. Because of their much larger size, it is suggested that the entire carcass would not have been brought back to the site. This is supported by the relative frequency of onager in the faunal sample (2%) – represented by only the limb elements. The very large aurochs, being more catholic in its habitat preferences, may have been more frequently encountered closer to Beidha. However, because of its great size, its remains also would not be expected to be very abundant and they are not (6%, all of which are limb elements).

4. A direct reading of table 32 indicates that aurochs provided the greatest amount of usable meat to the Beidha inhabitants whether calculated by the Minimum Number of Individuals (MNI) or One Bone equals One Individual (OBOI) method.[35] I believe, however, based on the subsequent prepottery Neolithic levels at Beidha where the samples are much larger, that this is probably more a reflection of small sam-

ple size than of what was actually going on at
Beidha.[36] Taphonomic processes (differential
survival and therefore the easier identification of
the remains of a large species) also most likely
contribute to the bias favoring aurochs.

5. Two wild species, boar (*Sus scrofa*) and
sheep (*Ovis orientalis*) have not been encountered
in the Natufian faunal assemblage. The small
size of the sample most likely accounts for the
absence of wild boar remains from the collection
– they were most likely present in the region.
But it should be noted that wild boar was not
very common in any of the Neolithic levels
either.

However the absence of wild sheep from the
collection is more problematical. This is because
they have recently been identified in Natufian
deposits at Wadi Judayid 2 in southern Jordan
(Henry and Turnbull 1985: 55-59), and at three
Epipaleolithic sites in the Negev (Davis *et al.*
1982)[37]. This is unexpected and should it hold
up to further scrutiny then the absence of sheep
at Beidha is at the moment inexplicable.

[35]Based on live weights from Walker (1964). The usable meat
from *Capra, Gazella, Equus* and *Bos* is generally considered roughly
50% of the live weight (Hole, Flannery and Neely 1969: 83;
Perkins and Daly 1968: 100; Perkins 1969: 177). In the case of the
Beidha material I think the live weight figure for *Bos* may be too
low and that for *Gazella* too high.

[36]In this regard the *Bos* sample from the early Natufian site of
Wadi Judayid 2 is also very small (6%) relative to the more
frequent remains of medium sized forms (84%) (Henry and
Turnbull 1985: table 3).

[37]It is my understanding that the assignment of the sheep remains
at Jericho to the prepottery Neolithic levels is somewhat in
question.

Appendix D.
The Natufian shells from Beidha

by David S. Reese

The Natufian levels at Beidha produced 74 marine shell fragments, samples coming from each of the excavation areas. The site is today located about 100 km from the Red Sea and some 180 km from the Mediterranean (these and all distances noted below are calculated as-the-crow-flies). Not only is Beidha closer to the Red Sea in absolute distance, but given the intervening terrain, it would have been an easier journey to reach the Red Sea.

Two of the genera present (*Nerita, Strombus*) are forms not found in the Mediterranean Sea and, therefore, must come from the Red Sea. In addition, many of the dentalia present are the large Red Sea species *Dentalium elephantinum*. It is quite likely that the remaining shells were also procured from Red Sea sources.

A catalogue of the material recovered from the Natufian of Beidha is presented in table 33. Most of the shells (59, 83%), come from the extensive excavations in 1958 and 1959.

By far the most numerous recent (non-fossilized) shell (62, 87%) is the tusk or tooth shell, *Dentalium*. These molluscs live buried in the sand or mud, and are naturally open at both ends. Eleven of the dentalia are fragments of complete shells, called here "beads". It is difficult, however, to know if the Beidha "beads" were intentionally made or are simply broken sections of complete shells. At other Natufian sites some *Dentalium* beads show signs of being cut from larger shells (Larson 1978). Twenty one (34%) of the complete Beidha dentalia are very worn and abraded, and it is possible that they were collected in this state on the beach. One is probably a fossil and another is burnt.

The remaining shells include three dove shells of two genera (*Pyrene, Columbella*), two from area K-2 and one from area J-2, with two holed. There are also single examples of *Nerita* (nerite), *Cypraea* (cowrie), *Strombus* (stromb), *Clypeomorus* (cerith), *Pecten* (scallop), and a straight *Vermetus* (worm tube). The vermetid closely resembles a dentalium shell, and was probably used in a similar manner.

The small number of coral fossil fragments and fossil dentalium are probably from the local Cretaceous limestone (Kirkbride 1966: 30, pl. XVIIB), and have not been modified by man.

It is clear that the dentalia, vermetid, and holed shells, served as decorative ornaments, and they represent the overwhelming majority of the Beidha sample (68 shells, 96%). The function of the remaining shells (dove shell, cowrie, and scallop) is less certain, although they may be fragments of ornaments that lack the pierced portion. Two of these shells are burnt; a situation that occurs at other Jordanian prehistoric sites.

The later aceramic Neolithic periods at Beidha have yielded over 600 other shells, mainly combrised of holed cowries, nerites, and bivalves (Kirkbride 1966: 28, pl. XVIB and personal analysis). The report on the Neolithic shell assemblage will be presented in a later volume.

Comparanda

Dentalium are generally considered to be one of the hallmarks of the Natufian culture. They are frequently found at Natufian sites, often in groups (particularly in burials), and presumably they were attached to headdresses or strung as armlets, girdles or necklaces (Reese 1982: 83-84). Their relative frequency, however, has rarely been quantified with regard to the other types of shells occurring in Epipaleolithic sites. Some comparative information follows.

In the Ras en Naqb in southern Jordan (Henry 1982), rockshelter J202 (about 40 km from the Red Sea) produced 15 shells from

Provenience	Species
F-1:2	1 *Nerita undulata* – open body
K-2 (all levels)	21 *Dentalium* – 8 water-worn, 7 "beads", 1 burnt
	1 *Pyrene testudinaria* – burnt
	1 *Columbella* – holed on body
	1 *Cypraea* – small lip fragment
J-2 (all levels)	31 *Dentalium* – 10 water-worn, 5 "beads"
	1 *Pyrene testudinaria* – small hole above mouth
	1 *Strombus* – open body, worn/abraded
	1 *Clypeomorus* – holed on lower body
	1 *Pecten* – fragment
	1 coral, 2 fragments -fossil
F-1:1 (1964)	5 *Dentalium* – 3 water-worn
	1 *Vermetus* – straight
H-4:55	2 *Dentalium* (Reg. #'s 2099, 2108, 2110)
C-01:2	3 *Dentalium* – 1 fossil? (Reg. #'s 2099, 2108, 2110)
C-01:3	1 *Dentalium* (Reg. # 2109)
C-01:4	1 *Dentalium* (Reg. # 2107)

Table 33. Natufian marine shells by provenience unit (N=73).

the late Hamran period of the Epipaleolithic, including five dentalia, one scallop, and one cowrie. The final Hamran occupation produced 41 shells, with 18 dentalia (44%, 2 burnt), four scallops, and one cowrie (personal analysis).

Also in the Ras en Naqb, the late Mushabian Epipaleolithic (level A) at Tor Hamar, J431 (Henry and Garrard 1988), about 70 km from the Red Sea, produced 212 marine shells, with 120 dentalia (57%). There are also numerous small holed gastropods, 14 burnt shells, and 14 scallop remains, two of which have slit holes below the umbo (bivalve "beak") (personal analysis).

In the Azraq Basin of eastern Jordan (Garrard *et al.* 1986, 1987), the late Epipaleolithic at Jilat 6 (170 km from the Mediterranean, 300 km from the Red Sea) produced 102 marine shells, with 57 dentalia (56%). The nearby late Epipaleolithic site of Jilat 8 produced seven dentalia out of ten shells recovered.

The Natufian site of Azraq 18 (200 km from the Mediterranean, 310 km from the Red Sea) produced 25 dentalia of 26 shells. Many of the dentalia are "beads", including a burnt one (personal analysis).

The early Natufian site of Wadi Judayid (J2) produced 70 marine shells, with 54 dentalia (77%, mainly beads, four burnt) and 11 *Nerita* (seven holed, others broken).

The early Natufian at Wadi Hammeh 27 near Pella in the Jordan Valley (80 km from the Mediterranean) produced over 150 dentalium, with 27 shells from a necklace in Burial XXJ. These include some water-worn examples, two burnt shells, one shell with red ochre on it, and one shell embedded in a gazelle phalange (Edwards 1987: 159, and personal communication).

In the early and late Natufian levels at Hayonim Terrace dentalia make up 646 of the 817 (Mediterranean) marine shells (79%, Reese 1982: 83-84). The Natufian of Hayonim Cave yielded 530 marine shells, with 490 (92%) dentalia. Of these *Dentalium*, at least 290 are Mediterranean (59%), 15 Red Sea (5%), and 185 unattributable (Tchernov 1974: 50). Both sites are about 15 km from the Mediterranean and over 350 km from the Red Sea.

To date 309 marine shells have been analyzed from 'Ain Mallaha (Eynan), located about 20 km from the Mediterranean and 340 km from the Red Sea. The collection includes 210

103

Mediterranean shells (68%), four Red Sea shells (one burnt), and 95 unattributable. Of the entire collection, 226 (73%) are *Dentalium*, all from Graveyard B and mainly early Natufian in date. There are also three fossil shells, including one late Natufian dentalium (Mienis 1987: 158, 161).

At the late Natufian site of Rosh Zin in the central Negev (70 km from the Mediterranean and about 150 km from the Red Sea), *Dentalium* make up 92% of the 304 shells, with about 59% from the Mediterranean, 33% from the Red Sea, and 7% unattributable (Tchernov 1976: 72-73). Henry (1976: 345, table 11-13) states, however, that there are over 338 dentalia and that most come from the Red Sea (Reese 1982: 85).

At the late Natufian site of Rosh Horesha, also in the central Negev (about 100 km from both the Mediterranean and the Red Sea) dentalia make up 93% of the 473 marine shells from the site (Mienis 1977: 348).

The Harifian village of Abu Salem in the Negev (105 km from the Mediterranean and 120 km from the Red Sea) produced 318 dentalia of 448 shells according to Mienis (1977: 348 and unpublished additions). Marks and Scott (1976: 57-58), however, mention that many more were recovered (over 500 dentalia alone), with roughly half from the Mediterranean and half from the Red Sea. *Dentalium* would therefore make up 71-79% of the collection. Abu Salem also produced 47 scallop remains, the most common shell after dentalia (Mienis 1977: 351).

The Harifian sites of Ramat Harif, Maaleh Ramon East, Har Arod, and others, also contained dentalia. Ramat Harif and Shluhat Harif also yielded scallops (Goring-Morris 1987: 322, 331, 364-365).

The Beidha sample shares a number of characteristics in common with the collections from the late Epipaleolithic and early Neolithic occupations mentioned above. In particular, dentalia dominate the sample at virtually all the sites. Furthermore, the closer a site is to a particular sea (the Mediterranean or the Red Sea), the higher the frequency of shells from that source. This reliance is not absolute, however, as there is typically a percentage of the shells from the other source.

Appendix E.
Chipped stone artifact classification

1. Blades: defined as flakes with length equal to, or greater than 2 times width
   a. complete
   b. large fragments still fitting above definition
      1. proximal fragment
      2. medial fragment
      3. distal fragment
   c. microblades: complete, less than 1 cm in length

2. Flakes
   a. complete
   b. large fragments
      1. proximal fragment
      2. lateral fragment
      3. distal fragment
   c. microflakes: complete, less than 1 cm in length

3. Indeterminate debitage
   a. small fragments with parallel sides & flake scars*
      1. proximal fragment
      2. medial fragment
      3. distal fragment
   b. other (chips)

4. Core trimming elements: defined as showing core preparation

5. Core tablets: special type of core trimming element (see Marks 1976: 374)

6. Microburin products
   a. microburins
   b. trihedral points
   c. Krukowski microburins
   d. Beidha Krukowski microburins

7. Primary elements: flakes or blades with greater than 50% cortex on the exterior

8. Burin spalls

9. Cores: raw material with 3 or more flake scars

10. Debris: angular fragments, with no recognizable interior or exterior surface

11. Tools

*This was only a provisional classification and ultimately these pieces were all placed in the blade and flake categories (see Chapter 5).

Appendix F.
Debitage, core, and chipped stone tool attribute analysis[38]

1. Length in mm. Defined as the maximum distance between the distal end and the platform

2. Width in mm. Measured at the mid-point perpendicular to the maximum length

3. Thickness in mm. Defined as the maximum distance between the interior and the exterior at the mid-point

4. Completeness of blank
   0. indeterminate
   1. complete
   2. proximal end missing
   3. distal end missing
   4. proximal and distal ends missing
   5. lateral edge missing
   6. other

5. Cortex amount (excluding platform)
   0. indeterminate
   1. none
   2. 1-10%
   3. 11-50%
   4. 51-99%
   5. 100%

6. Platform
   0. NA/indeterminate
   1. plain
   2. punctiform/lipped
   3. crushed
   4. cortical
   5. dihedral
   6. multiple facet

7. Lateral profile of blank
   0. NA/indeterminate
   1. incurving
   2. flat
   3. twisted
   4. rippled
   5. outcurving

8. Exterior flake scar pattern
   0. NA/indeterminate
   1. parallel
   2. expanding
   3. coverging
   4. radiating
   5. opposing
   6. parallel & transverse
   7. other

9. Distal shape of blank
   0. NA/indeterminate
   1. feathered, pointed
   2. feathered, blunt
   3. hinge fracture
   4. overshot

10. Skew class

11. Microburin notch location
    0. NA
    1. proximal left
    2. proximal right
    3. distal left
    4. distal right
    5. both ends
    6. indeterminate

12. Material
    1. flint: white, gray, blue
    2. chert: light brown
    3. chert: other (mainly cream & white)
    4. chert: speckled

[38]The raw data from the attribute analysis is available on diskette from the author.

106

13. Core exterior
    0. NA/absent
    1. battered cobble cortex
    2. rounded nodule cortex
    3. angular nodule cortex

14. Tool completeness
    0. NA/indeterminate
    1. complete
    2. proximal end missing
    3. distal end missing
    4. 1 indeterminate end missing
    5. proximal and distal ends missing
    6. lateral edge missing
    7. other

15. Position of retouch along margins
    0. NA
    1. left lateral edge
    2. right lateral edge
    3. indeterminate lateral edge
    4. bilateral
    5. proximal
    6. distal
    7. proximal and distal
    8. left lateral & proximal
    9. right lateral & proximal
    10. indeterminate lateral & proximal
    11. left lateral & distal
    12. right lateral & distal
    13. indeterminate lateral & distal
    14. left lateral, proximal & distal
    15. right lateral, proximal & distal
    16. indeterminate lateral, proximal & distal
    17. bilateral & proximal
    18. bilateral & distal
    19. bilateral, proximal & distal
    20. transverse
    21. indeterminate
    22. indeterminate lateral & 1 indeterminate end
    23. indeterminate end

16. Percentage of primary edge retouched
    0. NA/indeterminate
    1. 1-10%
    2. 11-50%
    3. 51-99
    4. 100%

17. Type of retouch backed edge (lateral)
    0. NA
    1. steep, abrupt exterior
    2. semisteep exterior
    3. semisteep interior
    4. bifacial (Helwan)
    5. bifacial (Helwan) and interior
    6. bipolar (alternate 1 & 1)
    7. flat invasive exterior
    8. steep on thin edges (Ochata)
    9. marginal
    10. alternate series, exterior & interior
    11. combination
    12. indeterminate
    13. other
    14. bifacial (varied platform location)
    15. bifacial (14) & interior
    16. exterior & bifacial
    17. bipolar (alternate series), abrupt & bipolar series

18. Shape of backed edge
    0. NA/indeterminate
    1. straight, parallel to unretouched edge
    2. straight, not parallel to unretouched edge
    3. concave
    4. convex (ends truncated)
    5. arched to point
    6. shouldered
    7. irregular
    8. pointed
    9. arched to 2 points
    10. indeterminate
    11. elongated, slightly convex

19. Shape of proximal end
    0. NA
    1. concave
    2. convex
    3. straight
    4. oblique, flat
    5. oblique, concave
    6. oblique, convex
    9. Krukowski microburin
    10. break
    11. unretouched
    12. other
    13. indeterminate
    16. modified base (distal or proximal)
    17. pointed
    18. negative Krukowski microburin
    19. irregular
    20. oblique acute

20. Microburin scar morphology
    0. NA/None
    1. microburin scar, indeterminate
    2. microburin scar, partially retouched, indeterminate
    7. negative microburin scar, exterior
    8. negative microburin scar, partially retouched exterior
    14. negative microburin scar, interior
    15. negative microburin scar, partially retouched interior

21. Type of retouch on proximal end
    0. NA/none
    1. steep, abrupt exterior
    2. semisteep exterior
    3. semisteep interior
    4. bifacial
    5. bifacial and interior
    6. bipolar (alternate 1 & 1)
    7. flat invasive exterior
    8. steep on thin edges (Ochata)
    9. marginal
    10. alternate series, exterior & interior
    11. combination
    12. indeterminate
    13. other
    14. minute "burin" blow
    15. break
    16. break with retouch

22. Angle of proximal truncation

23. Shape of distal truncation
    (same as 25)

24. Microburin scar location
    (same as 26)

25. Type of retouch on distal end
    (same as 27)

26. Angle of distal truncation

27. Edge damage on backed bladelet cutting edge
    0. none/NA
    1. present: light
    2. present: heavy

28. Sickle polish
    0. NA/none
    1. present: 1 side
    2. present: both sides

Appendix G.
Chipped stone core and tool typologies

Core type list*

Single platform blade cores
101. pyramidal (1/2 to 100% flaked)
102. subpyramidal (<1/2 of edge flaked)
103. face and edge
104. one face
105. thin edge
106. 2 thin edges
107. other

Opposed platform blade cores
108. same face
109. opposite face
110. pyramidal
111. other

90 degree platform blade cores
112. same face
113. different face
114. other

Flake cores
115. discoidal
116. single platform
117. multiplatform
118. other

Core fragment
119. blade
120. unidentifiable
123. flake
122. indeterminate

*See Henry (1973a: 66, 1976: 326), Marks and Larson (1977: 218)
and Tixier (1963) for complete definitions of these core types.

Tool type list (see figures 40-42)*

Scrapers
1. end scraper
2. bilaterally retouched end scraper
3. unilaterally retouched end scraper
4. double end scraper
5. ogival end scraper
6. circular end scraper
7. transverse end scraper on flake
8. rounded end scraper on flake
9. thumbnail scraper on flake
10. nosed end scraper
11. carinated scraper on flake
12. nucleiform/core scraper
13. double core scraper
83. side scraper
87. bilateral end scraper, steep retouch on sides
91. unilateral end scraper, steep retouch on side
92. denticulated scraper

Burins
17. dihedral
18. dihedral, offset
19. double dihedral
20. on break
21. on natural surface
22. transverse on natural surface
23. on straight truncation
24. on concave truncation
25. on convex truncation
26. on straight oblique truncation
27. on concave oblique truncation
29. transverse on lateral notch
30. multiple on snap
31. multiple on natural surface
32. multiple on truncations
33. multiple mixed
34. nucleiform
35. on interior surface

Notches and denticulates
36. large single notch (>7mm)
84. denticulate, multiple large notches
37. single small notch
38. single small notch with retouch
39. multiple small notches
40. multiple small notches with retouch
41. denticulate, small notches
42. small notched denticulate with retouch
86. small notch on break

Drills
75. perforator
76. multiple perforator
77. borer: bilaterally converging retouch

Retouched pieces
79. retouched piece (complete)
89. indeterminate retouched fragment

Multiple tools
14. end scraper with notch
15. scraper-burin
16. other

Truncations
43. single
44. double

Geometric microliths
45. lunate
90. lunate, asymmetric
46. triangle, symmetric
47. triangle, asymmetric
93. rectangle
94. trapeze

Nongeometric microliths
48. La Mouillah point
49. Harif point
50. microgravette point, laterally retouched, triangular cross-section
51. pointed piece bilaterally retouched primarily at tip (Falita point)
52. curved pointed piece, arched backed
53. arched backed with modified base
54. complete double truncated piece, symmetric
55. complete double truncated piece, asymmetric
56. complete piece with 1 truncation
57. complete piece, 1 truncation, modified base
58. complete piece, blunt, modified base

*See Tixier (1963) and Bar-Yosef (1970: 202-223) for definitions of most of the types. The figures are based after Bar-Yosef (1970: figures 5-8), and to some extent Goring-Morris (1987: Appendix II).

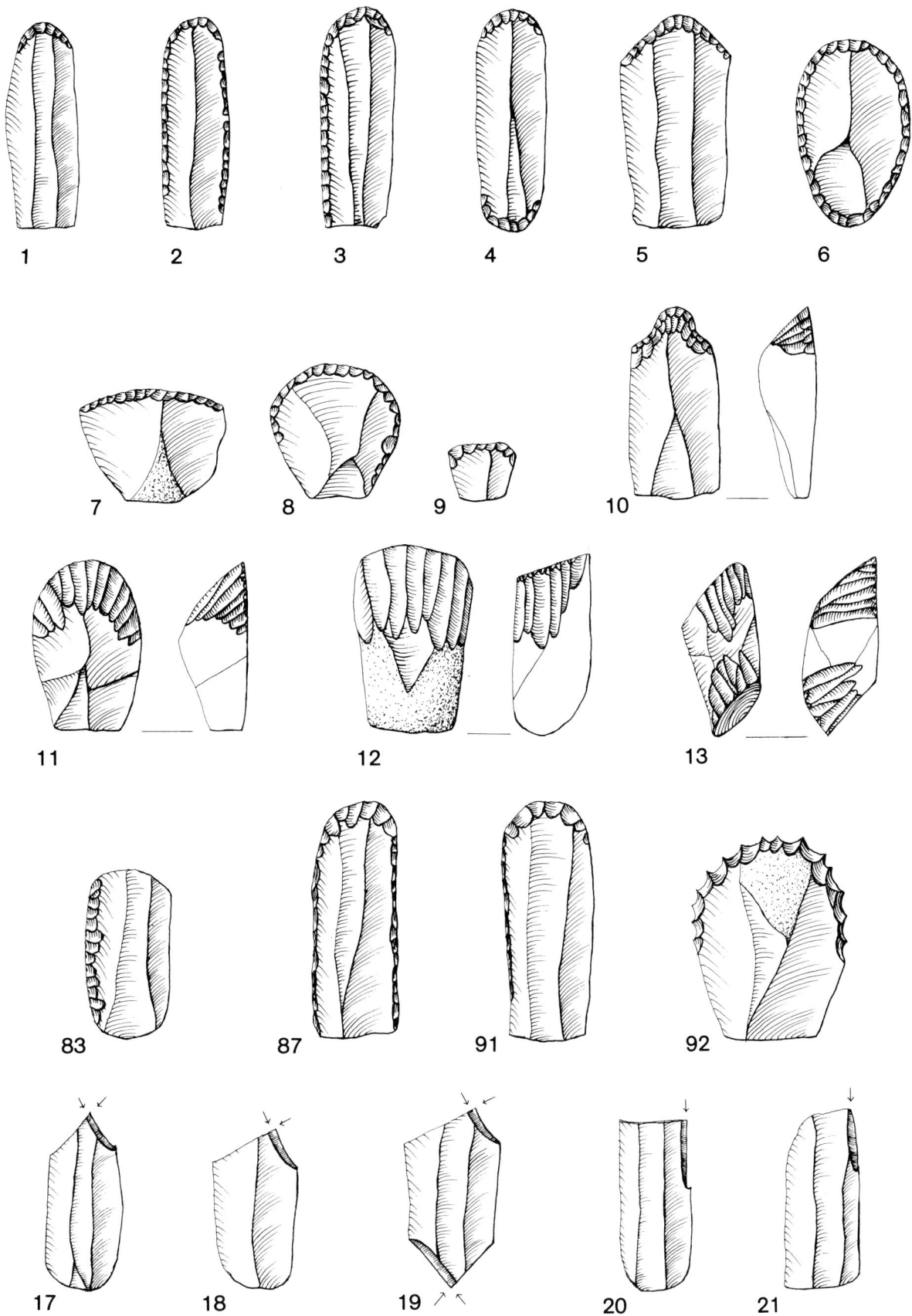

Fig. 40. Modal types for the chipped stone classification: scrapers and burins.

111

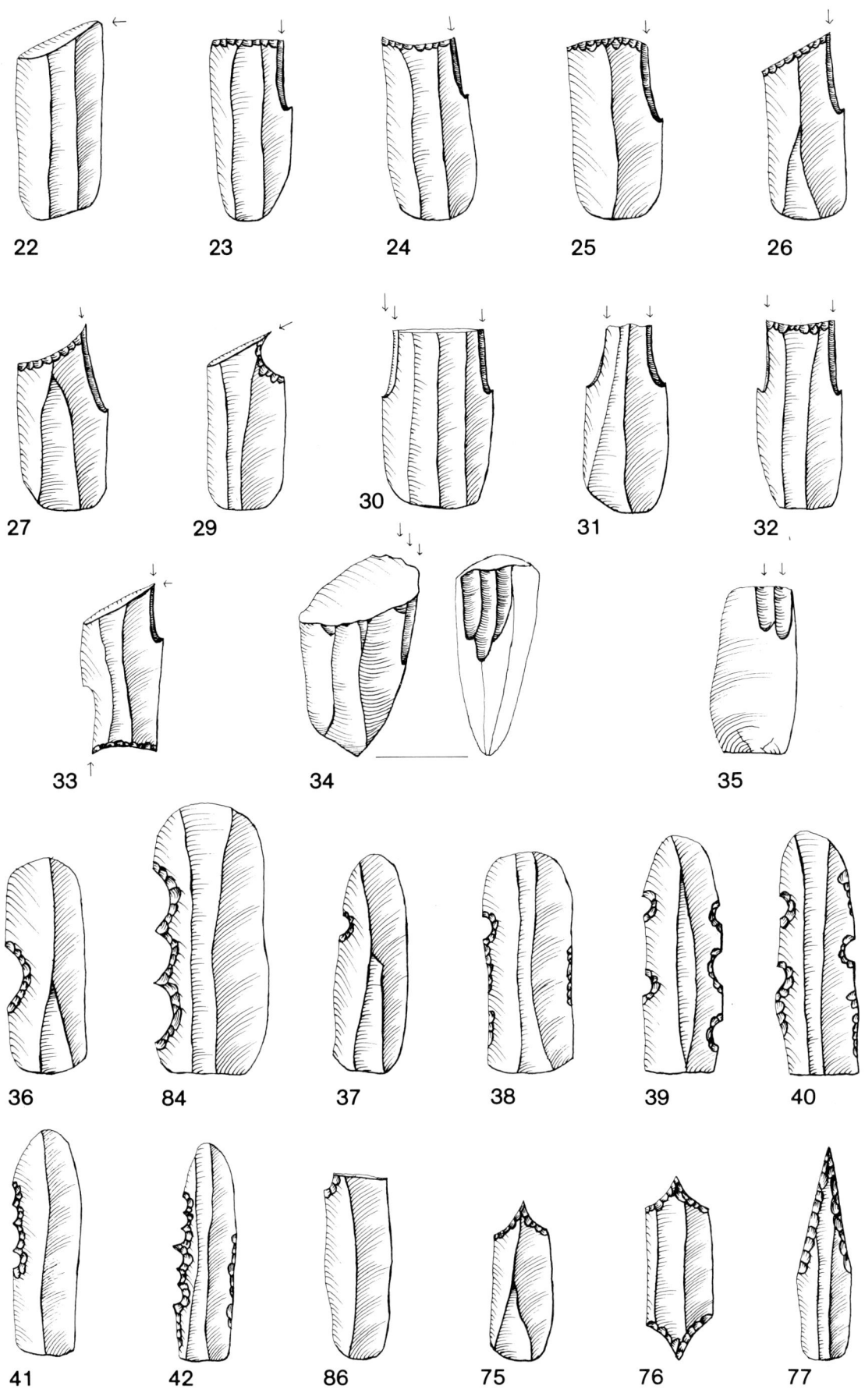

Fig. 41. Modal types for the chipped stone classification: burins (continued), notches and denticulates, and drills.

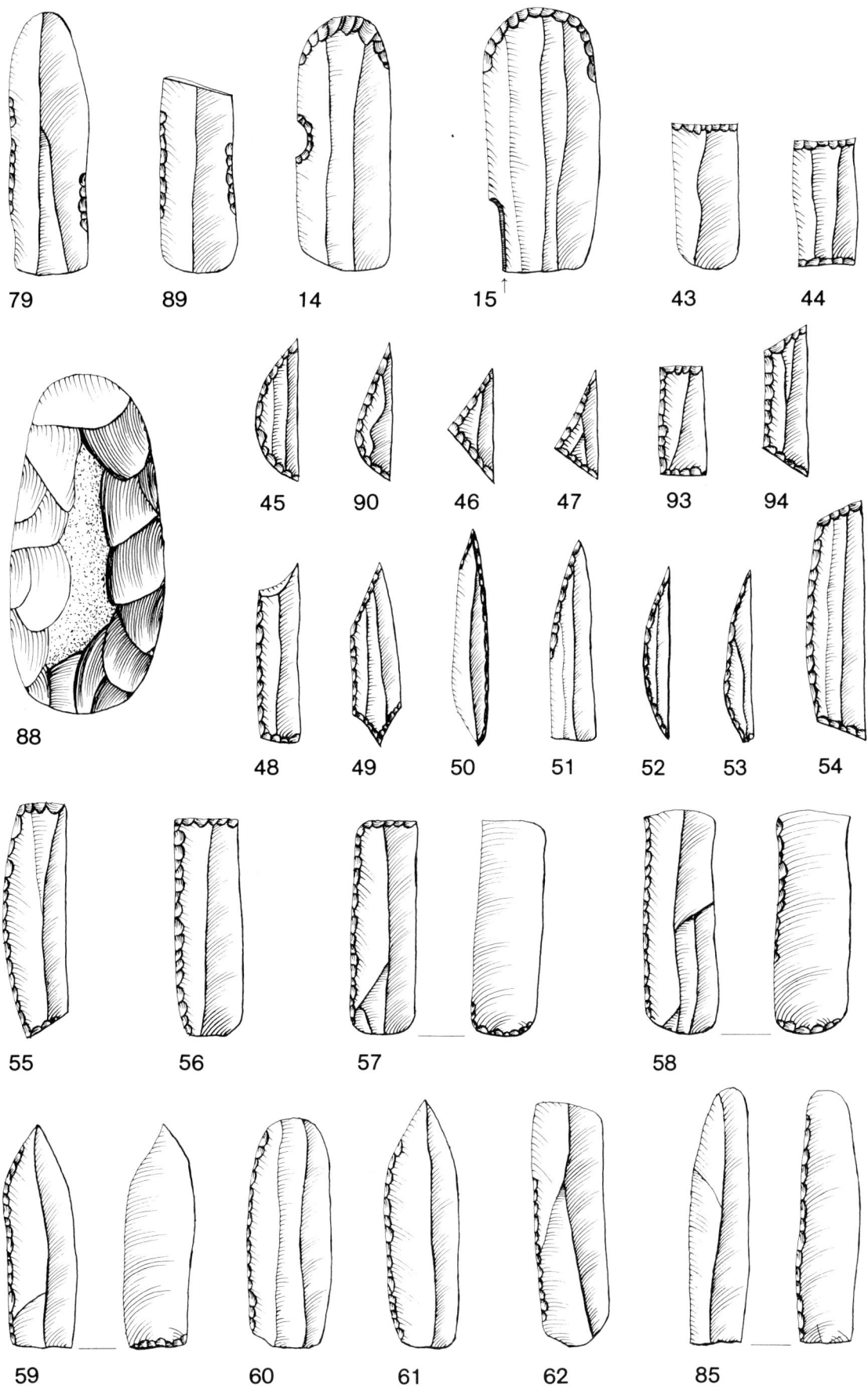

Fig. 42. Modal types for the chipped stone classification: retouched pieces, truncations, geometric microliths, nongeometric microliths, and a pick.

59. complete piece, pointed, modified base
60. complete piece, blunt, unmodified ends
61. complete piece, pointed, unmodified ends
62. complete piece, partially backed, no end modification
63. double backed piece
64. various backed pieces
85. interior retouched bladelet

Backed microlith fragments
65. proximal fragment with truncation
66. distal fragment with truncation
67. indeterminate fragment with truncation
68. medial fragment
69. proximal fragment without truncation
70. proximal fragment with base modification
71. distal fragment without truncation, blunt end
72. distal fragment without truncation, pointed end
73. partially backed fragment
74. indeterminate fragment

Various
78. sickle blade (unmodified)
80. battered piece
81. edge damaged piece
82. varia
88. pick

References

AL-EISAWI, D. M. 1985. "Vegetation in Jordan," in *Studies in the History and Archaeology of Jordan, II.* Edited by A. Hadidi, pp. 45-58. London: Routledge & Kegan Paul.

ANDERSON-GERFAUD, P. 1983. "A consideration of the uses of certain backed and "lustered" stone tools from late Mesolithic and Natufian levels of Abu Hureyra and Mureybet," in *Traces d'Utilization sur les Outils Neolithiques du Proche Orient.* Edited by M.C. Cauvin, pp. 77-105, Travaux de la Maison de l'Orient 5. Lyon: Maison de l'Orient.

ATKINSON K. AND P. BEAUMONT. 1973. The forests of Jordan. *Economic Botany* 25:305-311.

BAILEY, G., P. CARTER, C. GAMBLE AND E.H. HIGGS. 1983. "Epirus revisited: seasonality and inter-site variation in the Upper Paleolithic of north-west Greece," in *Hunter-Gatherer Economy in Prehistory.* Edited by G. Bailey, pp. 59-78. Cambridge: Cambridge University Press.

BANNING, E.B. AND I. KÖHLER-ROLLEFSON. 1987. Ethnoarchaeological survey in the Beidha area, southern Jordan. *Mitteilungen der Deutshen Orient Gesellschaft* 119:1-19.

BAR-YOSEF, O. 1970. The Epi-Paleolithic Cultures of Palestine. Unpublished Ph.D dissertation, Hebrew University, Jerusalem.

BAR-YOSEF, O. 1981. "The Epipaleolithic complexes in the southern Levant," in *Préhistoire du Levant.* Edited by J. Cauvin and P. Sanlaville, pp. 389-408. Colloques Internationaux du CNRS 598. Paris: CNRS.

BAR-YOSEF, O. 1983. "The Natufian in the southern Levant." in *The Hilly Flanks and Beyond.* Edited by T.C. Young Jr., P.E.L. Smith, and P. Mortensen, pp. 11-42. Oriental Institute Studies in Ancient Oriental Civilization 36. Chicago: University of Chicago.

BAR-YOSEF, O. 1987. "Direct and indirect evidence for hafting in the Epi-Paleolithic and Neolithic of the southern Levant", in *La Main et L'Outil. Manches et Emmanchements Préhistoriques.* Edited by D. Stordeur, pp. 155-164. Travaux de la Maison de L'Orient 15. Lyon: Maison de l'Orient.

BAR-YOSEF, O. AND D. ALON. 1988. *Nahal Hemar Cave.* 'Atiqot 18. Jerusalem: Department of Antiquities and Museums.

BAR-YOSEF, O. AND M.E. KISLEV. 1986. Earliest domesticated barley in the Jordan Valley. *National Geographic Research* 2:257.

BAR-YOSEF, O. AND E. TCHERNOV. 1966. Archaeological finds and fossil fauna of the Natufian and microlithic industries at Hayonim Cave (Western Galilee, Israel). *Israel Journal of Zoology* 15:104-140.

BAR-YOSEF, O. AND F.R. VALLA. 1979. L'évolution du Natoufien nouvelles suggestions. *Paléorient* 5:145-151.

BAR-YOSEF, O. AND J.C. VOGEL. 1987. "Relative and absolute chronology of the epipaleolithic in the south of the Levant," in *Chronologies in the Near East.* Edited by O. Aurenche, J. Evin and F. Hours, pp. 219-246. BAR International Series 379. Oxford.

BENDER, B. 1978. Gatherer-hunter to farmer: a social perspective. *World Archaeology* 10:204-237.

BETTS, A. 1986. The prehistory of the basalt desert, Transjordan: an analysis. Unpublished Ph.D. thesis, London University.

BETTS, A. 1987. Jebel es-Subhi: a Natufian site in eastern Jordan. *Paléorient* 13(1):99-103.

BINFORD, L.R. 1968. "Post-Pleistocene adaptations," in *New Perspectives in Archaeology.* Edited by S.R. Binford and L.R. Binford, pp. 313-341. Chicago: Aldine Press.

BINFORD, L.R. 1978. Dimensional analysis of behavior and site structure: learning from an Eskimo hunting stand. *American Antiquity* 43:330-361.

BINFORD, L.R. 1980. Willow smoke and dog's tails: hunter-gatherer settlement and archaeological site formation. *American Antiquity* 45:4-20.

BINFORD, L.R. 1982. The archaeology of place. *Journal of Anthropological Archaeology* 1:5-31.

BINTLIFF, J.L. 1982. "Paleoclimatic modeling of environmental changes in the east Mediterranean region since the last glaciation", in *Paleoclimates, Paleoenvironments and Human Communities in the Eastern Mediterranean Region in Later Prehistory.* Edited by J.L. Bintliff and W. van Zeist, pp. 485-527. BAR International Series 133. Oxford.

BODENHEIMER, F.S. 1958. The present taxonomic status of the terrestrial mammals of Palestine. *Bulletin of the Research Council of Israel* B 3-4:165-190.

BORDES, F. 1950. Principes d'une methode d'étude des techniques de débitage et de la typologie du Paléolithique ancien et moyen. *L'Anthropologie* 54:19-34.

BORDES, F. 1957. La signification du microburin dans le Paléolithique supérieur. *L'Anthropologie* 61:578-582.

BORDES, F. 1961. *Typologie du Paléolithic Ancien et Moyen.* Bordeaux.

BORDES, F. 1965. Utilization possible de côtés des burins. *Fundberichte aus Schwaben* 17:3-4.

BOTTEMA, S. AND Y. BARKOUDAH. 1979. Modern pollen precipitation in Syria and Lebanon and its relation to vegetation. *Pollen et Spores* 21:427-480.

BOUCHUD, J. 1987. "Les mammifères et la petite fauna du gisement natoufien de Mallaha (Eynan)". in *La Faune du Gisement Natoufien de Mallaha (Eynan) Israel.* Edited by J. Bouchud, pp. 13-114. Mémoires et travaux du Centre de Recherche Français du Jérusalem 4. Paris: Association Paléorient.

BRAIDWOOD, R.J. 1960. The agricultural revolution. *Scientific American* 203:130-148.

BREZILLON, M. 1968. *La Dénomination des Objects de Pierre Tailée.* IVe Supplement à Galla Préhistoire. Paris: CNRS.

BRINK, J. 1978. *An Experimental Study of Microwear Formation on Endscrapers.* Archaeological Survey of Canada, 83. Ottawa: National Museum of Man, Mercury Series.

BÜLLER, H. 1983. "Methodological problems in the microwear analysis of tools selected from the Natufian sites of el Wad and Ain Mallaha". in *Traces d'Utilization sur les Outils Néolithiques du Proche Orient.* Edited by M. Cauvin, pp. 107-126. Travaux de la Masion de l'Orient 5. Lyon: Masion de l'Orient.

BYRD, B.F. 1987. *Beidha and the Natufian: variability in Levantine settlement and subsistence.* Ph.D. Dissertation, University of Arizona, University Microfilms, Michigan.

BYRD, B.F. 1988. "The Natufian of Beidha: report on renewed field research," in *The Prehistory of Jordan.* Edited by A.N. Garrard and H.G. Gebel, pp. 175-197. BAR International Series 396. Oxford.

BYRD, B.F. 1989. The Natufian: settlement variability and economic adaptations in the Levant at the end of the Pleistocene. *Journal of World Prehistory* 3(2):159-197.

BYRD, B.F. AND G.O. ROLLEFSON. 1984. Natufian occupation in the Wadi el Hasa, southern Jordan. *Annual of the Department of Antiquities, Jordan* 28:143-150.

CAHEN, D. AND J. GYSELS. 1983. "Techniques et fonctions dans l'industrie lithique du groupe de Blicquy (Belgique)", in *Traces d'Utilisation sur les Outils Néolithiques du Proche Orient.* Edited by M. Cauvin, pp. 37-52. Travaux de la Masion de l'Orient 5. Lyon: Masion de l'Orient.

CAHEN, D. AND F. VAN NOTEN. 1971. Stone age typology: another approach. *Current Anthropology* 12:211-215.

CALLEY, S. 1984. Le débitage Natoufien de Mureybet: étude préliminaire. *Paléorient* 10(2):35-48.

CALLEY, S. 1986. *Technologie du Débitage à Mureybet, Syrie.* BAR International Series 312. Oxford.

CARR, C. 1984. "The nature of organization of intrasite archaeological records and spatial analytic approaches to their investigation," in *Advances in Archaeological Method and Theory, Vol. 7.* Edited by M.B. Schiffer, pp. 103-222. New York: Academic Press.

CAUVIN, J. 1977. "Les nouvelles fouilles de Mureybet (1971-1974) et leur significations pour les origines de la sédentarisation au Proche-Orient," in *Archaeological Reports from the Tabqa Dam Project-Euphrates Valley, Syria.* Edited by D.N. Freedman, pp. 19-48. Annual of the American Schools of Oriental Research 44.

CAUVIN, J. 1978. *Les premiers villages de Syrie-Palestine du IX-au VII Millenaire Avant J-C.* Série Archéologique 3, Collection de la Maison de l'Orient Ancien 4. Lyon: Maison de l'Orient.

CAUVIN, M. 1974. L'industrie natoufienne de Taibé dans le Hauran (Syrie). *Bulletin de la Société Préhistorique Française* 71:469-478.

CAUVIN, M., Editor. 1983. *Traces d'Utilization sur les Outils Néolithiques du Proche Orient.* Travaux de la Masion de l'Orient 5. Lyon: Masion de l'Orient.

CHILDE, V.G. 1935. *New Light on the Most Ancient East.* Hertford: Stephen Austin and Sons.

CLARK, G., J. LINDLEY, M. DONALDSON, A. GARRARD, N. COINMAN, J. SHULDENREIN, S. FISH AND D. OLSZEWSKI. 1988. "Excavations at Middle, Upper, and Epipaleolithic sites in the Wadi Hasa, west-central Jordan," in *The Prehistory of Jordan.* Edited by A.N. Garrard and H.G. Gebel, pp. 209-285. BAR International Series 396. Oxford.

CLARK, J.D. 1975-1977. Interpretations of prehistoric technology from ancient Egyptian and other sources. *Paléorient* 3:127-150.

CLARK, J.D., J.L. PHILLIPS AND P.S. STANLEY. 1974. Interpretation of prehistoric technology from ancient Egyptian and other sources. *Paléorient* 2:323-388.

116

CLOSE, A. 1978. The identification of style in lithic artefacts. *World Archaeology* 10:223-237.

CLUTTON-BROCK, J. 1971. The primary food animals of the Jericho Tell from Proto-Neolithic to the Byzantine period. *Levant* 3:41-55.

COQUEUGNIOT, L. 1983. "Analyse tracéologique d'une série de grattoirs et herminettes de Mureybet, Syrie (9ème-7ème millénaires)," in *Traces d'Utilisation sur les Outils Néolithiques du Proche Orient*. Edited by M. Cauvin, pp. 163-172. Travaux de la Masion de l'Orient 5. Lyon: Masion de l'Orient.

CRABTREE, D. 1972. *An Introduction to Flintworking*. Occasional Papers of the Idaho State University Museum 28. Boise.

CRABTREE, P.J., D.V. CAMPANA, AND A. BELFER-COHEN. 1987. A report on the first season of excavation at the late Natufian site of Salibiya I. Ms. on file, Department of Antiquities, Israel.

DARMON, F. 1987. Analyses polliniques de deux sites de la basse vallee du Jourdain: Fazael VIII et Salibiya IX. *Paléorient* 10(2):106-110.

DAVIS, S. 1981. The effects of temperature change and domestication on the body size of late Pleistocene to Holocene mammals of Israel. *Paleobiology* 7(1):101-114.

DAVIS, S. 1982. Climatic change and the advent of domestication: the succession of ruminant artiodactyls in the late Pleistocene-Holocene in the Israel region. *Paléorient* 8(2):5-15.

DAVIS, S. 1983. The age profiles of gazelles predated by ancient man in Israel. *Paléorient* 9(1):57-64.

DAVIS, S., N. GORING-MORRIS AND A. GOPHER. 1982. Sheep bones from the Negev Epipaleolithic. *Paléorient* 8(1):87-93.

DORST, J. AND P. DANDELOT. 1970. *A Field Guide to the Larger Mammals of Africa*. London: Collins.

EDWARDS, P.C. 1987. Late Pleistocene occupation in wadi al-Hammeh, Jordan Valley. Unpublished Ph.D. Dissertation, University of Sydney, Australia.

EIG, A. 1946. Synopsis of the phytosociological units of Palestine. *Palestine Journal of Botany* 3:183-247.

EMERY-BARBIER, A. 1988. Analyses polliniques du Quarternaire supérieur en Jordanie méridionale. *Palérient* 14(1):111-118.

EVANS, J. 1872. *The Ancient Stone Implements, Weapons, and Ornaments of Great Britain*. London: Longmans, Green, Reader, and Dyer.

FALL, P., C. LINDQUIST AND S. FALCONER. n.d. "Fossil hyrax middens from the Middle East: a record of paleovegetation and human disturbance," in *Fossil Packrat Middens: the Last 40,000 Years of Biotic Change in the Arid West*. Edited by P. Martin, T. Van Devender and J. Betancourt. Tucson: University of Arizona Press.

FISH, P.R. 1981. Beyond tools: Middle Paleolithic debitage analysis and cultural inference. *Journal of Anthropological Research* 37:374-386.

FISH, P.R. AND S.K. FISH. 1988. Modeling the transition: a comparative analysis. Paper presented at the SAA meetings, Phoenix, 1988.

FISH, S.K. 1985. "Prehistoric disturbance floras of the Lower Sonoran Desert and their implications," in *Late Quaternary Vegetation and Climates of the American Southwest*. Edited by B. Jacobs, P. Fall and O. Davis, pp. 77-88. American Association of Stratigraphic Palynologists Contribution Series 16.

FLANNERY, K.V. 1969. "Origins and ecological effects of early domestication in Iran and the Near East," in *The Domestication and Exploitation of Plants and Animals*. Edited by P.J. Ucko and G.W. Dimbleby, pp. 73-100. London: Aldine.

FLANNERY, K.V. 1973. The origins of agriculture. *Annual Review of Anthropology* 2:271-310.

FRITSCH, K.V. 1893. Die funde des Herrn Pater Gottfried Zumoffen Professors an der St. Josephuniversitat zu Beirut in den Höhlen am Fusse des Libanon. *Abhandlungen der Naturforschenden Gesellschaft zu Halle* 19(2):41-80.

GARRARD A.N. 1980. Man-animal-plant Relationships During the Upper Pleistocene and Early Holocene of the Levant. Unpublished Ph.D. dissertation, Darwin College, University of Cambridge, Cambridge, England.

GARRARD, A.N. 1984. "The selection of south-west Asian animal domesticates", in *Animals and Archaeology: 3. Early Herders and their flocks*. Edited by J. Clutton-Brock and C. Grigson, pp. 117-132. BAR International Series 202. Oxford.

GARRARD, A.N., A. BETTS, B. BYRD, AND C. HUNT. 1987. Prehistoric environment and settlement in the Azraq Basin: an interim report on the 1985 excavation season. *Levant* 19:5-25.

GARRARD, A.N., A. BETTS, B. BYRD, S. COLLEDGE AND C. HUNT. 1988. "Summary of paleoenvironmental and prehistoric investigations in the Azraq Basin," in *The Prehistory of Jordan*. Edited by A.N. Garrard and H.G. Gebel, pp. 311-337. BAR International Series 396. Oxford.

GARROD, D.A.E. 1932. A new Mesolithic industry: the Natufian of Palestine. *Journal of the Royal Anthropological Institute* 62:257-270.

GARROD, D.A.E. 1942. Excavation at the cave of Shukbah, Palestine, 1928. *Proceedings of the Prehistoric Society* 8:1-20.

GARROD, D.A.E. 1958. The Natufian culture: the life and economy of Mesolithic people in the Near East. *Proceedings of the British Academy* 43:211-227.

GARROD D.A.E. AND D.M.A. BATE. 1937. *The Stone Age of Mount Carmel, Vol 1.* Oxford: Claredon Press.

GEBEL, H.G. 1986. "Die Jungsteinzeit im Petra-Gebiet," in *Petra: Neue Augrabungen und Entdeckungen.* Edited by M. Lindner, pp. 273-308. München: Delp Verlag.

GEBEL, H.G. AND J.M. STARCK. 1985 Investigation into the stone age of the Petra area (early Holocene research): a preliminary report on the 1984 campaigns. *Annual of the Department of Antiquities of Jordan* 29:89-114.

GENDEL, P.A. AND L. PIRNAY. 1982. Microwear analysis of experimental stone tools: further test results. *Studia Praehistorica Belgica* 2:251-265.

GOLDBERG, P. 1981. "Late Quaternary stratigraphy of Israel: an eclectic view," in *Prehistoire du Levant.* Edited by J. Cauvin and P. Sanlaville, pp. 55-67. Colloques Internationaux du CNRS 598. Paris: CNRS.

GOLDBERG, P. AND O. BAR-YOSEF. 1982. "Environmental and archaeological evidence for climatic change in the southern Levant," in *Paleoclimates, Paleoenvironments, and Human Communities in the Eastern Mediterranean Region in Later Prehistory.* Edited by J.L. Bintliff and W. van Zeist, pp. 399-414. BAR International Series 133. Oxford.

GORING-MORRIS, A.N. 1987. *At the Edge: Terminal Pleistocene Hunter-Gatherers in the Negev and Sinai.* BAR International Series 361. Oxford.

GORING-MORRIS, A.N. AND O. BAR-YOSEF. 1987. A late Natufian campsite from the western Negev, Israel. *Paléorient* 13(1):107-112.

GOULD, R.A. 1967. Notes on hunting, butchering, and sharing of game among the Ngatajara and their neighbors in the West Australian desert. *Kroeber Anthropological Papers* 36:41-66.

GOULD, R.A., D.A. KOSTER AND A.H.L. SONTZ. 1971. The lithic assemblage of the Western Desert Aborigines of Australia. *American Antiquity* 3:149-169.

GROVES, C.P. 1974. *Horses, Asses and Zebras in the Wild.* Newton Abbot: David and Charles.

HARRISON, D.L. 1981. *The Mammals of Arabia.* London: Benn.

HAYDEN, B. 1977. "Stone tool functions in the Western Desert," in *Stone Tools as Cultural Markers: Change, Evolution, Complexity.* Edited by R.V.S. Wright, pp. 178-188. Canberra: Australian Institute of Aborigine Study.

HAYDEN, B. 1978. "Snarks in archaeology: or, interassemblage variability in lithics (a view from the Antipodes)," in *Lithics and Subsistence: the Analysis of Stone Tool Use in Prehistoric Economies.* Edited by D.D. Davis. Vanderbilt University Publications in Anthropology 20. Nashville.

HAYDEN, B. 1979. "Snap, shatter and superfractures: use-wear on stone skin scrapers," in *Lithic Use-Wear Analysis.* Edited by B. Hayden, pp. 207-229. New York: Academic Press.

HECKER, H.M. 1975. *The Faunal Analysis of the Primary Food Animals from Pre-pottery Neolithic Beidha (Jordan).* Ph.D. dissertation, Columbia University, University Microfilms, Ann Arbor.

HECKER, H.M. 1982. Domestication revisited: its implications for faunal analysis. *Journal of Field Archaeology* 9:217-236.

HELBÆK, H. 1959. Domestication of food plants in the old world. *Science* 130:365-372.

HELBÆK, H. 1964. First impression of the Çatal Hüyük plant husbandry. *Anatolian Studies* 14:121-126.

HELBÆK, H. 1966. "Appendix A: Pre-pottery Neolithic farming at Beidha, a preliminary report," in Five seasons at the Pre-pottery Neolithic village of Beidha, Jordan, by D. Kirkbride. *Palestine Exploration Quarterly* 98: 61-66.

HENRY, D.O. 1973a. The Natufian site of Rosh Zin, Negev, Israel: preliminary report. *Palestine Exploration Quarterly* 105:129-140.

HENRY, D.O. 1973b. *The Natufian of Palestine: its Material Culture and Ecology.* Ph.D. dissertation, Southern Methodist University, University Microfilms, Ann Arbor.

HENRY, D.O. 1974. The utilization of the microburin technique in the Levant. *Paléorient* 2:389-398.

HENRY, D.O. 1976. "Rosh Zin: a Natufian settlement near Ein Avdat," in *Prehistory and Paleoenvironments in the Central Negev, Israel, Vol. 1.* Edited by A.E. Marks, pp. 317-348. Dallas: Southern Methodist University.

HENRY, D.O. 1981. "An analysis of settlement patterns and adaptive strategies of the Natufian," in *Préhistoire du Levant*, edited by J. Cauvin and P. Sanlaville, pp. 421-432. Colloques Internationaux du CNRS, 598. Paris: CNRS.

HENRY, D.O. 1982. The prehistory of southern Jordan and relationships with the Levant. *Journal of Field Archaeology* 9:417-444.

HENRY, D.O. 1983. Adaptive evolution within the Epipaleolithic of the Near East. *Advances in World Archaeology* 2:99-160.

HENRY, D.O. 1985. "Preagricultural sedentism: the Natufian example," in *Prehistoric hunter-gatherers: the emergence of cultural complexity*. Edited by T.D. Price and J.A. Brown, pp. 365-381. New York: Academic Press.

HENRY, D.O. 1987a. The prehistory and paleoenvironments of Jordan: an overview. *Paléorient* 12(2):5-26.

HENRY, D.O. 1987b. "Topographic influence on Epipaleolithic land-use patterns in southern Jordan," in *Studies in the Archaeology and History of Jordan, III*. Edited by A. Hadidi, pp. 21-27. Jordan: Department of Antiquities.

HENRY, D.O. AND A. LEROI-GOURHAN. 1976. The excavation of Hayonim Terrace: an interim report. *Journal of Field Archaeology* 3:391-406.

HENRY, D.O., A. LEROI-GOURHAN AND S. DAVIS. 1981. The excavation of Hayonim Terrace: an examination of terminal Pleistocene climatic and adaptive changes. *Journal of Archaeological Science* 8:33-58.

HENRY, D.O. AND P.F. TURNBULL. 1985. Archaeological, faunal, and pollen evidence from Natufian and Timnian sites in southern Jordan. *Bulletin of the American Schools of Oriental Research* 257:44-64.

HILLMAN, G.C., S.M. COLLEDGE AND D.R. HARRIS 1989. "Plant-food economy during the Epipaleolithic period at Tell Abu Hureyra, Syria: dietary diversity, seasonality and modes of exploitation," in *Foraging and Farming: the evolution of plant exploitation*. Edited by Harris, D.R. and G.C. Hillman, pp. 240-268. London: Unwin Hyman.

HOLE, F., K.V. FLANNERY AND J.A. NEELY. 1969. *Prehistory and human ecology of the Deh Luran plain*. Museum of Anthropology Memoirs 1. University of Michigan, Ann Arbor.

HOOIJER, D.A. 1961. Ksar 'Akil, a Paleolithic rock shelter in the Lebanon. *Zoologische Verhandelingen* 49:1-67.

HOURS, F. 1974. Remarques sur l'utilization de listes-types pour l'étude du Paléolithique du Levant. *Paléorient* 2:3-18.

INIZAN, M.L. AND J. TIXIER. 1980. "Modifications possibles de la liste des types épipaléolithiques du Maghreb," in *Proceedings of the 8th Pan-African Congress of Prehistory and Quaternary Studies*. Edited by R.E. Leakey and B.A. Ogot, pp. 25-26. Narobi.

JELINEK, A.J. 1976. "Form, function, and style in lithic analysis," in *Cultural Change and Continuity: Essays in Honor of James Bennett Griffin*. Edited by C.E. Cleland, pp. 19-33. New York: Academic Press.

JUEL JENSEN, H. 1983. "A microwear analysis of unre-touched blades from Ageröd V," In *Ageröd V. An Atlantic Bog Site in Central Scania*, edited by L. Larsson, pp. 144-152, Acta Archaeologica Lundensta, series 8, no. 13. Lund, Sweden.

KEELEY, L.H. 1980. *Experimental Determination of Stone Tool Uses. a Microwear Analysis*. Chicago: University of Chicago.

KENYON, K. 1981. *Excavations at Jericho, Vol III, The Architecture and Stratigraphy of the Tell*. Edited by T. Holland. London: British School of Archaeology.

KIRKBRIDE, D. 1960. The excavation of a Neolithic village at Seyl Aqlat, Beidha near Petra. *Palestine Exploration Quarterly* 92:136-145.

KIRKBRIDE, D. 1966. Five seasons at the prepottery Neolithic village of Beidha in Jordan. *Palestine Exploration Quarterly* 98:5-61.

KIRKBRIDE, D. 1967. Beidha 1965: an interim report. *Palestine Exploration Quarterly* 99:5-13.

KIRKBRIDE, D. 1968a. Beidha: early Neolithic village life south of the Dead Sea. *Antiquity* 42:263-274.

KIRKBRIDE, D. 1968b. Beidha 1967: an interim report. *Palestine Exploration Quarterly* 100:90-96.

KIRKBRIDE, D. 1984. Beidha 1983: an interim report. *Annual of the Department of Antiquities, Jordan* 28:9-12.

KIRKBRIDE, D. 1985. "The environment of the Petra region during the Pre-pottery Neolithic," in *Studies in the History and Archaeology of Jordan II*. Edited by A. Hadidi, pp. 117-124. London: Department of Antiquities.

KURTEN, B. 1965. The carnivora of the Palestine caves. *Acta Zoologica Fennica* 107.

LARSON, P.A., JR. 1978. Ornamental beads from the late Natufian of southern Israel. *Journal of Field Archaeology* 5(1):120-121.

LECHEVALLIER, M. AND A. RONEN. 1985. *Le site Natoufien-Khiamien de Hatoula, près de Latroun, Israel*. Centre de Recherche Français de Jérusalem, 1. Jerusalem.

LEGGE, A.J. AND P.A. ROWLEY-CONLEY. 1987. Gazelle killing in stone age Syria. *Scientific American* 257:88-95.

LEROI-GOURHAN A. 1984. L'environment de Mallaha (Eynan) au Natoufien. *Paléorient* 10(2):103-105.

LUZ, B. 1982. "Paleoclimatic interpretation of the last 20,000 years record of deep sea cores around the Middle East," in *Paleoclimates, Paleoenvironments and Human Communities in the Eastern Mediterranean region in Later Prehistory.* Edited by J.L. Bintliff and W. van Zeist, pp. 41-61. BAR International Series 133. Oxford.

MAHER, L.J. 1972. Nomograms for computing 0.95 confidence limits of pollen data. *Review of Paleobotany and Palynology* 13:85-93.

MARKS, A.E., Editor. 1976. *Prehistory and Paleoenvironments in the Central Negev, Israel, Vol. 1, The Avdat/Aqev Area, Part 1.* Dallas: Southern Methodist University.

MARKS, A.E., Editor. 1977. *Prehistory and Paleoenvironments in the Central Negev, Israel, Vol 2, The Avdat/Aqev area, Part 2 and the Har Harif.* Dallas: Southern Methodist University.

MARKS, A.E., Editor. 1983. *Prehistory and Paleoenvironments in the Central Negev, Israel. Vol. 3, The Avdat/Aqev Area, Part 3.* Dallas: Southern Methodist University.

MARKS, A.E. AND P.A. LARSON, JR. 1977. "Test excavations at the Natufian site of Rosh Horesha," in *Prehistory and Paleoenvironments in the Central Negev, Israel, Vol. II.* Edited by A.E. Marks, pp. 191-232. Dallas: Southern Methodist University.

MARKS, A.E. AND T.R. SCOTT 1976. Abu Salem: Type site of the Harifian industry of the southern Levant. *Journal of Field Archaeology* 3(1):43-60.

MEHRINGER, P.J. 1967. "Pollen analysis of the Tule Springs area, Nevada", in *Pleistocene Studies in Southern Nevada.* Edited by H. Wormington and D. Ellis, pp. 13-200. Nevada State Museum Anthropological Papers 13.

MEINERTZHAGEN, R. 1954. *The Birds of Arabia.* Edinburgh: Oliver and Boyd.

MIENIS, H.K. 1977. "Marine molluscs from the Epipaleolithic Natufian and Harifian of the Har Harif, central Negev, Israel," in *Prehistory and Paleoenvironments in the Central Negev, Israel.* Edited by A.E. Marks, pp. 493-506. Dallas: Southern Methodist University.

MIENIS, H.K. 1987. "Molluscs from the excavation of Mallaha (Eynan)," in *La Faune du Gisement Natoufien de Mallaha (Eynan) Israel.* Edited by J. Bouchud, pp. 157-178. Mémoires et travaux du Centre de Recherche Français du Jérusalem 4. Paris: Association Paléorient.

MOORE, A.M.T. 1982. Agricultural origins in the Near East: a model for the 1980s. *World Archaeology* 14:224-236.

MORRIS, E.H. AND R.F. BURGH. 1954. *Basket Maker II Sites Near Durango, Colorado.* Carnegie Institute of Washington 604. Washington, D.C.

MORTENSEN, P. 1970. A preliminary study of the chipped stone industry from Beidha. *Acta Archaeologica* 41:1-54.

MOSS, E.H. 1983. *The functional analysis of flint implements: Pincevent and Pont d'Ambon.* BAR International Series 177. Oxford.

MUHEISEN, M., H.G. GEBEL, C. HANNSS AND R. NEEF. 1988. "Ain Rahub, a new final Natufian and Yarmoukien site near Irbid," in *The Prehistory of Jordan.* Edited by A.N. Garrard and H.G. Gebel, pp. 472-502. BAR International Series 396. Oxford.

NEEV, D. AND K.O. EMERY. 1967. The Dead Sea: depositional processes and environments of evaporites. *Geological Survey of Israel Bulletin* 41. Israel.

NEUVILLE, R. 1934. Le prehistorique de Palestine. *Revue Biblique* 53:237-259.

NEUVILLE, R. 1951. *Le Paléolithique et le Mésolithique du désert de Judea.* Archive de L'Institut de Paléontologie Humaine, Mémoire 24. Paris.

NEWCOMER, M.H. 1974. Study and replication of bone points from Ksar Akil (Lebanon). *World Archaeology* 6:138-153.

NEWCOMER, M., R. GRACE AND R. UNGER-HAMILTON. 1986. Investigating microwear polishes with blind tests. *Journal of Archaeological Science* 13:203-217.

NOY, T., A.J. LEGGE AND E.S. HIGGS. 1973. Recent excavations at Nahal Oren, Israel. *Proceedings of the Prehistoric Society* 39:75-99.

O'CONNELL, J.F. 1977. Room to move: contemporary Alyawara settlement patterns and their implications for aboriginal housing policy. *Mankind* 11:119-131.

O'CONNELL, J.F. 1987. Alyawara site structure and its archaeological implications. *American Antiquity* 52:74-108.

ODELL, G.H. 1981. The morphological express at function junction: searching for meaning in lithic tool types. *Journal of Anthropological Research* 37:319-342.

ODELL, G.H. AND F. ODELL-VEREECK. 1980. Verifying the reliability of lithic use-wear assessments by "blind tests". *Journal of Field Archaeology* 7:87-120.

OLSZEWSKI, D.I. 1986. *The North Syrian Late Epipaleolithic.* BAR International Series 309. Oxford.

OLSZEWSKI, D.I. 1988. The north Syrian Epipaleolithic and its relationship to the Natufian complex. *Levant* 20:127-137.

PERKINS, D. JR. 1966. "Appendix B: The fauna from Madamagh and Beidha, a preliminary report," in Five seasons at the Pre-Pottery Neolithic village of Beidha in Jordan, by D. Kirkbride. *Palestine Exploration Quarterly* 98:66-68.

PERKINS, D., JR. 1969. Fauna of Çatal Hüyük: evidence for early cattle domestication in Anatolia. *Science* 164:177-179.

PERKINS, D. JR., AND P. DALY. 1968. A hunter's village in Neolithic Turkey. *Scientific American* 219(5):97-106.

PERROT, J. 1962. "Palestine-Syria-Cilicia," in *Courses Toward Urban Life*. Edited by R.J. Braidwood and G. Willey, pp. 147-164. Chicago: Adline.

PERROT, J. 1968. La Préhistoire Palestinienne. *Supplément au Dictionaire de la Bible* 8:286-446.

PICHON, J. 1985. "Étude préliminaire de l'avifaune de Hatoula," in *Le Site Natoufien-Khiamien de Hatoula*. Edited by M. Lechevallier and A. Ronen, pp. 99-101. Centre de Recherche Français de Jérusalem 1. Jérusalem.

PICHON, J. 1987. "L'avifaune," in *La Faune du Gisement Natoufien de Mallaha (Eynan) Israel*. Edited by J. Bouchud, pp. 115-150. Mémoires et Travaux du Centre de Recherche Français de Jérusalem 4. Paris: Association Paléorient.

RAFFERTY, J.E. 1985. "The archaeological record on sedentariness: recognition, development, and implications," in *Advances in Archaeological Method and Theory, Vol. 8*. Edited by M.B. Schiffer, pp. 113-156. New York: Academic Press.

RAIKES, R.L. 1966. "Appendix C. Beidha prehistoric climate and water supply," in Five seasons at the Pre-Pottery Neolithic Village of Beidha in Jordan, by D. Kirkbride. *Palestine Exploration Quarterly* 98:68-72.

REINECK, H.E. AND I.B. SINGH. 1980. *Depositional Sedimentary Environments*. New York: Springer-Verlag.

REDDING, R.W. 1988. A general explanation of subsistence change: from hunting and gathering to food production. *Journal of Anthropological Archaeology* 7:59-97.

REDMAN, C.L. 1978. *The Rise of Civilization*. San Francisco: Freeman.

REESE, D.S. 1982. Marine and fresh-water molluscs from the Epipaleolithic site of Hayonim Terrace, western Galilee, northern Israel and other east Mediterranean sites. *Paléorient* 8(2):83-90.

RICE, G. 1975. *A Systematic Explanation of a Change in Mogollon Settlement Patterns*. Ph.D. dissertation, University of Washington. University Microfilms, Ann Arbor.

ROBERTS, T.J. 1977. *The Mammals of Pakistan*. London: Benn.

RUST, A. 1950. *Die Hölenfunde von Jabrud (Syrien)*. Neuemunster: Karl Wachhöltz.

SCHALLER, G.B. 1977. *Mountain Monarch. Wild Sheep and Goats of the Himalayas*. Chicago: University of Chicago.

SCHIFFER, M.B. 1972. Archaeological context and systemic context. *American Antiquity* 37:156-165.

SHEPPARD, P.J. 1987. *The Capsian of North Africa: Stylistic Variation in Stone Tool Assemblages*. BAR International Series 353. Oxford.

SIMMONS, A.H. AND G. ILANY. 1975. What means these bones? *Paléorient* 3:269-273.

SONNEVILLE-BORDES, D. AND J. PERROT. 1953. Essai d'adaptation de méthodes statistiques au Paleolithique supérieur. Premiers résultats. *Bulletin de la Société Préhistorique Française* 50:323-333.

STEKELIS, M. AND T. YIZRAELY. 1963. Excavations at Nahal Oren: preliminary report. *Israel Exploration Journal* 13:1-12.

SULLIVAN, A.P. 1987. Probing the sources of lithic assemblage variability: a regional case study near the Homolovi ruins, Arizona. *North American Archaeology* 8:41-71.

SUZUKI, C. AND T. AKAZAWA. 1971. Manufacturing technique of the stone artifacts from Palmyra, Syria. *Journal of the Anthropological Society of Nippon* 79:105-127.

TCHERNOV, E. 1966. Preliminary remarks on the faunal assemblage from Hayonim Cave. *Israel Journal of Zoology* 15:121-140.

TCHERNOV, E. 1974. "The animal remains," in *Hayonim Cave, Natufian cemetery and settlement remains*. Edited by Yedaya, M. Jerusalem: Bemaaravo shel Hagalil (Hebrew).

TCHERNOV, E. 1976. "Some late quaternary faunal remains from the Avdat/Aqev area", in *Prehistory and Paleoenvironments in the Central Negev, Israel, Vol. I*. Edited by A.E. Marks, pp. 69-73. Dallas: Southern Methodist University.

TCHERNOV, E., T. DAYAN AND Y. YOM-TOV. 1986. The paleogeography of *Gazella gazella* and *Gazella dorcas* during the Holocene of the southern Levant. *Israel Journal of Zoology* 34:51-59.

TIXIER, J. 1963. *Typologie de l'Épipaléolithique du Maghreb.* Mémoires du Centre de Recherches Anthropologiques. Paris: Préhistoriques et Ethnographiques, Alger.

TIXIER, J., M.L. INIZAN AND H. ROCHE. 1980. *Préhistoire de la Pierre Taillée: 1 Terminologie et Technologie.* Valbonne, France: Cercle de recherches et d'études préhistoriques.

TURVILLE-PETRE, F. 1932. Excavations in the Mugharet el-Kebarah. *Journal of the Royal Anthropological Institute* 62:271-276.

UNGER-HAMILTON, R. 1988. *Method in Microwear Analysis. Prehistoric Sickles and Other Stone Tools from Arjoune, Syria.* BAR. International Series 435. Oxford.

UNGER-HAMILTON, R. 1989. The Epi-paleolithic southern Levant and the origins of cultivation. *Current Anthropology* 30(1):88-103.

VALLA, F.R. 1975. *Le Natoufien: une Culture Préhistorique en Palestine.* Cahiers de la Revue Biblique 15. Paris: Gabalda.

VALLA, F.R. 1984. *Les industries de silex de Mallaha (Eynan).* Mémoires et Travaux du Centre de Recherche Français de Jérusalem 3. Paris: Association Paléorient.

VALLA, F.R. 1987a. "Chronolige absolue et chronologies relatives dans le Natoufien," in *Chronologies of the Near East.* Edited by O. Aurenche, J. Evin and F. Hours, pp. 267-294. BAR International Series 379. Oxford.

VALLA, F.R. 1987b. "Les Natoufiens connaissaient-ils l'arc?," in *La Main et l'Outil. Manches et emmanchements prehistoriques.* Edited by D. Stordeur, pp. 165-174. Travaux de la Maison de l'Orient 15. Lyon: CNRS.

VALLA, F.R. 1988. Les premiers sédentaires de Palestine. *La Recherche* 199:576-584.

VAUFREY, R. 1951. "Étude paléontologique. 1. Mammiferes," in *Le Paléolithique du Desert de Judée.* Edited by R. Neuville, pp. 198-217. Archives de l'Institut de Paléontologie Humaine. Mémoire 24.

VOLKMAN, P. 1983. "Boker Tachtit: core reconstructions," in *Prehistory and Paleoenvironments in the Central Negev, Israel, Vol 3.* Edited by A. E. Marks, pp. 127-190. Dallas: Southern Methodist University.

VON DEN DRIESCH, A. 1976. *A Guide to the Measurement of Animal Bones from Archaeological Sites.* Cambridge, Mass: Peabody Museum Bulletin I.

WAECHTER J. 1948. The excavations at Ala Safat, Transjordan. *Journal of the Palestine Oriental Society* 21:98-103.

WALKER, E.P. 1964. *Mammals of the World, Vol. 2.* Baltimore: John Hopkins.

WHITE, J.P. 1968. "Ston naip bilong tumbuna," in *La préhistoire et tendances.* Edited by D. de Sonneville-Bordes, pp. 511-516. Paris: CNRS.

WILMSEN, E.N. 1968. Functional analysis of flaked stone artifacts. *American Antiquity* 33(2):156-161.

WRIGHT, G.A. 1971. Origins of food production in southwest Asia: a survey of ideas. *Current Anthropology* 121:447-470.

YELLEN, J.E. 1977. *Archaeological Approaches to the Present: Models for Reconstructing the Past.* New York: Academic Press.

ZOHARY, D. AND P. SPIEGEL-ROY. 1975. Beginnings of fruit growing in the Old World. *Science* 187:319-327.

ZOHARY, M. 1940. Geobotanical analysis of the Syrian desert. *Palestine Journal of Botany* 2:46-96.

ZOHARY, M. 1962. *Plant life of Palestine.* New York: Roland Press.

ZOHARY, M. 1973. *Geobotanical Foundations of the Middle East, I and II.* Stuttgart: Fisher Verlag.

أفضل ما يمكن وصف البيضا النطوفية به هو أنها كانت موقع تخيم قصير المدى أو موسمي تم اعادة استعماله لفترة طويلة من الزمن. إن الدليل المحدود على التغيّر المكاني بين وحدات المصدر في عينات الأدوات الحجرية المصنعة، ونوع النشاطات المتمثلة في جموع الحجارة المصنعة الكبيرة، خاصة بالنسبة للنشاطات المتعلقة بالصيد، ووجود المواقد الصغيرة وامكنة الشي الكبيرة وفقدان العناصر المنسوبة عادة للاستيطان الدائم مثل أدوات الجرش والطحن الكبيرة والمعالم الانشائية كالبيوت وأمكنة التخزين والمدافن تدعم هذا التفسير.

استنادا على قلة الأدلة على جمع النباتات ونشاطات الاستهلاك في منطقة كانت غنية بالموارد النباتية، أقترح بان البيضا لم تستوطن خلال الفترات التي توفرت فيها هذه الموارد، أي الربيع وأوائل الصيف للحبوب والبقول والخريف لموارد الجوز، ويرجح أنها استوطنت خلال الشتاء والصيف لعدم توفر النبات خلال هاتين الفترتين والاضطرار على التوجه على الصيد.

رغم أن معلوماتنا عن التأقلم خلال الفترة النطوفية في منطقة البتراء ما زالت شحيحة، غير انه من المحتمل ان الاستيطان كان قد تميز ببعد أمكنة التخيّم عن بعضها البعض، وأن نظام الاستقرار الحولي من تجمع وتشتت موسمي قد خلق مستوطنات كبيرة وأخرى صغيرة. كانت أمد البقاء في أماكن معينة وانتقال المخيمات تتزامن مع توفر الموارد المحلية خاصة إذا أخذنا بالاعتبار الاختلاف الكبير في الارتفاع الجغرافي. من المحتمل أن التجمع كان خلال فترات وفرة الموارد، وتشمل الربيع إلى أوائل الصيف والخريف. مواقع التجمع هذه، غير المكتشفة بعد،قد تكون في مناطق الغابات المرتفعة. بالإضافة لا بد من وجود مخيمات مجموعات صيد الطرائد في منطقة مسطح الصخر الرملي ووادي عربة.

لا تعطي أدلة المعيشة المحدودة المتوفرة من البيضا أية دلائل على القيام بزراعة النباتات أو تدجين المواشي (وهذا ارتكازاً على بحث هكر). لذا فإن الدور الذي لعبته المنطقة في الخطوات الأولى نحو انتاج الغذاء لا يزال غامضا.

توحي لنا تحاليل التنسيب بتتابع تصغيري في صناعة الأدوات، بدأ بإنتاج قطع طويلة مستدقة النصل ثم نَصُل أصغر وأدق إلى مرحلة نهائية تميزت بقطعها القصيرة والعريضة أبعادها قريبة إلى أبعاد الشظايا. غير أن فئات مخلفات النصل والشظايا تتداخل إلى حد بعيد من ناحية صفات الحجم وشكل أثلام الشظايا وخواص الأسطح. بالرغم عن هذا فإن عدد النَصُل يزيد قليلاً عن عدد الشظايا، والنصل بمعناها الضيق غير شائعة. وكانت النَصُل هي النوع المفضل من المخلفات المستخدمة لتصنيع الأدوات وتتفاوت أحجامها بشكل كبير بين جموع الأدوات.

هنالك مجموعتان من المتغيرات في صفات اللقى ضمن الموقع يبدو أن لهما مغزى بالنسبة لسلوك ما قبل التاريخ، حيث يظهر تغير ملحوظ في العدد النسبي للنوي وفي نسبة المخلفات إلى الأدوات بين بعض مناطق الحفريات. ليس بالإمكان تحديد فيما إذا كانت هذه الفوارق متعلقة بتغيرات في نسب تصغير النوي أو أماكن طرح المواد الخام المستهلكة. بالإضافة إلى هذا فإن النماذج المجمعة من الاستيطان النطوفي المتأخر في المنطقة C-10 تختلف عن النماذج الأخرى في عدة نواحي تشمل نسبة النُصُل إلى الشظايا وطول الأدوات الهلالية الشكل. ويبدو أن هنالك علاقة زمنية لهذه الفوارق.

يفيدنا ملحق هكر (الملحق c) بأن الماعز كانت أكثر الحيوانات استغلالاً خلال الفترة النطوفية في البيضا. لا تشير الدلائل الى أن الماعز كانت قد دجنت، وتم التعرف على نوعين منها هما الماعز البري والبدن أو تيس الجبل اللذين كانا بلا شك يحتلان كوتين طبيعيتين مختلفتين في البيئة المحلية الوعرة. كان الغزال الذي ربما تم صيده في وادي عربه ثاني الأنواع من حيث العدد، ويبدو أن تواجد الثور البري والأخدر أو حمار الوحش كان نادرا.

رغم القيام بعمليات تعويم عينات التربة لجمع المخلفات المتفحمة في عامي ١٩٦٤ و ١٩٨٣، لم تجمع أية مواد نباتية يمكن التعرف عليها من الفترة النطوفية في البيضا.

الأدلة شحيحة على استخدام أدوات الجرش والطحن لتصنيع الحبوب والجوز، حيث لم يتم العثور سوى على حجري تصنيع هما كسرة مدقة (يد هاون) من الحجر الرملي وحجر يدوي قرصي الشكل (أحادي الوجه).

هنالك نوعان من المعالم الانشائية في البيضا النطوفية هما المواقد وأمكنة الشيء، وقد تم اكتشاف خمسة مواقد ومكانين للشي. تتخذ المواقد اشكالاً دائرية الى بيضاوية تتراوح أقطارها بين ٣٥ و ٦٠ سم، أما أماكن الشي فهي اكبر حجما حيث تصل أقطارها إلى ٢,٥م وتحوي عظام حيوانات وكانت قد صفت حجارة كبيرة داخلها وخارجها. رغم امتداد منطقة الحفريات لم يعثر على معالم أخرى من الفترة النطوفية في البيضا مثل الجدران أو المباني أو اماكن التخزين أو الأرصفة الحجرية كما لم يعثر على أية مدافن.

يمكن تقدير امتداد المستوطنة النطوفية في البيضا على أساس توزيع مجسات الحفر التي عثر فيها على مخلفات سكنية في موضعها الأصلي أو منقولة، ويبدو أن مساحة المخلفات التي ما تزال في موضعها الاصلي تقارب ٦٠ في ٤٠ اي ٢,٤٠٠ مترا مربعا تتضمن اقساما من المستوطنة الحالية. وبما أن سيل عقلات قد قام بجرف الجزء الغربي من المستوطنة، فإن امتداد الموقع في تلك الناحية ليس مؤكداً غير أن اسقاط مساحة ٤,٠٠٠ مترا مربعا ليس بمستبعد. إن إمتداد المخلفات الباقية في موضعها الاصلي لا يعكس بدقة عدد السكان الذين اقاموا في البيضا في أي من الاوقات، وبالأحرى فإن الموقع كان قد استوطن مراراً عدة في سلسلة من مناطق السكن المتداخلة مما أدى الى تكون مساحة استيطانية أعيد استخدامها وتشكيلها مراراً.

إن تعدد أصناف الأدوات الحجرية المشغولة الممثلة في البيضا تدل على تعدد النشاطات التي كانت قائمة في الموقع، وكان هنالك تركيزا كبيراً على اعادة تجهيز الأدوات للصيد وتصنيع جلود الحيوانات. ينبع هذا الاستنتاج عن وفرة الأدوات الحجرية الهندسية الصغيرة والمكاشط العلوية. كما يبقى الدليل على جمع الحبوب والجوز شحيحا وذلك لقلة وجود الأدوات الحجرية غير الهندسية الصغيرة وندرة نُصُل المناجل وقلة أدوات الجرش والطحن.

تقدم هذه الدراسة تقرير السيدة كيركبرايد النهائي حول الحفريات الأثرية في المستوطنة النطوفية في البيضا في جنوب الأردن. ولقد نتجت الأبحاث عن ثمانية مواسم ميدانية بين عامي ١٩٥٨ و ١٩٨٣ تم العمل خلالها بترخيص ودعم من دائرة الآثار الأردنية التي نود أن نشكر مسؤوليها وموظفيها لدعمهم الحثيث والمستمر.

كان هنالك اهتماماً كبيراً بالمجتمعات الحضارية لنهاية عصر البليستوسين المسمى بالنطوفي منذ أن عرفته السيدة دورثي غارود عام ١٩٣٢، وذلك انطلاقاً من الحفريات في مغارة الشكبه في وادي النطوف ومغارة الواد في جبل الكرمل. ولقد أدى الادراك لمركز الفترة النطوفية الحيوي في تتابع التطور البشري، من مجتمعات الصيد والقطاف المترحلة إلى مجتمعات القرى المستوطنة، إلى جمهرة من الأبحاث خلال الخمسين عاماً اللاحقة.

كان البحث في البيضا (التي سميت اصلاً بسيل عقلات) في منطقة الصخور الرملية الوعرة قرب البتراء هو الاول من نوعه في موقع نطوفي في الاردن. ومن هنا فلقد أعطى التصورات الأولى عن تأقلم الانسان مع البيئة خلال الفترة النطوفية في النصف الشرقي من جنوب شرق المتوسط، وعن فيما إذا كانت أنماط تأقلمه في هذه المنطقة مماثلة لأنماط التأقلم المعروفة في المناطق الغربية. واليوم وبعد ثلاثين عاماً تبقى معرفتنا بتغير انماط التأقلم في نهاية عصر البليستوسين محدودة. ان البيضا هي الموقع الوحيد المؤكد تأريخه للفترة النطوفية الذي تم حفره في منطقة البتراء في جنوب الأردن، ولم تجر حتى الآن سوى ابحاث تمهيدية في المواقع العائدة الى الألف السابق والألف اللاحق للنطوفية.

يميل البحث الأولي في البيئة القديمة في منطقة البيضا، المتمثل في دراسات فيلد (الملحق A) وفش (الملحق B)، الى تأكيد الجزم بأن المناخ في الفترة النطوفية كان أبرد مما هو عليه الآن وبأن الرطوبة الفعلية كانت أعلى. ويشير ارتفاع القعر في وادي الغرب خلال الفترة النطوفية الى أن الغطاء النباتي كان أكثر كثافة في الوديان الطمية القاطعة لمسطح الصخر الرملي وبأن الغابات المفتوحة والمناطق الانتقالية كانتا أوسع انتشاراً من وقتنا الحالي. ولقد لعبت مصادر المياه الموسمية أو الدائمة في جوار البيضا دوراً حيوياً في توضيع الموقع، ونتج عن نظام الطقس والتمنطق الارتفاعي الشاسع لجموع النباتات، أي اختلاف انواعها نتيجة الفروق الشاسعة في الارتفاع الجغرافي، تنوع في المصادر الغذائية التي شملت النباتات البرية الصالحة للأكل بالإضافة إلى حيوانات القطعان (خاصة ذوات الحوافر).

كشفت الحفريات في البيضا عن ٥٤ متراً مربعاً من الفترة النطوفية وهي ثاني أوسع مساحة مكشوفة ضمن المواقع المعاصرة في الأردن (كون وادي الحمة أوسعها). بلغ معدل سماكة الطبقات السكنية في الجزء المركزي من الموقع بين ٠,٤م و ٠,٦م حيث صنفت ثلاثة مراحل من الرواسب ضمن تتابع زمني متعاقب. أما في طرف الجزء الشمالي من الموقع فلقد ظهر تسلسل طبقي مختلف، حيث كُشف عن مرحلتي استيطان تفصلهما طبقة من الرواسب الطبيعية. تبلغ سماكة مرحلة الاستيطان السفلى في هذه المنطقة ٠,١٥م وتحوي على جموع لقي أثرية مماثلة لتلك التي اكتشفت في مناطق أخرى من الموقع. تمثل هذه المرحلة مستوطنة نطوفية تم تأريخها بواسطة الكربون المشع الى ١٢,٠٠٠ عام قبل الحاضر، ويبدو أن هنالك فاصل زمني طويل بين مرحلتي الاستيطان السفلى والعليا في طرف الموقع الشمالي حيث تم تأريخ المرحلة العليا، رغم صغر العينة المكتشفة، إلى الفترة ما بين النطوفية المبكرة والمتأخرة.

تم تركيز التحليل على الأدوات الحجرية الواسعة الانتشار وذلك بسبب تحدد مجال واختلاف انواع اللقى المكتشفة، ولقد تم بشكل خاص فحص تقنية مراحل تصنيع الأدوات من الحجر الخام أو السابق التصنيع وطبيعة الادوات المنمقة بالتفصيل. وجد أنه قد تم استغلال الحصي الصواني المحلية العالية الجودة، وكان يتم تحضير النوي، ومعظمها وحيدة السطح، في مكان آخر. استعمل «الشرت» أحياناً، وهو حجر صواني غير نقي، ويتمثل هذا الحجر فقط في بعض الأدوات التي جلبت للموقع وطرحت هناك. لم يقم صانعو الأدوات الحجرية سوى بالقليل من تحضير النوي أو تجديدها، لكن رغم ذلك فلقد قاموا باستغلال مكثف للنوي من ناحية تصغيرها.

التخيّم النطوفي في البيضا

التأقلم خلال عصر البليستوسين المتأخر

في جنوبي شرق المتوسط

بريان ف. بيرد
المقدمة للسيدة ديانا كيركبرايد
بمساهمة
جون فيلد ـ سوزان فش ـ هوارد م. هكر ـ ديفيد س. ريس

منشورات جمعية جوتلاند الأثرية